The Which? Guide to Going Digital

About the author

Roy Brooker is the Principal Scientist at Consumers' Association's Research and Testing Centre at Milton Keynes. Along with other experts at the centre he tests all the latest goods and services – often before they are available to the public – and reports on them for *Which?* magazine.

Acknowledgements

The author and publishers would like to thank the staff of the electronics department at the Research and Testing Centre for their help on the book. Thanks too to the research staff at Consumers' Association for their contributions.

The Which? Guide to Going Digital

Roy Brooker

Which? Books are commissioned and researched by
Consumers' Association and published by
Which? Ltd, 2 Marylebone Road, London NW1 4DF
Email address: books@which.net

Distributed by The Penguin Group:
Penguin Books Ltd, 27 Wrights Lane, London W8 5TZ

First edition June 2001

British Library Cataloguing in Publication Data
A catalogue record for this book is available from the British Library

ISBN 0 85202 849 0

Editorial and production: Robert Gray, Nithya Rae
Cover and text design by Kysen Creative Consultants
Cover image by Paul Wootton
Line drawings by Mark Winson, Saxon Graphics Ltd

Typeset by Saxon Graphics Ltd, Derby
Printed and bound in Great Britain by Clays Ltd, Bungay, Suffolk

Contents

* An asterisk next to the name of an organisation in the text indicates that the address can be found in this section

Introduction

Exciting and baffling – and happening now: the digital revolution cannot be ignored. Entertainment, work, communications and many everyday goods and services are changing, or about to change, dramatically, and this book explains how they will affect you and your bank balance.

Surveys conducted by Consumers' Association (CA) have consistently highlighted low levels of awareness among the general public of the availability, benefits and costs of digital products and services. Even those who know about such technologies are not particularly enthusiastic about them: many people feel that developments such as the Internet and digital television have little to offer them personally, and that the advantages of these advances are of little relevance or are outweighed by cost.

Digital television is one area where lack of knowledge, apathy and general confusion are rife. The government and the large broadcasting companies are very keen for the public to switch to the new digital services. In spring 2001 CA carried out a survey to find out what percentage of the British population was interested in receiving digital TV. The results were revealing: roughly a quarter of the population currently has digital TV, but nearly half of all consumers have not even investigated getting such a service, and a quarter does not ever want to get it.

Why should so many people be so uninterested in digital technology? After all, 'going digital' seems to be an inevitability and, with all the new services on offer, surely we should be more keen on them? The main reason is obvious: it is hard for us to be excited about something we know little about. It is a sad fact that many of the suppliers and promoters of the 'digital future' have made a pretty poor job of communicating the new technology to the consumer. Furthermore, the media has not conveyed extensively or accurately explanations of digital technology and the effect it is likely to have on our lives. It is hard to work out which products or services are worth having, even if we are aware of them. Moreover, even digital technology has its share of turkeys: there are many potential 'dead ends' in terms of redundant technologies and inadequate services for consumers who rush headlong into the digital age, as users of WAP phones will testify.

A clearer understanding of what 'going digital' means will help consumers make up their minds. At CA's Research and Testing Centre we test the very latest digital products and services: we are therefore well placed to explain what are, and will be, available in the fields of entertainment, information-gathering, shopping, home automation, photography, working from home and communications. In this guide we set out what they do and disentangle the genuine advantages of these developments from the hype spread by government and industry. Most importantly, we include valuable buying advice (of the sort that only an independent research-based body such as CA can provide) that will help readers make decisions about what systems to go for by comparing them (e.g. video-recording systems in Chapter 1).

Does digital imply better quality?

The impression that 'digital' equals 'better quality' arose partly from the fact that the digital compact disc got rid of the noise and crackles that were a feature of vinyl records. However, improved quality is not the whole story. Digital technology can be used to provide new and more products and services, not just better ones. So the digital engineers and the big companies that sell digital systems have to choose between quality, quantity and innovation. For example, with digital TV, they can increase quantity (e.g. more channels) rather than quality or they can provide new services (e.g. electronic shopping). Alternatively, they can attempt to achieve a balance of the three elements. Given this degree of variation, consumers need to be abreast of developments so we can choose the products and services that best suit our needs.

The benefits of digital technology

Although some of the digital products and services currently on the market, particularly mobile phone and television services, are commercially driven, it would be wrong to assume that digital technology is simply a gimmick to extract more money from unwary consumers. Quite apart from the attractions highlighted earlier, digital technology can make our daily domestic lives more comfortable, enjoyable and secure, as the chapter on home automation (Chapter 6) shows. Moreover, digital electronics is also 'green' electronics. If digital systems are implemented and managed responsibly, their energy consumption can be made much lower than their analogue equivalents (see Appendix II).

The ever-changing nature of digital technology

Nearly every day, newspapers and the broadcast media have some new development in digital technology to report. Indeed, just as *The Which? Guide to Going Digital* went to press, ONdigital, one of the three main digital TV systems in the UK, announced a change of name to ITV Digital. Rather confusingly for the consumer, ITV Digital transmits not only commercial TV but BBC and subscription TV as well.

Also in spring 2001, apparently in a bid to help consumers buying new TVs, high-street shops have been stocking sets sporting a 'DVB' logo on them. Again, it is debatable whether such a move will in fact assist anyone. It is not clear what DVB *means* (it *stands for* digital video broadcasting) because, as is explained in Chapter 1, viewers do not need a special TV set to receive digital broadcasting – any TV can be converted into a digital TV with the right equipment.

In keeping with the spirit of this topic, a web site (www.whichdigitalguide.co.uk) has been set up to answer questions that may arise after a reading of this book.

Despite the state of flux of the digital market, this guide explains clearly which digital technologies are being used in different areas of our everyday lives, and what the general trends are, thus arming consumers with the knowledge and advice needed to make informed decisions in what is a confusing hi-tech market.

Chapter 1

Entertainment

Since the 1950s developments in electronics have changed the face of home entertainment in the UK. Until the advent of digital technology, radios, televisions and hi-fi systems underwent a steady evolution.

Radios became smaller and more portable, and the move to higher frequencies gave listeners interference-free and hi-fi quality stereo reception.

Television progressed from low-definition black-and-white screens to high-definition colour. At the same time, the reliability and screen quality of the television set itself improved. The number of terrestrial TV stations steadily increased too: from just a single public service channel, through the addition of a commercial channel in 1955, to four channels in 1982. Analogue satellite television made its appearance in the UK in 1989. The domestic video-cassette recorder, introduced in 1975, enabled users to record television programmes for viewing at a later time, as well as to play video cassettes from elsewhere, as long as they used the same recording systems.

Music entertainment in the home progressed from bulky radiogram devices, playing crackly, brittle 78 rpm records, of which a single Beethoven symphony would occupy several sides, to micro-grooved long-playing records offering high fidelity and stereo, and finally to the remarkable quality and convenience of digital compact discs.

A common theme is evident in these developments: they are all improvements in quality brought about by technical developments. The recent – and continuing – digital revolution has also led to better-quality products, but more significantly, it has brought other changes: a broader range, different methods of delivery and new sources of entertainment and associated services.

Since the 1990s, the digital revolution has resulted in a much more rapid development of gadgets and has also introduced new services. This chapter looks at the new digital world of home entertainment, explaining what the products are, how they function, what their advantages are over older appliances, and what to look for when you are buying them. It will also explain the options for linking these together and the sharing of resources, such as high-quality home-cinema systems.

Digital radio

The concept of digital radio, or digital audio broadcasting (DAB), dates back to 1990. The BBC first began broadcasting its national networks on digital channels in 1995, with coverage reaching just 20 per cent of the UK; by 1997 this was over 50 per cent. However, in spite of much publicity and at least a couple of official launches, there was little interest among the public. This was hardly surprising, as no one was making any DAB receivers.

The other problem with DAB in the early days was that it was not immediately obvious what its benefits would be. In fact, in addition to the improved sound quality, DAB has several advantages:

- clearer and more convenient reception in cars
- automatic tuning of stations
- display of 'text' information on a panel
- room for many more radio stations, so certain types of music or information programmes can have dedicated stations.

DAB has now started to take off. The year 2000 saw the manufacture of several home hi-fi and in-car receivers, and the DAB broadcasting network expanded rapidly. The two national networks are the BBC network, which broadcasts all its national stations plus the World Service and is planning to open four more specialist stations during 2001, and Digital One,* a national commercial network which comprises Classic FM, ITN News, Virgin and several other speech and music stations.

During 2000, eight local networks were also opened around the UK, and a total of over 35 local and regional networks are planned to open by mid-2002. As each of these networks can carry five or more local commercial and BBC stations, the choice of radio stations is expanding significantly.

What is available on national digital radio

Station name	Comments
BBC Radio 1	
BBC Radio 2	
BBC Radio 3	
BBC Radio 4	
BBC Radio 4 LW	Long-wave version
BBC Five Live	
Five Live Sports+	A 'secondary' sports service
BBC World Service	
Virgin	Pop music
One Word	Spoken word, books, poetry
Planet Rock	Rock music
Classic FM	Classical music
Core	Modern pop
Life	Contemporary pop
ITN News	
Primetime	Easy listening
Talk Sport	
Bloomberg-Talk Money	Finance and business news

Technically, DAB employs several of the latest digital techniques. The audio signal is digitised first, in much the same way as it would be for a compact disc. However, to broadcast the signal in this form would not be practical because it would require too large a chunk of the allocated radio spectrum. So, the digitised signal then undergoes a process called 'digital compression' (see box), which reduces the amount of radio spectrum required. In another digital process, this audio signal is mixed with signals from several other radio stations and the group transmitted together in one radio channel. Such groups are called 'ensembles'. For example, most national BBC stations are mixed together into one 'BBC' ensemble: this ensures most efficient use of the available radio spectrum.

Availability of local/regional networks on DAB

Region	Number of stations available and when
Birmingham	5
Manchester	8
Greater London	18; more to follow
Glasgow	7
S. Yorkshire	7
Tyne & Wear	7
Cardiff & Newport	8
Wolverhampton	9
Liverpool	8
Edinburgh	8
Leeds	7 (May 2001)
Teesside	7 (June 2001)
Bristol/Bath	9
Coventry	9
Central Lancs	8 (Sept 2001)
Northern Ireland	10 (Sept 2001)
Central Scotland	9 (May 2001)
Humberside	8 (Sept 2001)
North-East (region)	9 (June 2001)
Severn Estuary (region)	(Feb 2001)
West Midlands (region)	(Mar 2001)
North-West (region)	(Apr 2001)
Aberdeen	(Apr 2001)
Southend/Chelmsford	(June 2001)
Ayr	(July 2001)
Bournemouth	(Sept 2001)
Dundee/Perth	(Sept 2001)
Exeter/Torbay	(Oct 2001)
Bradford/Huddersfield	(Nov 2001)
Peterborough	(Dec 2001)
Inverness	(Jan 2002)
South Hampshire	(Feb 2002)
Norwich	(Mar 2002)
Yorkshire	(May 2002)

Source: Digital One and the Radio Authority, February 2001. Note: The actual numbers of stations and dates may be subject to change. In most cases, a BBC local station will be included in the above local networks.

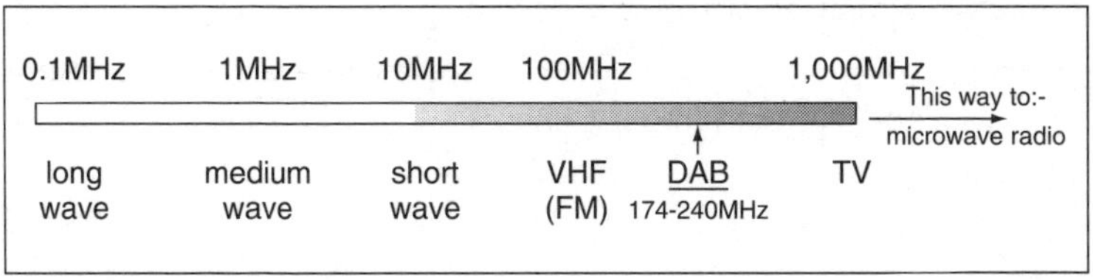

0.1MHz	1MHz	10MHz	100MHz		1,000MHz	This way to:- microwave radio
long wave	medium wave	short wave	VHF (FM)	DAB 174-240MHz	TV	

The broadcast radio spectrum showing where the new DAB services are positioned

Digital compression of sound

When an electrical audio signal is digitised, it is converted into a data stream of '1's and '0's – the binary system also used for computer data. However, the amount of data has to be reduced in order for it to fit into the allocated radio channels. This is done before transmission, without it having any significant audible effect on the received sound.

Several computational techniques are used to achieve this, but the most interesting is the one that exploits the psycho–acoustic property of our ears. If we are experiencing a loud sound at a particular frequency, our hearing will ignore (or mask) any quieter sound at a nearby frequency. Digital compression electronics makes use of this effect and discards such lower-level signals, thus reducing the amount of data that needs to be transmitted. The degree of compression can be varied but at its best the technique has little or no effect on the quality of the sound transmitted. The compression system used for DAB is called MPEG audio. Alternative but similar systems are used for mini-discs and MP3 players.

There is another technical advantage to DAB. In the past, with analogue radio, it was impossible to transmit a national radio (or television) station on one single frequency throughout the UK. This is because the different transmitters required to cover different areas would have interfered with one another if they had been on the same frequency. This resulted in very inefficient use of the radio spectrum, limiting the number of stations that could be fitted into the band, and, for car-radio listeners, the need constantly to re-tune their radios as they moved between transmitter areas.

For DAB a new modulation system called coded orthogonal frequency division multiplex (CODFM, see box below) has been developed, which allows each station or ensemble to have the same frequency throughout the UK. This means that listeners will not have to re-tune their radios or rely on complicated tuning systems such as radio data system (RDS, see below). In fact, they will no longer have to worry about tuning – they can simply select the station they want from a menu.

A single interference-free channel for the UK

By using a modulation system called coded orthogonal frequency division multiplex broadcasters are now able to broadcast national radio on a single channel throughout the UK. While analogue radio works by using a single frequency carrier within a channel to carry the programme, CODFM uses a very large number of low-data-rate carriers packed closely together in the single channel. For example, a total of 1,500 carriers can be used in the 1.536 MHz bandwidth. The lower-data-rate transmissions are less susceptible to interference, so not only does this allow a single channel to be used throughout the country (the so-called single frequency network, SFN), it also eliminates local signal reflections and cancellations which so often spoil analogue reception.

Coverage

In September 2000 DAB services were available in over 75 per cent of the UK, and by summer 2002 the coverage is expected to be as high as 85 per cent. It is not clear when coverage will approach 100 per cent. You can find out whether DAB is available in your area now or will be in the near future by contacting Digital One or BBC Reception Advice.*

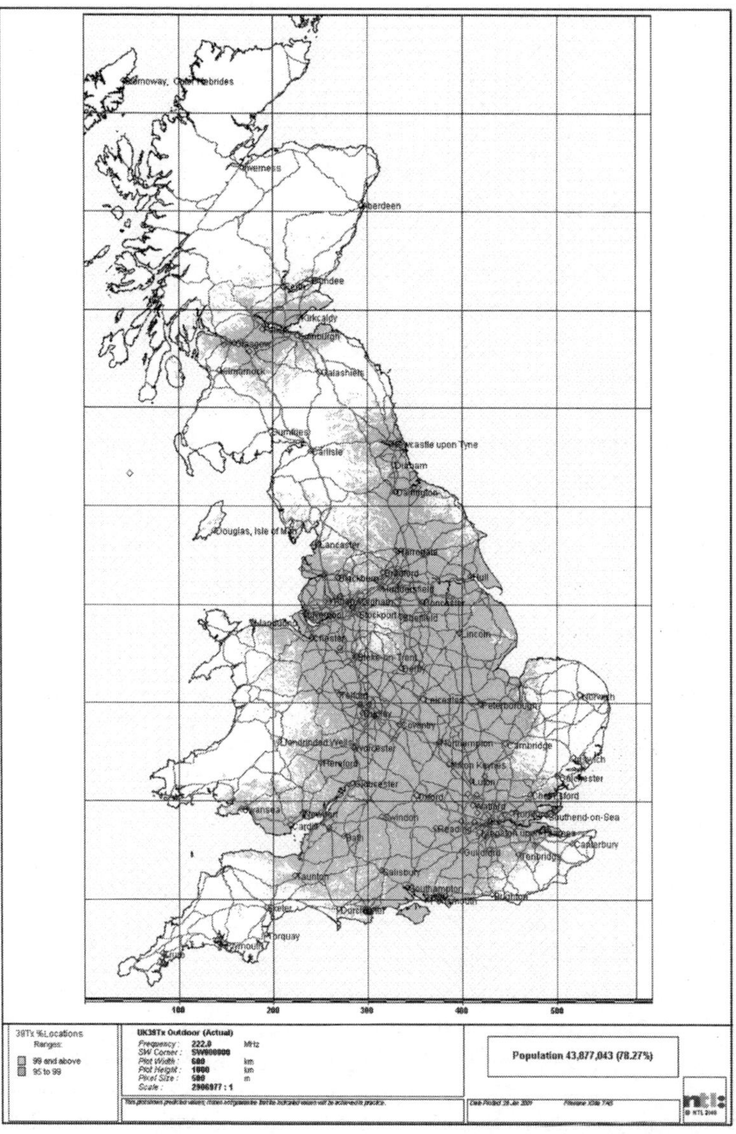

Map of UK showing coverage of digital radio reception. Map supplied by ntl and Digital One at the beginning of 2001 showing current and predicted coverage for the near future. Only the BBC's national multiplex is available in Northern Ireland.

Additional services

As well as the much increased number of radio stations, new services are available too. Many of them are similar to those seen on FM radios equipped with RDS: some can display, on the small front panel screen, the name of the station and small amounts of other text, such as details of the programme you are listening to or record titles and artist information. Also, as with RDS, while you are listening to one station, the radio can 'grab' news or local traffic information from other stations by re-tuning to them (you can select what types of bulletins you want) and then return to the original station. On DAB these services will be gradually improved.

Much more comprehensive 'data' services, now at the experimental stage, are planned for the future. On a DAB radio with a larger front panel screen than is currently available, dedicated 'data' channels could bring you news, sports, business and weather information. These would be displayed rather like a web page, in effect providing pictures and text, as well as sound, via the radio.

Radio data system (RDS)

One big problem with FM radio for motorists was the need to keep re-tuning the station while travelling, which was necessary because a national radio station on the FM band needed to transmit on different frequencies in different areas of the UK in order to avoid the various transmitters interfering with one another. A solution to this problem was developed. Called RDS, it works by transmitting inaudible digital codes along with the analogue radio signal. In an RDS-equipped radio, these codes tell the radio what frequency to tune to as the car travels from one area to another.

RDS is also used by the BBC to automatically re-tune a car radio if a local traffic bulletin is being broadcast on another BBC station and then return to the original station when the bulletin has finished. RDS also allows a limited amount of digital text to be transmitted with each station and this is used to display the station name.

The RDS system is also available on hi-fi tuners and is a useful but slightly limited feature. It works satisfactorily in cars but is sometimes complicated to set up. DAB transmissions offer similar but enhanced services and are easier to use.

Typical front-panel display on a DAB radio receiver

How do you receive digital radio?

Like all things digital, there is no one simple answer to this – you have a choice.

Stand-alone DAB hi-fi tuners

These are only just coming on the market and are expensive, costing anything between £300 and £800. They can be connected to your system of hi-fi separates in the usual way. If your hi-fi system is a single package, you may still be able to add a DAB tuner to this if the system has external input sockets (typically labelled AUX).

Some hi-fi DAB tuners are available with analogue FM tuners built in, which may be useful if your favourite local station has not moved to DAB yet.

You will also need an aerial. If you live near a transmitter (contact Digital One to find out), a piece of wire dangling down behind the tuner will be sufficient to give a perfect signal. If you live further away, you will need a special DAB aerial. Known as 'band III' aerials, they cost about £20 and should be available from any good aerial installer. The aerials are slightly taller than a TV aerial but normally have only a single vertical element, and, hence, are not very conspicuous (in areas of weaker reception they may have to have additional elements). They may work from within a loft, but

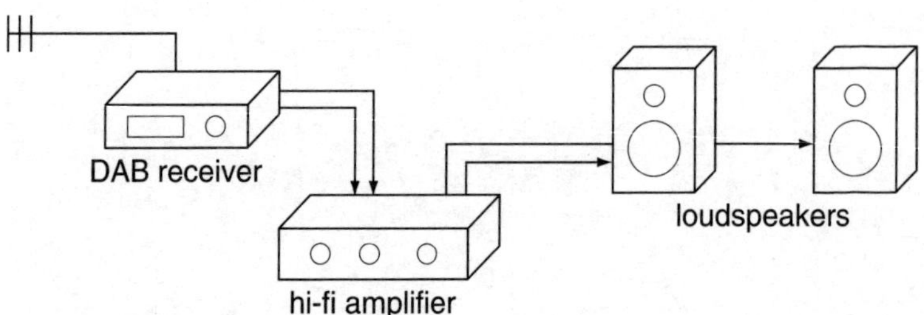

Simple DAB set-up for hi-fi listening

mounting on a roof is preferable. For details of a DAB aerial installer local to you, contact the Confederation of Aerial Installers (CAI).*

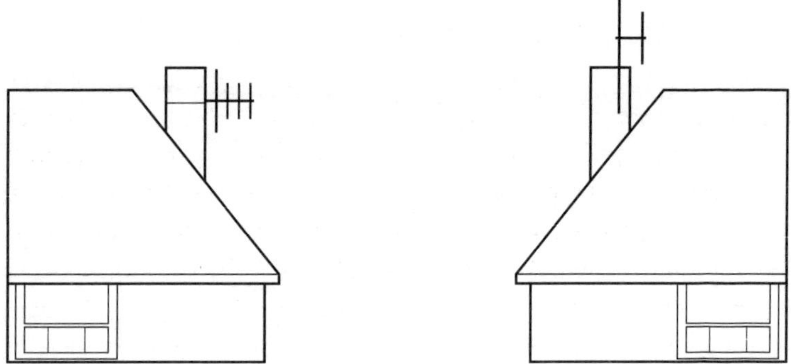

Typical band III (DAB) rooftop aerials

In-car DAB

This is where the technical benefits of DAB really come into their own. Reception in cars is clearer and the problems of signal interference and fading have been virtually eliminated, so long as you are in a designated reception area. The car DAB receivers do not have to be re-tuned to alternative frequencies as you travel across the country, and regular traffic and news services are being introduced. Many of these services are already provided in up-market car radios equipped with the RDS system, but the DAB system should be more reliable and versatile.

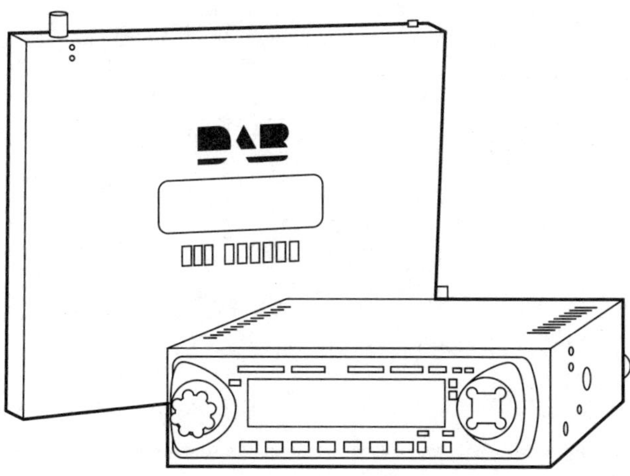

A typical DAB box and radio for the car

Current in-car DAB receivers, which are expensive, consist of two boxes. One is a conventional-looking car radio with analogue tuner and tape or CD player. The other box is the DAB receiver that has to be installed – perhaps out of sight behind the dashboard, for example. You also have to have a special aerial installed outside the car. This is smaller than a normal car aerial. However, you will probably want to keep your conventional car aerial as well because DAB coverage still does not cover the whole of the UK. In an area where there is not sufficient signal, DAB car radios will automatically switch to the equivalent analogue transmission if it is available for that station.

On your computer

Psion, a computer company best known for making personal organisers, has introduced an unusual-looking DAB receiver called the WaveFinder that plugs into any computer with a universal serial bus (USB) socket. The gadget enables people to select and listen to radio stations by clicking on icons on the screen while using the computer. The WaveFinder is also capable of receiving teletext-style pages of text information which are displayed on the computer screen along with the radio broadcasts. It is possible that this type of DAB receiver will be built into computers in the future.

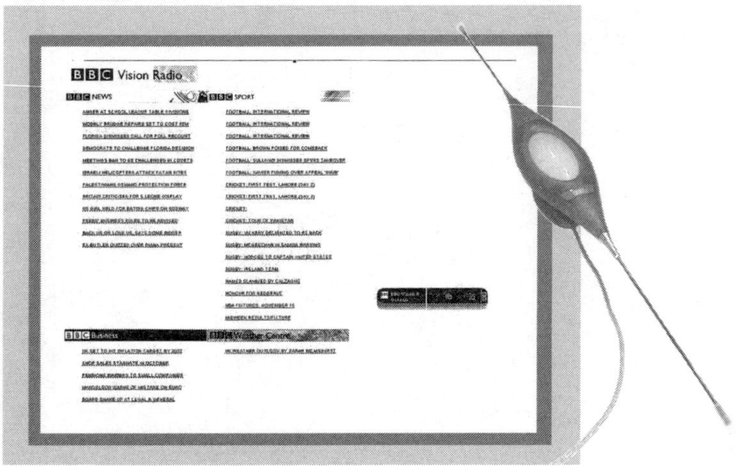

DAB text and Psion WaveFinder

DAB via satellite

If all this sounds expensive and too much trouble, there is a simpler solution. People who receive digital television from satellite already have access to many digital radio stations. These include all the BBC stations and a good many of the national commercial DAB stations. You can listen to these radio stations either through your TV loudspeaker or by connecting the Sky digital TV receiver directly to your hi-fi in a similar way to connecting a DAB tuner to your hi-fi as shown above.

Subscribers who use a Sky digital TV set-top box have a bonus: up to 44 extra subscription radio stations from a company called Music Choice. These are best described as 'themed' radio stations. Each station broadcasts just one type of music (say, jazz, pop, various genres of rock, or classical) with no announcers or advertisements – just continuous music. The title and artist of each piece of music being played is displayed on the TV screen. Subscribers to Sky digital TV get ten of these themed stations as part of the package, but they have to pay extra to subscribe to the other 34.

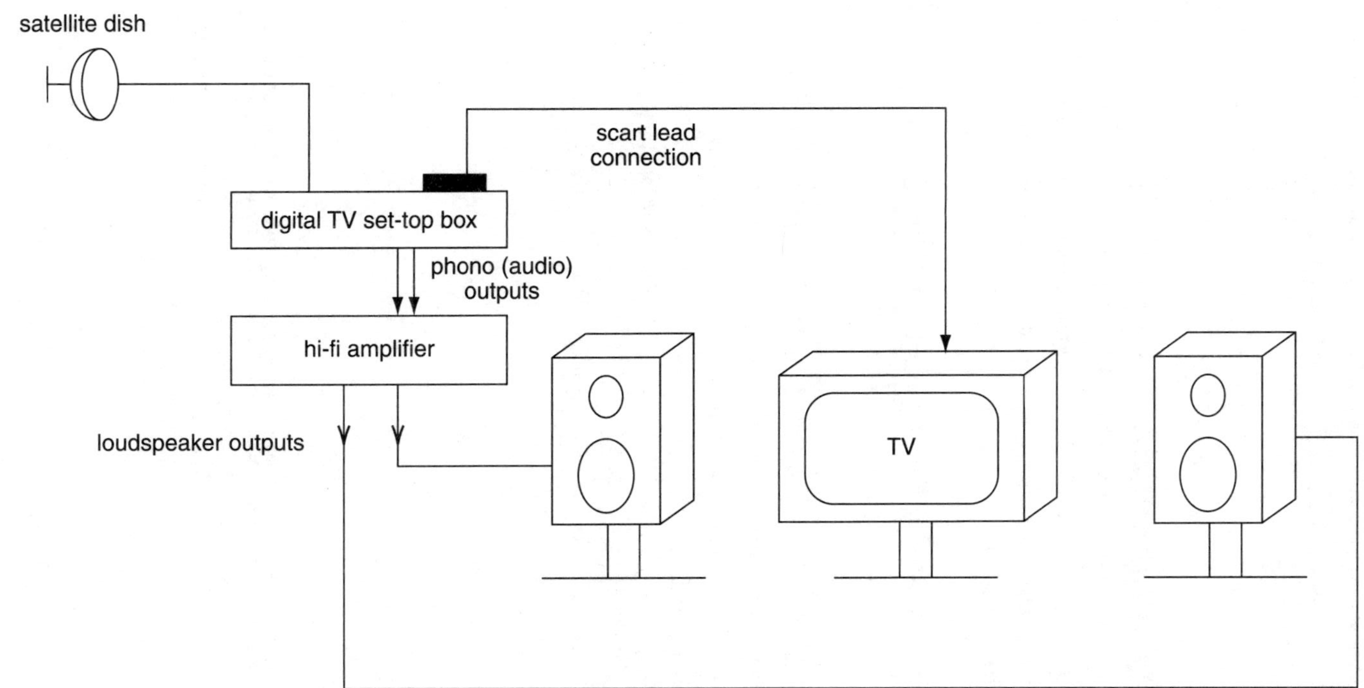

A digital receiver and dish linked to a TV and hi-fi system

You And Yours

With Liz Barclay and Anna Hill. Includes an investigation by RADIO4's Farming Today team on the government's handling of foot and mouth. Call in for free on 0800 044 044. Weather follows.

914 BBC R4 FM 12.55pm Fri 6

NOW You And Yours

Search Channel Search Favourite

Now playing on......
SYMPHONIC 11
Joyeuse Marche
Chabrier, Royal Philharmonic Orchestra

music choice

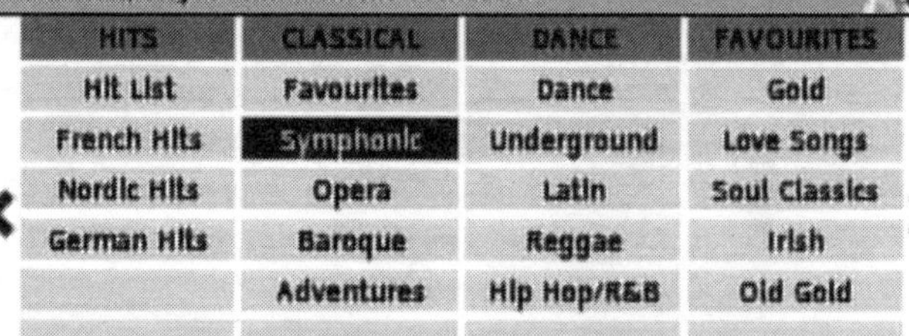

HITS
CLASSICAL
DANCE
FAVOURITES
Hit List
Favourites
Dance
Gold
French Hits
Symphonic
Underground
Love Songs
Nordic Hits
Opera
Latin
Soul Classics
German Hits
Baroque
Reggae
Irish
Adventures
Hip Hop/R&B
Old Gold

Choose channel & press SELECT

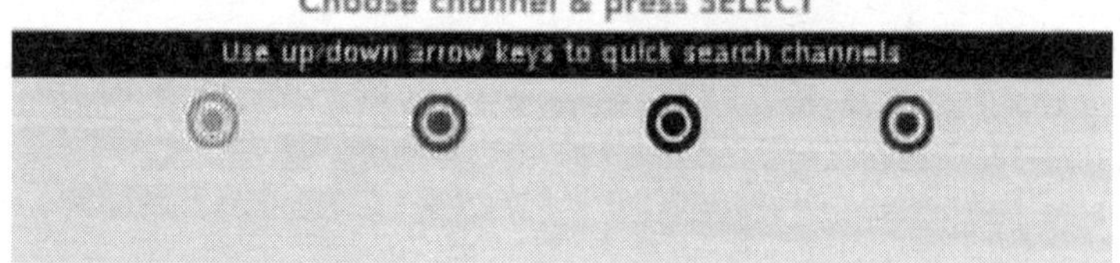

Use up/down arrow keys to quick search channels

Examples of information displayed on the TV screen from a satellite digital radio channel. Top: BBC radio; bottom: part of the Music Choice menu of themed radio channels

Sound quality

The quality of the sound from DAB receivers and Sky digital TV boxes is impressive. Hi-fi experts may argue about the differences in quality between receivers, and whether it is in fact better than the state-of-the-art analogue FM receiver. Certainly high-quality transmissions from BBC Radio 3 and Radio 4 are technically more accurate from DAB than from their analogue equivalents. However, the differences are fairly subtle.

One thing is certain: listeners to DAB do not suffer from variable reception quality. If you can pick up the signal, then you are guaranteed good quality.

For details on whom to contact to find out what you can receive on digital radio, see the address list at the back of this book.

Digital television

As will already be evident, the advent of digital radio has been something of a quiet revolution. The introduction of digital television has been quite the opposite. Broadcasters, TV equipment manufacturers and even the government have all been encouraging us to 'go digital'. In fact, we appear to have little choice in the matter: the government wants to switch off the analogue transmitters by the end of the decade. Before it does that, it has to ensure that 95 per cent of households in the UK have switched to digital.

Digital TV promises to bring us more than plain old TV programmes. It will be *interactive* and will bring together, or *converge*, other entertainment and communication activities in our homes. In the meantime, it is worth knowing how the whole package fits together and how it is being sold to us.

Who is behind the digital TV revolution?

The traditional approach to getting television programmes to our homes has been fairly fragmented. In the UK, programmes were made and transmitted by three main broadcasters, BBC, ITV companies and Channel 4. Electronics manufacturers designed and made the actual receivers, and high-street retailers sold them to the consumer. For the television picture to be available in the home, an aerial had to be fitted to the occupier's roof, by an independent aerial installer.

Today, digital TV is organised and marketed as a complete service – as a 'vertically integrated model'. The sáme individual companies still exist but they do not operate independently. For example, a broadcaster such as BSkyB* or ONdigital* will specify and commission the receiving equipment from the manufacturers, such as Pace or Amstrad, and may even supply it directly to the customer or will control how the retailer sells it. It will even be responsible for getting the aerial (or dish) installed.

Integration of this order comes with certain disadvantages. One is the limited choice it gives consumers: you cannot, for example, easily choose which 'brand' of digital TV receiver you get. Another is that certain programmes or channels may sign exclusive deals with one provider – this is a particular problem with some sporting events. Integration has the effect of slowing down the development of new ideas: for example, all Sky digital TV set-top boxes, regardless of the manufacturer or the style of the case, are near identical on the inside. An individual manufacturer cannot introduce new developments without the co-operation or permission of others. The positive side of integration for the consumer is that upgrading to digital TV is becoming cheaper. The providers of the service subsidise the cost of the receiving equipment. Indeed, they may even give it away, on condition that you sign up to the service for a specified time.

There are a number of competing digital TV service providers to choose from:

- ONdigital, which transmits services **terrestrially** and can be received via a conventional TV aerial
- BSkyB Digital, which broadcasts from a **satellite** and is received via an external dish
- Telewest and ntl, both of which offer digital TV via **cable**.

Why upgrade to digital TV?

The first thing to consider is whether you want to upgrade or not. You do not have to do anything yet. Regular, analogue terrestrial TV broadcasts will continue for many years, so although the government intends switching it off at some time in the future, there is no immediate urgency to upgrade now. Subscribers to Sky's analogue satellite services will have already made the decision to switch to digital as Sky is planning to switch off this service in the very near future. If you are not especially interested in receiving all the new channels and services offered by digital TV and do not want to pay for a subscription, it may be wise to hang on for as long as possible. This is because it is possible that low-cost digital upgrade kits will eventually be developed so you can receive the free-to-air broadcasts on your existing TV without having to pay a subscription. At present this equipment is still being developed. Another reason to wait for a while is that the next generation of digital set-top boxes or integrated TV receivers will be more versatile than the existing ones.

Upgrading to digital TV is quite simple and has the advantage of providing access to many more channels and extra services. Contrary to some early newspaper reports, there is no necessity to buy a new TV – you will be able to receive the digital service on your existing TV. The only reason you may consider buying a new set is to get a widescreen TV to obtain the full effect of the increasing number of programmes being broadcast in that format on digital TV. In this case you have the choice of getting a widescreen TV plus set-top box or an integrated widescreen TV with the digital receiver built in.

Quality or quantity?

It is a common perception that going digital leads to higher quality and more convenience. Comparing the compact disc to the vinyl LP would seem to confirm this. But, as digital electronic techniques have developed, the situation is not quite as straightforward. Going digital gives policy-makers a choice: to go for better picture or sound quality, greater quantity, or even a combination of both. The current digital TV systems in the UK and continental Europe have gone primarily for the greater quantity option. There are good economic reasons for doing this, for both the industry and the consumer. To make a significant improvement in quality using digital TV would mean switching to a system known as HDTV (high-definition TV), which in turn would necessitate a major upgrade of the broadcasters' studio equipment and their programme-making techniques. An HDTV picture is made up from 1,250 horizontal lines compared with the 625 lines on current TVs, so it would also mean that we would all have to buy expensive high-definition televisions in order to appreciate the improved quality.

What the current digital TV service gives us is a larger number of TV channels and new services with a technical quality level comparable with existing analogue services. If you are already receiving a good-quality analogue signal from your rooftop aerial, you will hardly notice any change in the quality. However, many viewers are unable to achieve the full potential of the analogue service because of local reception difficulties. In these cases, digital TV *will* provide a quality improvement.

Poor-quality digital pictures or sound

It is often said that with digital sound and video you get either a good-quality picture or nothing at all. It is true that digital pictures and sound do not *gradually* deteriorate as the signal becomes low or suffer interference in the way that analogue pictures do. So in theory grainy pictures should not occur. However, some viewers have found that digital TV reception can be poor, with the picture freezing periodically for a few seconds or breaking up into little squares. This problem, which affects digital terrestrial TV in particular, is almost always caused by a faulty aerial or aerial cable. Digital satellite TV is less likely to suffer in this way, but if it does happen it probably means that the satellite dish has got out of alignment and needs to be re-aligned. Exceptionally heavy rain could also result in poor-quality reception on satellite TV.

Limitations of the current digital TV systems

People who have already upgraded to digital TV have found a few limitations. One of the main ones is the way in which digital TV interfaces with a video-cassette recorder (VCR). The VideoPlus system that makes programming a VCR easy may no longer work or it may need some complicated setting up. The popular programme delivery control (PDC) system on most modern VCRs, which adjusts recording times to allow for programmes running late, does not work with current digital TV receivers. The automatic widescreen selection signal is not sent to the VCR. And, most inconveniently, you cannot watch one programme while recording another – something that people with analogue TVs have been able to do for years.

There is a short-term solution to most of these problems in the case of the five existing terrestrial channels. If you keep your old analogue aerial connected to your VCR, you can use PDC, VideoPlus and watch a digital channel while recording an analogue one.

Another issue that needs to be addressed is how to get digital TV on second or portable TVs in the house without having to get a second set-top box or subscription.

Future developments, such as the personal video recorder (PVR), will resolve most of these limitations (see pages 47–50).

How does digital TV work?

Technically, digital TV employs several of the latest digital techniques. First, the sound and vision electrical signal is digitised, in much the same way as a music signal is digitised for a CD. To broadcast the signal in this form would not be practical because it would require too large a chunk of the allocated frequency spectrum. So, the digitised signals are then compressed (see box), to reduce the amount of the radio spectrum required. This digitised TV signal is mixed with signals from several other TV stations and the group is transmitted in one TV channel. Such groups are called 'multiplexes'. For example, most national BBC stations are mixed together into one 'BBC' multiplex.

Widescreen television

Prior to the introduction of digital TV, Channel 4 experimented with an analogue-based widescreen system called Pal+, but it has been the change to digital TV that has been the real impetus for widescreen. There is some confusion about what widescreen TV really means. True widescreen images offer a greater area of picture left and right. They are not the normal picture stretched to fit a

Digital compression of pictures

A digitised picture is split up into a large number of tiny squares. Each of these is coded and given a number comprised of '1's and '0's which mathematically describes the colour and brightness of the square. This produces a tremendous amount of data for each frame of the TV picture. It is necessary to reduce the number of digital data bits in order to transmit the pictures in the allocated frequency band.

Computation makes it possible to discard some of these data bits before transmission without it being noticed on the received picture. One method, for example, where a group of data bits are all the same, as might happen in a picture with a patch of blue sky, is to send only the code for one pixel together with instructions of how many times it should be repeated. Another method is to reduce the number of frames transmitted. A moving TV picture is similar to a film: it comprises a sequence of 'frames', each one slightly different, to give the impression of motion. The digital compression computations are able to detect those parts of the picture which have changed in successive frames, owing to motion, and those which have not changed, because they are static. Only the changed parts of each frame need to be transmitted. What this means is that a picture containing a lot of detail and movement cannot be compressed as much as a still picture with little detail in it, so the degree of compression is constantly changing. Things can go wrong if the picture has too much detail and movement. The compression electronics can 'run out of steam' and the effects of the compression can be seen on the screen (loss of detail, jerky movement or the picture breaking up into little square blocks).

The sound is also compressed, in the way described for digital radio (see page 13). This system of compressing sound and picture is called MPEG2.

wider screen, making everyone look as if they have put on weight. Unfortunately, many people think widescreen means a stretched picture because most high-street shops, when displaying their widescreen TVs, used to do exactly this. (They either did not understand how to set up their TVs or they did not have access to proper widescreen programmes.)

True widescreen programmes are broadcast all or most of the time by a few TV stations, notably BBC Choice and BBC News 24. All the terrestrial channels broadcast widescreen if the programme was made in widescreen. Viewers with standard 4:3-sized TVs will see these widescreen programmes satisfactorily but they will miss some of the picture at each side. To minimise this effect, for some programmes the picture is made slightly narrower vertically (a 14:9 format), leaving narrow black bands at the top and bottom of the screen.

If you have a widescreen TV, it is important to make sure both it and your digital TV set-top box are set up correctly. In the set-up menu of the set-top box you should select widescreen (or 16:9) mode. On the TV too you should select the correct widescreen mode. Unfortunately no standard terminology exists for this: different TV manufacturers give it different names. To make matters worse, many widescreen TVs have an array of 'incorrect' settings, some designed to 'fill the screen' irrespective of what the broadcaster intended. So it may be a matter of experimenting to find the 'correct' setting. If set correctly, a standard (4:3 ratio) picture will not fill the screen and a true widescreen (16:9 ratio) picture will. The correct selection should happen automatically so long as you connect the equipment using scart leads.

What is a scart lead?

A scart lead is a standardised, 21-pin cable designed for connecting together separate pieces of domestic TV and video equipment. It is used throughout Europe but is rarely found in other parts of the world.

The advantage of the scart lead is that one connection system can carry all video and audio formats needed. Hence, a scart lead carries stereo sound, standard video, and high-quality RGB or 'S' video (systems in which some component colours are transmitted separately instead of being mixed into one composite signal). Additionally, it can carry special control signals to select automatically the appropriate TV input whenever you play a tape or DVD and to select the correct widescreen format.

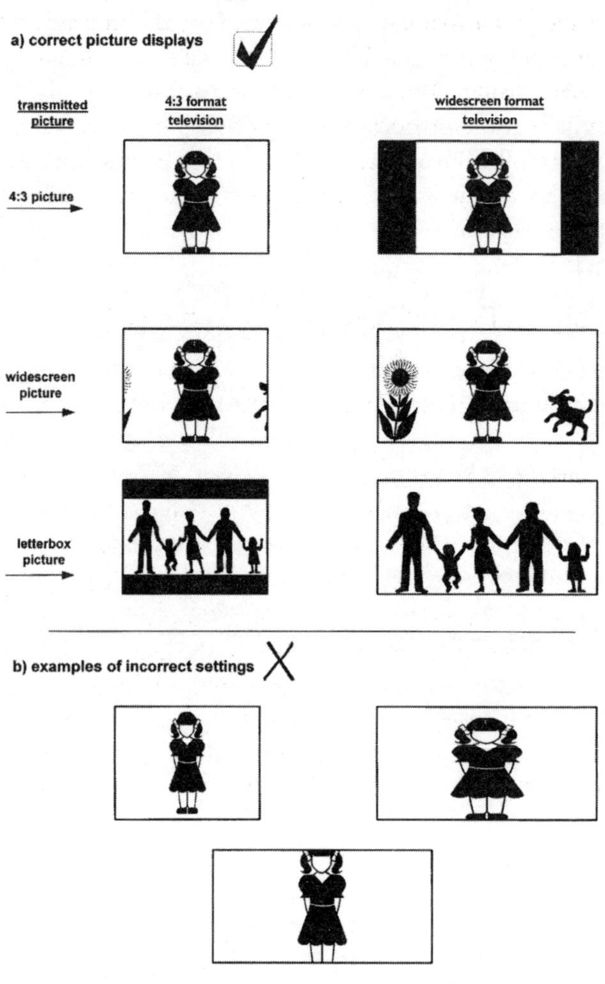

How normal and widescreen pictures should (and should not) appear on standard and widescreen TVs

Surround sound

With so many film channels available now on television, you would expect the latest surround-sound technology to be incorporated into digital TV. This is not the case. True, the sound being transmitted with digital TV is digital sound, but then so is the NICAM sound transmitted with analogue TV. Home cinema surround sound is transmitted with films, but it is the old Dolby Pro-Logic version. This is an analogue process whereby the 'centre' and 'surround' channels are blended into the normal stereo channels, to be decoded later using a Pro-Logic decoder. As this is already done by the filmmakers, the broadcasters do not have to do anything other than broadcast the normal stereo. This system works, but it is not as impressive as the digital surround systems discussed later in this chapter (see pages 56–9).

Which digital TV service should you choose?

This section looks at the three main systems that provide digital TV: satellite, terrestrial and cable. Each system has its pros and cons.

Digital satellite television (DSTV)

Digital satellite television is transmitted using a satellite system operated by a Luxembourg-based company, Société Européenne des Satellites (SES), or Astra as it is most commonly called. The satellite channels are leased by a consortium of programme and service providers including the BBC and BSkyB, but because the main subscription services and customer interfaces are handled by BSkyB the whole service is generally thought of as being operated by Sky. Subscribers to this service have access to hundreds of TV channels.

What TV channels are provided?

Forty or so channels are available free of charge. For some of the others you have to pay either a monthly subscription or a fee for each programme you watch. Most of the subscription channels are bundled into groups. You pay different subscriptions for different groups. This means you cannot pick and mix the channels you want. The broad categories of channels and bundles available are described below.

- Four of the **terrestrial channels** – BBC1, BBC2, Channel 4 and Channel 5 – are available via digital TV. These are free-to-air, which means viewers do not have to pay subscription charges. In addition to these four are some new free-to-air channels covered by the BBC's licence fee – BBC Choice (entertainment), BBC

What different digital TV services offer

Station descriptions	Satellite	Terrestrial	Cable	Comments
BBC Network*	Y#	Y#	Y	
ITV and ITV2	N#	Y#	Y	Expected on satellite in the future
Channel 4, Channel 5	Y#	Y#	Y	
Other general entertainment	20	7	17	e.g. Sky One, E4 and repeats of comedy, drama, soaps, etc.
News	5#	1#	5	
Sports	7	5	4	Terrestrial best for UEFA Champions League
Documentary	14	1	9	
Music	10	1 (MTV)	7	
Film	13	3	5/13	Most require separate subscription. Number available on cable depends on where you live
Box-office films: number of channels	82	5	50	A film can be on several channels with staggered start times
typical choice of films/evening	35	4	12	
Children's entertainment	10	2	5	Mainly cartoons. Disney on cable & satellite only
Shopping	10#	2#	4	
Adult	6	3	3	Late night. Requires separate subscription/pay-per-view
Miscellaneous & specialist**	24	1 (Money)	4	Some require special subscription
Film 4 package	Y	Y	Y	Separate subscription required. One channel only on terrestrial
Manchester United TV	Y	N	N	Separate subscription required
Racing channel	Y	N	Y	Separate subscription required
Arts channel	Y	N	Y	Separate subscription required
Radio stations	82	N	20	
Interactive shopping & services	Y	N	Y	
Dynamic teletext	Y	Y	N	
Internet access on TV	N (planned)	Y	Y	Separate modem box required*

* This includes BBC1, BBC2, BBC Choice (entertainment), BBC Knowledge (documentaries), BBC News 24, BBC Parliament (sound only on terrestrial).
** This includes community, religious and ethnic stations.
# All or most available without subscription.
Notes: Not all cable areas carry all services. Some channels broadcast for only part of the day.
Numbers are given as guides only: actual numbers may change as new stations are added.
Regional variations are available for ITV, BBC Choice, BBC Radio 4 and S4C. Check with supplier for availability in your area.

Knowledge (documentaries), BBC News 24 and BBC Parliament. Note that none of the ITV channels is currently available via satellite, but this is likely to change during 2001.

- **Additional free-to-air stations** These are not covered by the licence fee but viewers do not have to pay any subscription charges. They include news and information services from the likes of ITN and CNN, shopping channels such as QVC, specialist, religious and ethnic services. There are approximately 20 such channels.
- **Basic subscription channels** You can elect to subscribe to all or part of the basic group of channels. These include: 20 entertainment channels showing a mix of old programmes from the BBC, commercial channels and American TV, plus some original programming and studio chat shows; 5 news and sports channels; 11 factual and documentary channels; 8 children's channels (mainly cartoons); and 8 popular music channels. New channels are added from time to time.
- **Premium channels** For an additional monthly subscription you can add some or all of the following to your basic package: 12 film channels (a range of popular films which are repeated regularly throughout the month) and 3 sports channels showing major sporting events.
- **Stand-alone subscription channels** Some broadcasters prefer you to subscribe to their channels separately, not as part of a Sky package. These include three Film 4 (independent films) channels; Disney Channel; MUTV (a channel dedicated to Manchester United football team); a small number of ethnic Asian channels; and a small number of 'adult' channels.
- **Pay-per-view (box office) channels** These are film channels that you do not have to subscribe to. Instead, you select a film from the electronic programme guide (see below), and book it in advance. You will be charged between £1.50 and £3 per movie. For this technique to work your digital TV receiver needs to be connected to your telephone line so that you can be billed automatically. Over 70 pay-per-view film channels are available, each showing a certain film several times a day. Furthermore, many films are shown on more than one of these channels, so you can catch the start of the film every 15 minutes, for example.

What other services are provided?

- **Electronic programme guide** Known as EPG, this gives the full schedule of the channels several days in advance, including a programme synopsis. In the future, the EPG could become more interactive, enabling viewers to select in advance programmes for recording.
- **Interactive programmes** DSTV occasionally broadcasts programmes that allow the viewer to 'interact' with the programme. For example, for some sporting events you are given the option of selecting different camera angles, asking for action replays or calling up instant statistics. If the digital TV receiver is connected to a telephone, it is possible to use this link, together with your remote control, to take part in quiz shows, for example, by registering your vote or answer (usually from a multiple choice list) or even requesting a music video.
- **Shopping** DSTV also offers an interactive shopping and information service called OPEN (see Chapter 3).
- **Teletext** DSTV carries the conventional teletext service that viewers are familiar with from analogue TV. This system is very popular but it does have limitations. The quality of pictures is very limited. Moreover, the data has to be split across many pages and you cannot scroll down pages as you can on a computer, so finding the page you want can be quite time-consuming. However, a new digital teletext type service is being introduced (see box below). On the digital satellite service this is provided by the BBC and BSkyB in two ways: as a general teletext service for all Sky channels and as an added extra to the Sky News channel, which provides a text news service plus some small-screen video clips of earlier news items.
- **Radio stations** A wide selection of national radio stations and 'themed' radio stations is available.
- **Email** Electronic mail is also available – see Chapter 4. The phone charges for using the email service is the local telephone call rate plus 1p per minute, which is a little more than for the other systems.

Digital teletext

Teletext on digital TV has superior presentation to that of teletext on analogue TV. The pages incorporate good-quality pictures, photographs, and sound and video clips, and, more importantly, you can scroll down pages on the screen.

The new teletext services on digital TV are often referred to as 'digital teletext'. This is a convenient way of distinguishing it from the original teletext service but it would be wrong to assume that the original service was an analogue one. In fact, the original teletext service was arguably one of the first digital services to be introduced to the home – long before the compact disc, which is often thought of as the first digital product for consumers. The characters and graphics on the screen were created digitally. Like NICAM stereo TV sound, it was a digital system that was 'piggybacked' on to an analogue service.

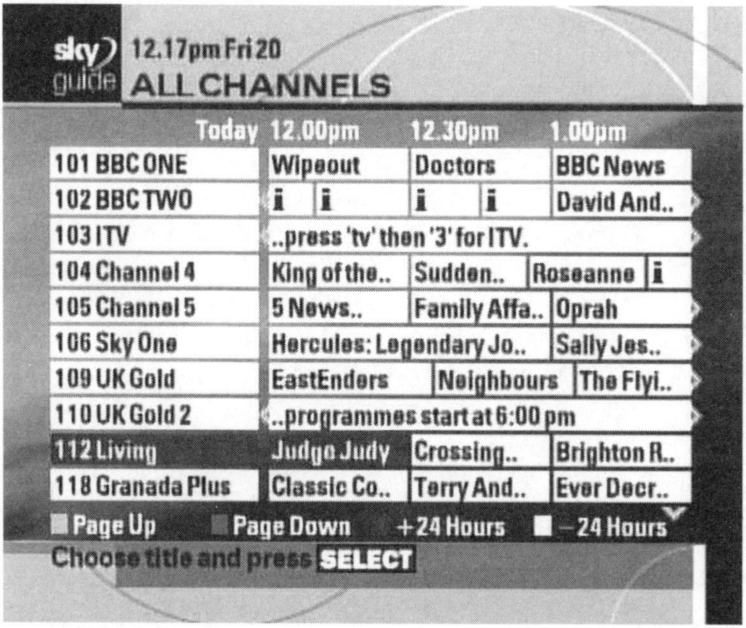

sky guide 12.17pm Fri 20
ALL CHANNELS
Today 12.00pm 12.30pm 1.00pm
101 BBC ONE | Wipeout | Doctors | BBC News
102 BBC TWO | David And..
103 ITV | ..press 'tv' then '3' for ITV.
104 Channel 4 | King of the.. | Sudden.. | Roseanne
105 Channel 5 | 5 News.. | Family Affa.. | Oprah
106 Sky One | Hercules: Legendary Jo.. | Sally Jes..
109 UK Gold | EastEnders | Neighbours | The Flyi..
110 UK Gold 2 | ..programmes start at 6:00 pm
112 Living | Judge Judy | Crossing.. | Brighton R..
118 Granada Plus | Classic Co.. | Terry And.. | Ever Decr..
Page Up Page Down +24 Hours –24 Hours
Choose title and press SELECT

Sky Digital's on-screen EPG. Viewers can scroll ahead to view the programme schedule for several days and down for more channels

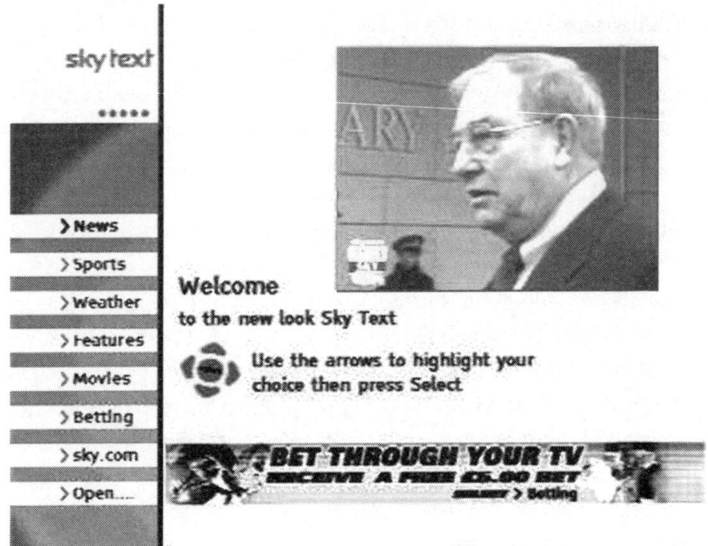

Digital teletext

How do you subscribe?

You can subscribe to DSTV by phoning BSkyB, or by visiting a local high-street retailer. You will not be given a set-top box straight away: an engineer will deliver and install it a few days (or weeks) later. This generally means that you have no choice about which brand of set-top box you get. In theory this should not matter, because all the boxes are built to the same specification. However, some brands improve the performance of their boxes before others do: for example, some boxes have a faster-responding EPG than others, which is an advantage.

You have to pay an installation fee of about £40 for digital satellite television, which includes the fitting of the satellite dish, and sign a direct debit form to pay for the subscription cost of the TV package you choose. Interestingly, you do not have to pay anything for the box itself. This is true even if you do not subscribe to any TV services. You can elect to have only the free-to-air channels, and still get the box so long as you sign a contract with the interactive shopping service OPEN. With this option, you will have to pay about

£100 for the installation and you may have to convince the retailer that this is what you want to do.

If you elect to subscribe to Sky channels, you will be sent a smart card to put into your set-top box. This will identify you and what bundles of programmes you are entitled to. You will not be able to use this card in any other box. If you opt for the free-to-air channels only, you will have to request a free-to-air card by phoning Sky Digital. The card will be sent to you within a few days at no charge.

How is the system connected up?

The installers should make all the necessary connections for you. The diagram below shows a typical arrangement if your TV and VCR have scart sockets.

The normal TV aerial is retained in order that you can receive ITV channels (not yet available on satellite) and so that you can record terrestrial analogue channels on your VCR while watching a different programme on digital satellite.

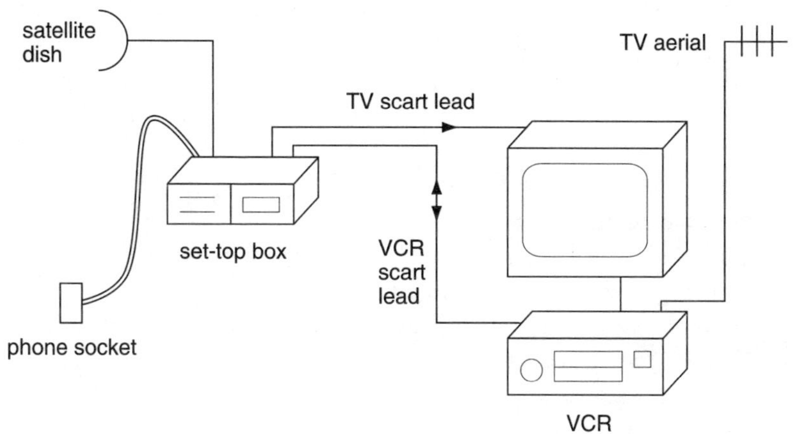

Set-up for digital satellite systems

Composite video and RGB

On analogue TV the electrical signal that carries the picture information is a bit of a compromise. It has to mix the monochrome and colour information into one signal – a 'composite video' signal. This was done so that it would be compatible with both colour and black-and-white TVs. The side effects of this process are a very slight loss of fine detail in the picture and the strange phenomenon known as 'cross colour', which is better known as the rainbow effect you see when, for example, a newsreader wears a striped shirt.

Digital TV systems do not have this problem as the broadcast signal keeps the colour signals separate. This signal is called an RGB (Red Green Blue) and produces better clarity of colour.

The scart lead can carry both the composite video and the RGB signal. The TV should automatically select the better RGB signal but some TVs may require you to configure this manually.

It is necessary to connect the set-top box to your telephone line so that you can take advantage of the shopping services from OPEN and automatically order 'box office' films and other special events.

Digital terrestrial television (DTTV)

Who operates the service?

The DTTV service is operated by a company called ONdigital, which is responsible for subscriptions and transmitting programmes. Several different broadcasters, including the BBC, ITV and Sky, provide the programmes.

Who can receive it?

Unlike satellite TV, a terrestrial service cannot cover the whole of the UK in one go: it needs to build up a network of transmitters. However, the fact that digital terrestrial channels use the same frequencies as analogue TV channels has helped somewhat. The main difficulty is making sure that the new low-power digital transmitters and the higher-power analogue ones do not interfere with one another. DTTV is being built up gradually, so you may find that you are not yet within the service area. To find out if you are, contact ONdigital with your postcode. At the beginning of 2001, DTTV covered about 75 per cent of the UK population, but it will be several years before the target of 94 to 99 per cent coverage is reached.

What TV channels are provided?

DTTV has had to squeeze its channels into the already crowded conventional TV broadcast bands. This means that it currently has less space (bandwidth) than the two other services, cable and satellite. Nevertheless, DTTV is a more efficient system than conventional analogue TV. In the space occupied by one analogue TV channel the system can fit five or six digital channels of comparable quality. Moreover, the transmitter power required is a fraction of that required for equivalent analogue coverage.

ONdigital offers the following TV channels:

- All the **terrestrial channels** – BBC1, BBC2, ITV (regional), Channel 4, S4C and Channel 5 – are available via digital TV. These are free-to-air, which means no subscription charges have to be paid. In addition to these are some new free-to-air channels – BBC Choice (entertainment), BBC Knowledge (documentaries), BBC News 24 and BBC Parliament (sound only), ITV2 and a limited service from ITN (news).
- **Basic subscription channels** There are about 18 basic subscription channels to choose from. You can elect to subscribe to all or part of the basic group of channels. These are mainly general entertainment channels such as Sky One and E4.
- **Premium channels** For an additional monthly subscription you can add some or all of two film and three sports channels to your basic package.
- **Stand-alone subscription channels** Some broadcasters prefer you to subscribe to their channels separately, not as part of an ONdigital package. These include Film 4 (independent films) and a couple of 'adult' channels.
- **Pay-per-view (box office) channels** These are film channels that you do not have to subscribe to. Instead, you select a film from a menu, and book it in advance. You will be charged about £3 per movie. For this to work your digital TV receiver needs to be connected to your telephone line so that you can be billed

automatically. There are five pay-per-view film channels, each showing a certain film several times a day. Some showings are in widescreen format.

What other services are available?

- **Digital teletext** The dedicated teletext channels are: BBC Text, Teletext, ONview and Channel 4 Text. These teletext services also have programme guides, but they are not as comprehensive as the satellite or cable EPGs and cover only a 24-hour period. BBC Knowledge provides its own text service that gives background details and contacts to do with programmes being broadcast on that channel.
- **Games** Two channels are dedicated to arcade-style interactive games.
- **Email** An email service, called ONmail, is provided as a part of the ONdigital package.
- **Internet access** A full Internet access service, called ONnet, is available as an optional extra. This needs a special add-on modem and an extra monthly subscription. This service is discussed in more detail in Chapter 4. An enhanced email package, ONmail+, is provided as a part of this Internet service.

How do you subscribe?

You can take out a subscription to ONdigital at most high-street electrical stores. You will be given a set-top box to take home straight away. Once connected up and tuned in you should get all the free-to-air services. A phone call is needed to get your chosen subscription channels working.

Alternatively, for about £80 you can opt for the pre-paid option and get a set-top box plus one year's subscription to six of the basic channels. You do not need to set up any subscription unless you want to add extra channels.

Interestingly enough, while a digital satellite set-top box belongs to you, a digital terrestrial set-top box remains the property of ONdigital, and, in theory, you have to return it to the company if you stop subscribing or do not extend the pre-paid subscription after the year.

How do you connect up the system?

Unlike digital satellite, you will probably have to connect up the system yourself, but it is quite straightforward. The diagram below shows a typical arrangement if your TV and VCR have scart sockets.

ONdigital promotions claim that DTTV can be received using a conventional TV aerial. However, the chances are that your existing aerial will not be good enough and you will have to have a new, wideband aerial fitted. If this proves to be the case, ONdigital will fit one for free.

> **TV aerials**
>
> Conventional TV aerials are divided into groups known as A, B, C/D and W. Each group is designed to pick up TV signals in only one part of the TV broadcast band to reject signals outside its band. This is done to reduce the effects of interference from neighbouring transmitters. Digital TV does not suffer from this type of interference. In order to fit all the new digital TV multiplexes into the TV band without clashing with the existing analogue service, in some parts of the UK broadcasters have had to make use of the whole band, not just frequencies in the local group. This means that an aerial will reject some of these multiplexes. In order to get all the digital channels it is necessary to fit a wider-band aerial, which covers two or more groups.

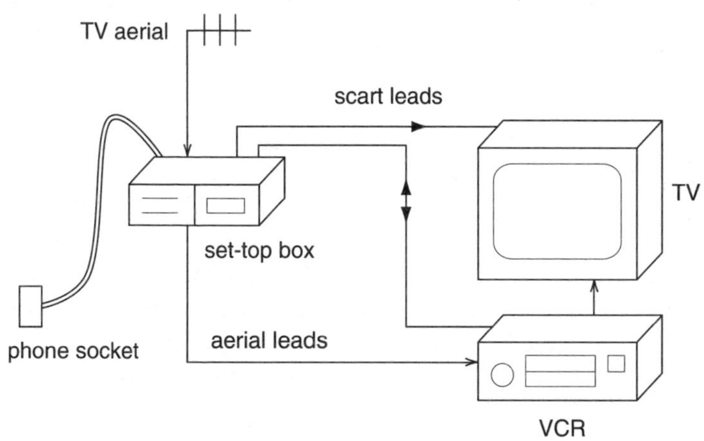

Set-up for digital terrestrial systems

Digital cable television (DCTV)

Cable TV started rolling out a digital TV service only at the beginning of 2000, so it has a bit of catching up to do. Digital cable has the potential for greatest capacity (bandwidth) and so could fit in more channels without loss of quality. Moreover, cable is a two-way system so the same connection can be used for telephones and high-speed Internet access as well as interactive TV services.

Digital cable does not cover the whole of the UK, and is generally restricted to built-up areas. To find out whether you have a local cable, phone the ITC* or contact a cable company direct (see address list at the back of the book).

Who operates the service?

There are two main digital cable operators in the UK which are gradually upgrading their systems for digital: ntl and Telewest. These two companies have taken over most of the smaller cable operators.

What TV channels are provided?

The TV channels offered may vary between cable companies, but the range is broadly similar to – and slightly smaller than – that from satellite TV. A typical listing from Telewest, taken at the end of 2000, comprised the following channels.

- All the **terrestrial channels** – BBC1, BBC2, ITV (several regions), Channel 4 and Channel 5 – plus the new free-to-air channels: BBC Choice (entertainment), BBC Knowledge (documentaries), BBC News 24, BBC Parliament, ITN and ITV2. Although these are free-to-air channels you still have to pay a monthly fee to receive them via a cable box.
- **Basic subscription channels** You can elect to subscribe to all or part of the basic group of 55 channels. As in the case of satellite TV, these include a mix of general entertainment, music, documentary and children's channels.
- **Premium channels** For an additional monthly subscription you can add up to four sports channels and between four and eleven film channels. The actual number you can choose from varies, depending on where you live and what cable company you have access to.

- **Pay-per-view (box office) films** These are film channels that you do not have to subscribe to. Instead, you select a film from the electronic programme guide and book it. You will be charged about £3 per movie. You have the equivalent of 50 channels for this, typically offering a choice of 12 different films starting at staggered times.
- **Other channels** These include a couple of ethnic channels, three 'adult' channels and a 'local information' channel – something the other systems do not offer.

What other services are available?

Initially, not all of the following services were available to all digital cable customers, but they are gradually being introduced.

- **Electronic programme guide** This offers a full schedule of programmes, including synopses. At present, where this service is available, it is limited to 24 hours' worth of information, but it could expand to cover several days in the future.
- **Shopping** Digital cable TV also offers an interactive shopping and information service. Compared to the satellite equivalent, this service is a little easier to use and has more shops to choose from. This is covered in more detail in Chapter 3.
- **Teletext** Teletext does not appear to be a priority with the cable companies and even the provision of the old-style teletext service is patchy. Teletext-style information pages are provided in the interactive shopping area but they do not appear to be as versatile as the newer-style 'digital' teletext on terrestrial and satellite.
- **Telephone** Cable companies can supply you with a phone line as part of the package you sign up for, so it may save money to use their telephone service.
- **Email** A free email system is available from both cable companies.
- **Radio stations** A selection of about 20 local and national stations, including BBC stations, is usually available.

Buying guide for digital television

Which of these three systems, digital satellite TV, digital terrestrial TV or digital cable TV, is best for you? Your choice may be limited by where you live because digital terrestrial and digital cable do not cover the whole of the UK, but digital satellite reaches just about everywhere. In practice it may be difficult in some areas to obtain permission to install a satellite dish but because the DSTV dishes are now smaller and neater than they used to be this is becoming less of an issue. It is worth noting that dishes do not always have to be fixed unattractively to the front of your house. They can often be located more discreetly – on the roof, for example – so long as they have a clear line of sight in a southerly direction. Unfortunately, dish installers will not necessarily do this automatically; you will have to request it.

Free-to-air packages

If you want to go digital but do not want all the hassle of subscription channels, it is possible to go for a free-to-air package (see above). The most advantageous free-to-air option is from BSkyB because it will give you a set-top box and dish for free, even if you do not subscribe to any Sky channels. All you have to pay is £100 to have the dish fitted. You will have to sign a contract with its shopping service OPEN saying you will connect the box up to your telephone, but there is no commitment to use the service or buy anything. The only drawback of this option is that (at the time of going to press) you cannot get ITV or ITV2 from satellite, but you can still get ITV from your old analogue aerial until this issue is resolved. You will also get a number of other free-to-air channels such as CNN, ITN, Sky News, a classic movies channel (TCM), various shopping channels and some other specialist channels. Alternatively, you can get a free-to-air option using a digital terrestrial box, but this is expensive as you have to buy the box outright, at a price of at least £300.

Subscription channels

If you want the largest choice of channels available, digital satellite is the best bet, although cable is not far behind.

If you want digital TV but prefer a more modest selection of subscription channels, ONdigital offers a quite straightforward entry into digital TV. You may have to have your TV aerial upgraded, but this should be done free of charge.

If you want to play with interactive TV services and use online TV shopping, digital satellite or digital cable are the ones to go for. If you live in a digital cable area, this is the best option, as these services are convenient and versatile to use. Digital terrestrial TV does not provide this type of interactive service, but it does offer Internet access on your TV as an optional extra, so if you do not have a home computer, you could consider it.

Set-top box or integrated TV?

So far this chapter has looked only at set-top boxes as the means of receiving digital TV. However, widescreen televisions with a digital TV decoder built in are now available. Buying such a TV certainly offers a neater solution, and minimises the number of external cables and setting-up procedures, but it has some drawbacks.

First, there is a limited number of TVs to choose from, and most of them can receive only digital terrestrial; none of them has a built-in receiver for digital cable. Second, the digital receiver built into these models may not be the latest version and in some cases upgrading it can be difficult. If in the future you want to change from DTTV to DSTV, or you wanted the latest technology such as built-in PVR (see below), you would still have to get a set-top box. Once the digital TV market has stabilised, an integrated TV will be an attractive proposition, but in the meantime a set-top box offers more versatility.

New developments

Two important new developments will solve most of the limitations of digital TV highlighted earlier (see pages 26–7).

The quad LNB satellite dish

Digital satellite broadcasters have developed a four-channel receiver, which uses a 'quad LNB' satellite dish and gives four separate satellite feeds into a house. The LNB (low noise block) is the part of the dish that sits at the end of the protruding arm which picks up the signal that is bounced off the dish.

The four-channel feed allows digital TV to be distributed throughout the house and be tuned to different channels simultaneously. For example, one channel could feed the main TV, another a VCR or other video-recording device, a third a TV in the bedroom or kitchen, and a fourth connected to a computer for Internet access via satellite. Broadcasters could well fit these new dishes as a matter of course to new subscribers, even if the latter do not fully utilise them at first, as it is cheaper than re-visiting the house later to put up a new dish.

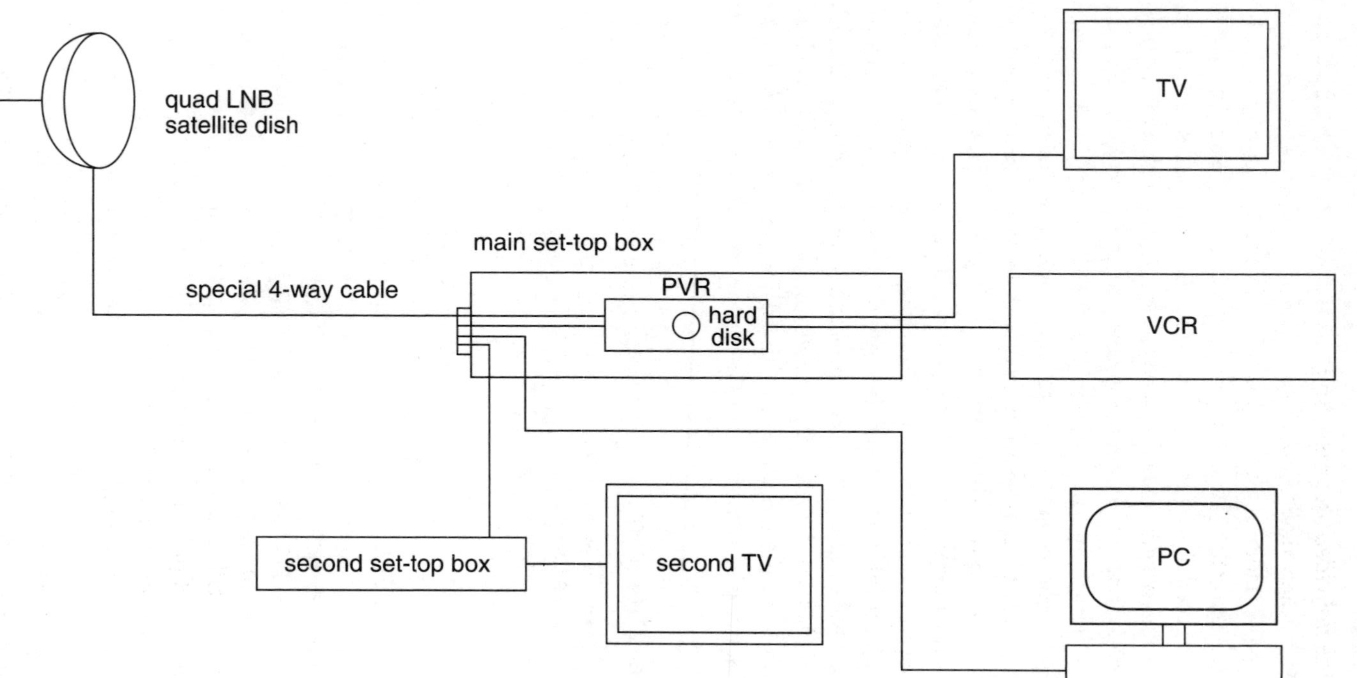

Schematic diagram of the quad LNB system

The personal video recorder (PVR)

The second new development is the PVR, a strong contender for replacing the traditional VCR. The PVR is simply a computer hard-disk drive adapted for recording video. The disk cannot be removed from the recorder, so it is no good for playing pre-recorded films or for recording programmes for keeping. It is very much a temporary recording system. However, it has three unique features.

- A PVR is constantly in 'record' mode, storing the previous half-hour of the programme you are watching live. This means that so long as your set-top box is tuned to the TV channel you want, you do not have to watch the programme until you are ready. You could go and make a cup of tea and come back ten minutes later to see the start of the programme. This also means that, while you are watching the programme, you can skip boring bits or adverts until you catch up with the live broadcast. Similarly, if the phone rings while you are watching a programme, you do not have to miss any of the programme (or hurriedly look for a blank bit of tape) – all you have to do is hit the 'pause' button. When you return you can continue where you left off, while the PVR continues recording ahead to the end of the programme.
- A PVR links to an electronic programme guide which it receives either off-air (e.g. from a digital satellite TV service) or by downloading it via the telephone line. This guide has details of programmes on all channels for at least one week ahead. You can programme the PVR to record the programmes that you want by selecting them using the on-screen EPG. This means that if there are any changes in the programme schedule the PVR will still catch it. You can also instruct it to record all episodes of a series of programmes and it will do this automatically, irrespective of any changes in day or time of transmission.
- The most talked-about feature of a PVR is that you can 'tell' it what type of programmes you like and do not like, and after you have programmed it a few times it 'learns' your preferences. This way it can 'recommend' programmes to you and can predict what you want and will record a programme it spots on the schedule that you may have missed. If all this sounds a bit like 'Big Brother', you will be relieved to know that you still have full

control of the system and that the broadcasters guarantee that none of what the PVR has learnt about you is passed back to them.

In the UK the first PVR box was launched at the end of 2000 under the brand name TiVo.* It consists of a fairly large box that connects to a TV and set-top box. Costing about £400, it is very similar to models available in the USA. TiVo downloads via the telephone the EPG it requires to be able to do its timer recordings, for which you pay either a subscription of £10 per month or a one-off payment of £200. The TiVo boxes are manufactured by Thompson and marketed by Sky, and the regular programme guides are supplied by TiVo.

The TiVo box works with analogue TV, digital terrestrial TV and digital satellite TV.

You can select the level of picture quality you want. Four levels are available on a TiVo box: at the best quality you get about 12 hours' worth of recording, and at the lowest quality (suitable for 'talking heads' types of programme, where there is not much movement) you get 40 hours. As you can mix recording qualities, you can end up with something between these two values. In the (unlikely) event of your filling up the disk, TiVo will delete the 'low-priority' recordings, including those it had suggested itself.

Tests done on TiVo for *Which?* magazine indicate that its ability to record all episodes of a series is impressive. Its intelligent 'learning' capability takes some time to settle in, and so although it does come up with some good recommendations of programmes to record, some of its choices are rather strange. TiVo's success in this respect depends on the ability of the programme suppliers to 'tag' their programmes with useful descriptors. Simply calling a show a 'comedy' or a 'documentary' does not give TiVo much to go on. The tests found that if TiVo was used by several members of a family with different tastes in programmes, it tended to concentrate on one or two of them and ignore the others. Being more selective in the types of programmes they watched resulted in a better performance from TiVo.

The main problems with some early TiVos were that they suffered occasional jerky pictures and sound, and often lost the end of a programme that was running late. These issues are being

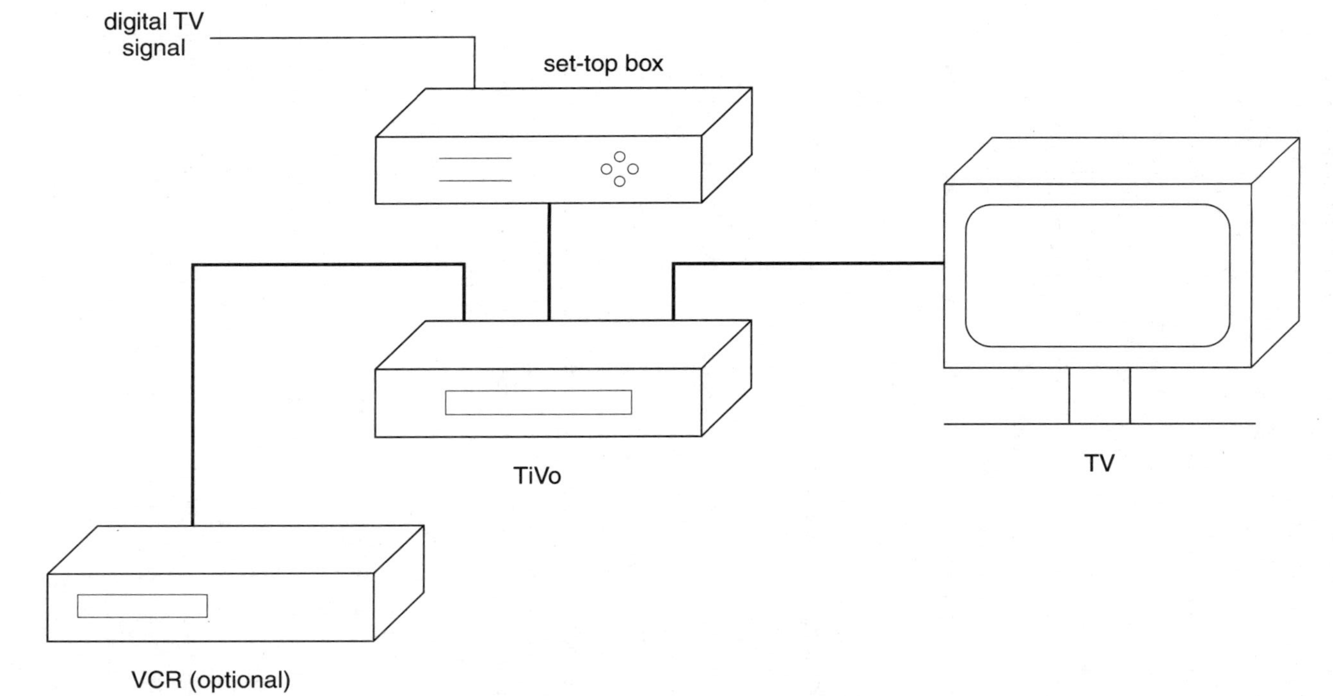

How a TiVo box is connected to your digital TV system

addressed, and it is likely that newer models of TiVo and built-in PVRs will be better still.

To some extent, the TiVo box is a bit of a stop-gap device as it has a couple of drawbacks: it is bulky, and it needs to get its EPG from the telephone line at extra cost. Technically, too, it has some limitations: its video input and output signals are in analogue form, although it is debatable whether this significantly affects picture quality.

The newer PVR devices will be built into set-top boxes, initially suitable only for digital satellite TV. These will be 'all digital' systems and use BSkyB's broadcast EPG. They will also make use of the four-channel capability of the new set-top boxes and record one channel while you are watching another.

Products for people with visual and hearing impairments

New products are being developed to help people with a visual impairment or hearing difficulties get more out of digital TV. If you already have a digital TV set-top box or integrated TV you may have noticed an unused connector or slot at the back. This is designed to take plug-in modules, such as an audio description module. As well as relaying normal TV sound, the audio description module gives a description of the scene being shown to help visually impaired people to picture the image. This can be heard either through headphones so that it does not disturb other viewers, or it can be connected to a hi-fi system. The system relies on the broadcaster supplying the extra audio information. This technology could also be used for other interesting applications such as dual-language TV, so different viewers could watch the same programme in different languages.

Another product being developed is a module that will supply signing for the hard of hearing. This would mean the superimposition of a small video picture of a person signing on the screen. Automatic signing, with a virtual person doing the signing, is also likely to be developed.

Home hi-fi and video

The introduction of digital audio compact discs in 1982 was a significant development. CDs caught on very quickly, not just because of the better sound quality they offered but also because of their ruggedness and convenience of use. Moreover, they were made to a universal standard.

Surprisingly, for the next ten years or so there were few new digital innovations for the home and those that were introduced failed to catch on. In the mid-1980s Sony and some other VCR manufacturers introduced PCM digital audio recording using specially adapted VCRs and later in that decade a small digital tape recorder called DAT. Although these developments were intended for domestic use, they were successful only in the professional field. In the late 1990s, Philips introduced the digital compact cassette recorder (DCC) that could record on cassette tapes that were mechanically the same shape as the conventional analogue cassette. DCC machines could therefore handle analogue and digital cassettes, but despite that they failed to catch on. The reasons these products were not successful was their high price and the fact that they suffered from the disadvantages of magnetic tape.

Since the late 1990s, however, there has been a torrent of new digital playback and recording systems for video as well as audio.

This next section covers all the digital audio and video developments that became available in the late 1990s and the early 2000s, including digital versatile disc (DVD) and digital video recorders, and audio systems such as MP3 and Dolby AC3.

One thing is certain: these digital systems can no longer be treated as separate entities. For the true 'digital home' in the future, the hi-fi system, the TV, the video recorder and even the computer system will 'converge' – become interconnected.

DVD players

A DVD player is used primarily for playing back full-length feature films on the television. It offers higher quality than videocassettes and is more convenient and versatile. A DVD player looks just like a standard CD player, except for the scart sockets at the back, and you can quite easily play standard audio CDs on it as well as DVDs. The diagram on page 52 shows a typical set-up of a DVD player and TV.

Most new home computers come with DVD players fitted. These players are primarily intended for playing DVD-ROMS containing games or other software rather than films. However, with the right MPEG digital decoder plug-in card or MPEG decoder software, such as WinDVD, it is possible to watch DVD films on a computer monitor.

As with digital TV, the best picture quality from a DVD player is obtained by connecting it with a scart lead and configuring the TV input for RGB or 'S'. The TV may select this automatically. If connected correctly the TV will automatically select DVD when a disc is inserted. As with digital TV you also need to tell the DVD player what type of TV you have – standard 4:3 or widescreen 16:9. An on-screen set-up menu for the DVD player is available where you can select this. If you used a scart lead for the connection, the correct screen setting will be selected for the film automatically.

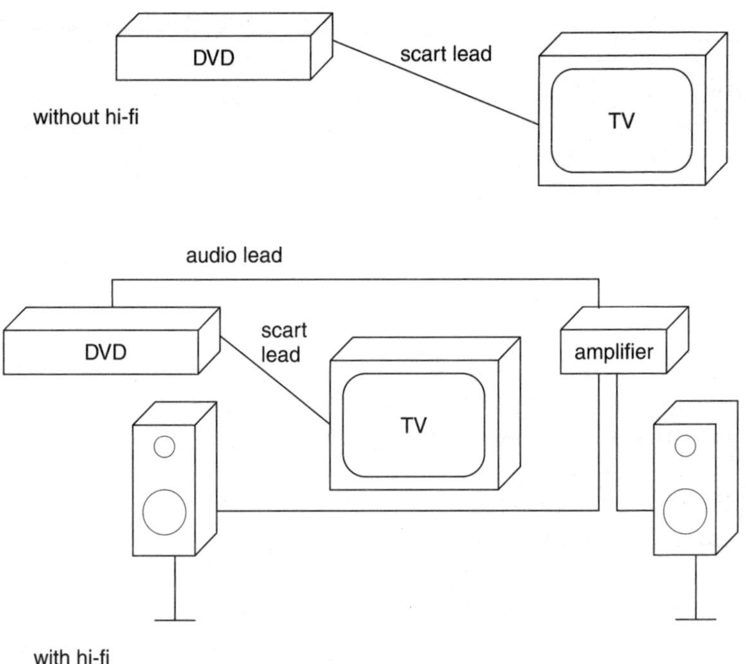

Two typical arrangements for connecting up a DVD player

Widescreen confusion

For the TV industry, the 4:3 ratio screen is standard and 16:9 ratio is widescreen. For the film industry 16:9 (approximately) is standard, and widescreen can mean ratios of anything from 2:1 to 2.35:1. When you buy a DVD film you have to look at the back of the box to see what ratio has been used to transfer the film to DVD. In the USA it is common to find DVD films available to match both 4:3 and 16:9 TVs but so far in the UK they are either one or the other.

If the film has been transferred as standard 4:3 it will look good on a standard TV but with some picture loss at the sides; it will not, however, fill a widescreen TV.

If the film has been transferred as 16:9 it will look good on a widescreen TV and fill the screen, but it will most likely be letterbox shape (black bands top and bottom) on a standard TV.

If the film was made in one of the *cinema*'s widescreen formats and transferred in this form to DVD (this pleases the purists), it will not even fill a widescreen TV and will have black bands top and bottom. It will look very narrow on a standard TV.

Previous attempts to introduce films on optical disc to the UK market, had been pretty disastrous. In 1980 Pioneer and Philips introduced the laser disc in Europe. This was an analogue-based system offering a limited amount of user interactivity. In spite of numerous re-launches, its appeal was restricted to the film-buff market, whose enthusiasts preferred it to videotape because of its higher quality. But, for most users, the large size (the discs were 12-inch and so the players were correspondingly large) and the difficulty of getting films (the choice of films in Europe was relatively small) outweighed the advantages.

In 1993 various companies introduced CD-sized video discs. Philips's VideoCD format was the most widely available. This system uses a digital video compression format called MPEG1, which is of a noticeably lower quality than that possible with the MPEG2 format used by digital TV and DVDs. A film was typically spread over two discs. Combined CD audio and VideoCD discs were also released containing pop videos. The lower-quality digital compression and the limited choice of films were not appreciated by the enthusiasts, and for most consumers the fact that they could not record on the discs meant such discs could not compete with videotapes. Therefore, the system never really took off. However, they do have a legacy: all of today's DVD players will also play back VideoCDs.

Fitting information on a disc

Since the introduction of the audio CD in 1982 a number of technical developments have helped to increase the storage capacity for data (music, video, computer programs, etc.) on a single disc.

DVDs use the digital compression of audio and video signals explained previously. In addition, two important factors have helped the DVD.

First, more advanced optics and lasers have enabled smaller 'pits' (data bits) to be recorded on the disc and allowed the tracks to be narrower. Second, a DVD is a dual-layer disc. The recorded side has two layers, one on top of the other, sandwiched between transparent plastic layers. The playback laser can change its focus so it picks up just one layer at a time. When it reaches the end of one layer, it automatically re-focuses and continues playing the second layer, usually without the viewer noticing the break. Thus, the playing time of a disc is doubled. It is also possible to record on both sides of a DVD and so a dual-layer double-sided disc is possible.

A single-layer disc can accommodate about two hours of high-quality video and so a film such as *Titanic*, which is over 3 hours long, will easily fit on one side of a dual-layer DVD with room to spare for extra material.

So, why in the year 2000 did the DVD catch on in such a big way? Several factors contributed to its popularity: the system was universally adopted throughout the world by many different hardware and software manufacturers, which meant that there would be no shortage of titles; the picture quality was good; the price was low; and both the players and discs were of a convenient size. The final thing that guaranteed success in the UK was that the video rental shops started to stock DVD films. The only drawback with DVDs at present is the fact that you cannot record on the discs, but that is set to change in the near future.

The advantages of DVDs are several: they can support subtitles in different languages, including subtitles in English (for foreign films) and special subtitling for the hard of hearing. They can support different soundtracks, in different languages, including audio description for the blind or partially sighted. Because a film is divided into chapters, it is easy to locate a particular scene from a menu at the start of the film. In addition, because of the high capacity of the DVD it is often possible to include extra background information about the film including interviews and details about how it was made.

It is not just films that you get on DVD: classical concerts, TV series, pop videos, documentaries, etc. have all been released on DVD. There are also some special audio-only DVDs that claim to offer better quality than CDs, but these systems, aimed at the hi-fi enthusiast, have not yet caught on in a big way.

All films have a high-quality stereo soundtrack, of course, but many have something extra: a digital surround-sound system called Dolby AC3 (see 'Home-cinema systems', below).

Regions

The film industry likes to control the release of films throughout the world. This was not too much of a problem in the early days of video owing to the different analogue TV formats used in different parts of the world. Videotapes from the USA could not be played on UK VCRs and TVs, and *vice versa*. In recent years advances in electronics have broken this barrier. With the launch of DVD, the film industry needed to find a way of keeping control of its local market. The solution was to code DVD discs with a region. Hence, in the USA, DVD players were coded region 1 and would play only region 1 discs. Similarly, in Europe players sold in the shops were region 2 and so would play only European region 2 discs. In all there are six regions plus a region 0 used for old films, music videos or any other material that does not need to be regionalised. This is a good idea in theory, but it was not long before electronics experts found out how to convert players so they could play discs from any region. Now, the process known as 'chipping' is considered quite normal, and when buying a DVD player you could ask the retailer to do it for you. (Chipping invalidates the manufacturer's guarantee but the retailer often takes over the guarantee.) There are also several low-priced DVD players on the market, imported from China, that are supplied as a 'multi-region' player. So, with a multi-region player and an Internet connection, you can buy DVDs from the USA, where the choice is much greater than in the UK.

Home-cinema systems

Home cinema is an audio-video system that re-creates quite effectively the surround-sound experience of modern cinemas. The home-cinema effect is created by using extra audio channels – in addition to the usual left and right channels that you have with stereo. One of them is a centre channel with a loudspeaker that sits near the TV and so 'anchors' centre-stage sounds, such as the dialogue, to the picture. There is also the surround channel and surround speaker(s). They provide all the sound effects that creep up from behind, such as explosions or background music.

You can buy fairly modest home-cinema systems with some of the loudspeakers built in to the TV. At the other extreme, enthusiasts use large projection TVs, six large loudspeakers and lots of amplifier power.

Analogue home cinema

Analogue home-cinema systems have been around for some time. They use a system known as Dolby Pro-Logic, which was something of a compromise, with the surround- sound channel and the centre-channel having to be mixed in with the normal left and right stereo channels in order to record it in stereo for TV broadcasting or videotape. A Pro-Logic decoder then had to be used to extract the surround and centre information. The results were very convincing, but the digital AC3 system (see below), as used on DVDs gives a worthwhile improvement in sound quality and surround effect.

Tests on analogue home-cinema systems by *Which?* magazine showed that the cheaper systems were often disappointing. It is therefore worth spending a little extra to get a system based on separate components, but you do not need to spend a fortune to get good results. It is also possible to upgrade a hi-fi system to a sur-

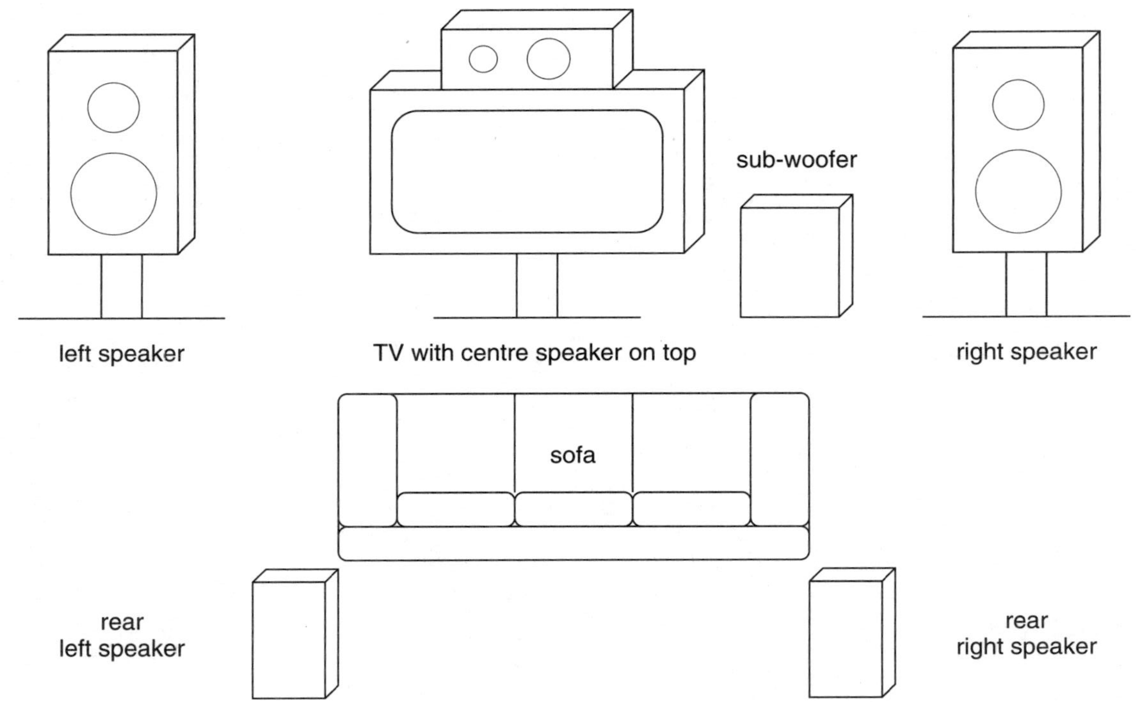

Typical digital surround system

round system but this does not always work well. Best results are obtained when all the speakers in the system are acoustically matched and this may not be the case when you are adding to an existing system.

Digital home cinema

The digital home-cinema system, Dolby AC3, is what is known as a 5.1 system. This means it uses five surround speakers plus one special speaker for very low frequencies.

Most modern films on DVD have a normal stereo soundtrack and an AC3 digital-surround soundtrack. You can choose which one to use, depending on what sort of audio system you have. How impressive the surround sound is depends largely on the type of film and how much effort the film-makers put into creating it. Not surprisingly, some of the most spectacular surround sound is found on action movies; a costume drama, on the other hand, would have only ambient sounds coming from the surround channel. Nevertheless, the overall effect is usually good.

In the UK, viewers cannot get digital surround from films shown on digital TV because the broadcasts do not carry AC3 digital surround. However, they do usually still have the analogue, Pro-Logic surround-sound system in the stereo channels, so, when buying a new surround system, it is worth making sure it has both AC3 and Pro-Logic.

There is a rival system to Dolby AC3, called DTS, but so far only a handful of discs exist using this format.

Home cinema has been slow to catch on in the UK but is very popular in the USA. As DVD players become more popular, home-cinema systems may become more widespread in the UK.

Tests on surround-sound systems for *Which?* magazine showed that that they offer a significant enhancement to the experience of watching films. The newer digital AC3 system in particular gets viewers more involved with the film. However, the effectiveness of the surround sound depends to a large extent on the soundtrack and the type of film. Big blockbuster action movies are more likely to benefit from surround sound than a romantic or a comedy film. So, if you are keen on films, particularly big-budget action spectaculars, you should seriously consider getting a DVD player and a home-cinema system.

Surround sounds and quadrophonics

In the 1970s several hi-fi companies and broadcasters worked on a system called quadrophonics. It consisted of having four speakers, one in each corner of a room, and was seen as the natural development of the two-speaker stereo system. The idea was to re-create the natural ambience of music and the concert hall. (In those days most audio developments were made with classical music in mind.) There was even talk of being able to position the listener in the middle of the orchestra. The buying public was not convinced. Having – and paying for – four large loudspeakers was a problem; another was that there were at least four rival systems to contend with.

Cinema surround is quite different because it was designed for effect rather than for re-creating acoustic accuracy. To this end, it succeeded and made a visit to a suitably equipped cinema even more exciting. AC3 brings the system into the home very effectively. The rear channel speakers are often called the 'effect' speakers and do not have to be as large as the main speakers. The centre speaker is sometimes called the 'dialogue' speaker: its job is to focus the sound on what is happening at the centre of the screen, which is usually dialogue.

What you hear has less to do with the 'acoustic accuracy' sought after by quadrophonics and more to do with what the film makers want and what they think sounds good or exciting.

Buying guide for home-cinema systems

- **TV-based system** You can get a home-cinema system that is partially built into a new TV, but you have to take care that this is not just a low-cost compromise. In particular, the front-centre (dialogue) speaker needs to be of good quality, and the front-left and -right speakers should not be built into the TV as they should be positioned at a reasonable distance from the screen. TV-based home-cinema systems also tend to be of the old analogue Pro-Logic design.

- **Component system** A better bet is to buy a dedicated DVD home-cinema system. For upwards of £1,000 you can get state-of-the-art systems with fairly large speakers and powerful amplifiers. Even a more modest outlay, say about £500, can get you a well-designed package of separate components based around bookshelf sized speakers. This can sound quite impressive if all the speakers are well matched. An even larger, floor-standing 'sub-woofer' speaker will take care of all the lower frequencies that the main speakers cannot handle. This speaker can be hidden away, behind the TV, for example. Such systems give impressive sound but are often considered too obtrusive for most living rooms.
- **Package system** The most popular type of home-cinema system is one that is less obtrusive. Many systems in the major high-street shops rely on very small, stylishly designed speakers rather than traditional wooden boxes. These small systems can give surprisingly good results if well designed; a sub-woofer speaker is essential. You should expect to spend about £700 or more for such a system (including the DVD player and all the electronics) if you want good results.
- **Upgraded hi-fi system** You could upgrade an existing hi-fi system to home cinema, but the results are often disappointing unless you can tonally match the new centre and rear speakers with your existing speakers – this is particularly important for the centre-front speaker.

Whichever system you choose and however discreet and stylish it may look in the shop, remember there will be a lot of speaker cables running around the room which will have to be hidden away.

Video recorders

Video recorders too are going digital, with some interesting new features. Digital VCRs are already available in the UK: Sony and Panasonic produce them using a system called DV (digital video), which can use either three-hour DV tapes or one-hour mini-DV tapes. The mini-DV tape is used by most digital camcorders.

Meanwhile, Philips and JVC have launched a rival system called D-VHS. This is also a cassette-tape-based system. The tapes used are identical to the normal analogue VHS cassettes except that they have special-grade tape inside. The advantage of this system is that it will play old VHS or SVHS tapes as well. It can record up to 21 hours of good-quality digital video on to a single tape. Unfortunately, the special tape is rather expensive (at £25 each) and so, at current prices, you do not save any money by getting so much on the tape. Moreover, the D-VHS players cannot do freeze-frame or slow-motion playback.

Both types of digital video recorders cost in excess of £1,000. The picture quality on both systems is excellent, although DV is the better of the two, and is limited only by the quality of the TV itself. There is no degradation of picture quality when you make a recording or copy a recording.

The disadvantage of both the DV and the D-VHS system is the inconvenience of having to wind through tapes to find a recording that you want. So these tape-based systems are unlikely to provide serious competition for the PVR (see above) and the recordable DVD.

Recordable DVD

Pioneer launched its first DVD player/recorder in Japan in early 2000. Being the first of its kind, it was expensive, bulky and in short supply. However, it made the point that recordable DVD was possible and that the discs are re-recordable (that is, they could be used over and over again, just like a videotape). DVD recorders should be available in the UK by the end of 2001.

Recordable DVD has several advantages.

- The recorder creates a menu at the start of each disc, so it is easy to find the recording that you want quickly.
- It is very easy to edit the recordings. You can erase selected parts of recordings (the adverts or announcements, for example) and you can rearrange the order of the recordings on the disc. Unlike linear tape systems, there are no annoying gaps when you erase parts of the disc. The blank space gained is available for the addition of more recordings to the end of the disc. These simple editing features will make recordable DVD particularly attractive for camcorder users.

- You can select what level of quality you want. The Pioneer recorder has 32 quality levels to choose from. The highest level of quality is probably better than you get from digital TV, but it gives only one hour's worth of recording on a disc. The lowest level of quality is fairly poor, similar to LP mode on an analogue VCR, but it gives eight hours' worth of recording on one disc.

A big problem at the moment is that different versions of recordable DVDs exist. Some of these are for recording computer data (DVD-RAM), but even in the area of recording video, different systems are being proposed. One of the reasons for this is that it is technically difficult to make a home DVD recorder that produces discs that can then be played on normal DVD players. A recent development by Philips, called DVD+RW, claims to have solved this but when this book went to press the product had not appeared on the market.

Another issue is to do with the ability to make good-quality copies of films and TV programmes. Because of the nature of digital signals, it is very easy for DVD makers and broadcasters to put 'anti-copying' codes into the data to prevent the recording of certain programmes. Pre-recorded DVDs, TV box-office film channels and even some sporting events already do this, so in the future we may find that the number of programmes we are allowed to record is reduced. PVR devices do not have this problem because broadcasters are not worried about viewers making time shift, temporary copies.

It seems very likely that recordable DVDs will have a place in the digital home, perhaps as a complement to the PVR. The DVD player/recorder would be used for playing back pre-recorded films and for making recordings of TV shows that you want to keep (you can easily copy non-copy-protected programmes from a PVR on to a DVD recorder). The PVR would be used for time-shifting and temporary recording. It seems unlikely that any digital-tape-based system could compete with this partnership.

One area where a DVD recorder could come into its own is for copying digital camcorder recordings. The copies will be of high quality of course, but also, once all the camcorder clips have been copied on to the disc, it is easy to cut, edit and juggle them to produce a finished, edited film. To do this with analogue or digital tape systems requires loads of cables, several readings of the instruction manual(s) and loads of patience.

Comparison of different video-recording systems

System	Advantages	Disadvantages	Manufacturers
D-VHS	Up to 21 hours on one tape. Will also record and play analogue VHS/SVHS tapes.	Expensive and bulky. Have to wind tape to find recordings. Tapes are expensive. No freeze-frame or slow motion.	JVC Philips Thompson
DV	Small. Compatible with DV camcorder tapes and good for editing them. Very good quality recordings.	3-hour tapes are expensive. Have to wind tape to find recordings.	Sony Panasonic
Recordable DVD-video	Versatile medium. Easy to index and locate recordings. Easy to edit and crop recordings. Very good quality recordings.	Expensive. Compatibility with other DVD players and recorders in question.	Philips, Pioneer (Not in the UK until late 2001)
PVR	Unique features such as ability to record all episodes of a series, delay live TV and learn your preferences. Ideal for television addicts	Not intended for permanent recording or for playback of pre-recorded videos. Need to subscribe to electronic programme guide.	TiVo (available now) Pace, Nokia (later in 2001)
Solid state recorders	Small and robust.	Not available yet.	

Entertainment from the Internet

Among other things, the Internet is a means of accessing music, video and radio stations. The most popular method of storing music on the Internet is in the form of MP3 files. Many web sites specialise in supplying these files. MP3 music is sometimes from new rock bands that do not have official recording contracts. They 'post' their music on the Internet to distribute it. Western classical music and jazz are available too. Some record companies also supply their music in MP3 format over the Internet but you have to pay to download it. Not all MP3 sites are lawful: some openly supply or distribute copyrighted material. To counter this, some record companies are promoting alternative digital formats for their recordings – Windows Media Audio (WMA) and Open MG, which is used by Sony. These types of files cannot be digitally copied but even if the use of these formats grows, it is unlikely to have an impact on the distribution of MP3 files over the Internet because the MP3 format is now so well established.

The most popular MP3 site on the Internet is www.mp3.com. Western classical and jazz music is available from www.gmn.com, but typing 'MP3' into an Internet search engine will bring up thousands of sites ranging from authorised sites to illegal pirated music stations and from professional artistes through to complete amateurs.

Downloading MP3 files can take some time on a standard 56K modem connection. Typically, three minutes of music can take up to four minutes to receive. Once you have downloaded an MP3 file to your computer, you can play it using special MP3 software and your computer's soundcard. The software is available over the Internet. One of the most popular MP3 recorder/player applications is RealPlayer,* which can be downloaded for free. Alternatively, you can transfer it to an MP3 player, a small personal-stereo type device. This type of player stores the files either internally or on a removable memory card. If your computer is equipped with a recordable CD-ROM drive, you can store MP3 files on a CD. You cannot play this CD on a conventional CD player, but MP3-compatible CD players are beginning to appear on the market.

MP3 players contain no moving parts and can be quite small, so it is no surprise that they are beginning to appear combined

MP3 file format

The music in an MP3 file is heavily digitally compressed. The number of digital bits necessary to record one second of good-quality music in MP3 is approximately one-eleventh of that needed for one second of music stored on a conventional audio CD. How much space an MP3 file takes up on your hard drive and how quickly it downloads depend on the amount of compression, which can be altered by changing the 'data rate'. The fewer bits per second, the less space a file takes up on the hard drive or in the MP3 player's memory. However, the more you compress a file, the more rapidly its audio quality deteriorates. Most MP3 files come at a data rate of 128Kbps (that is, 128,000 digital bits per second). At this data rate you get what is often described as 'near-CD' quality.

The compression system used is similar to that described in the section on digital radio (see page 13). The digitisation process used to make a normal CD is accurate but very inefficient. On a CD even long passages of silence would be methodically digitised! The MP3 system is cleverer. It does not digitise anything it does not need to. In fact, it has been programmed to mimic the human ear's psycho-acoustic properties. It does not bother to digitise any part of the music signal that will be 'masked' by louder parts of the music of a similar pitch. The result is a high-quality signal, virtually indistinguishable from that of a CD. Not all hi-fi purists agree with this, but as MP3 files are so convenient and tend to be used in portable players anyway, this is hardly important.

MP3 files can also store song titles, lyrics and other data, which is very handy.

with other digital devices, particularly those that use memory cards. You can already buy cameras and watches with built-in MP3 players.

Internet radio stations

Many conventional radio stations broadcast their programmes via the Internet, while many new radio stations have started up as Internet-only stations. To listen to these stations on your computer,

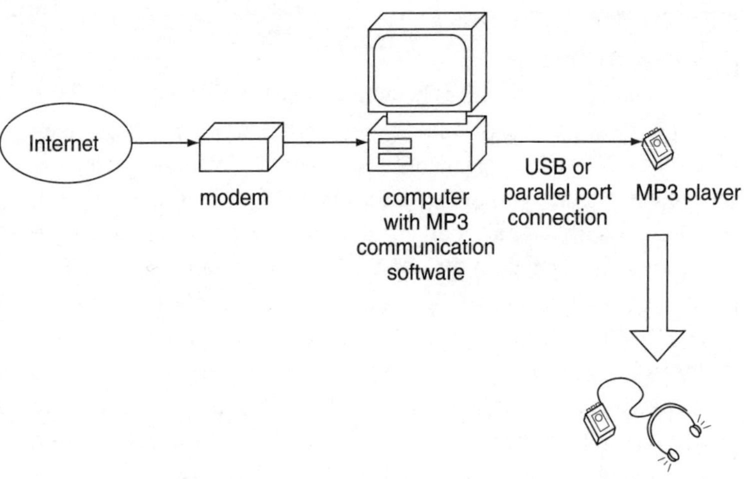

How MP3 files are downloaded and played

you need special software such as Real Audio Player or the latest version of Windows Media Player. This, in conjunction with your Internet browser, enables you to listen 'live' to radio on the Internet. The catch is that because it is live rather than a file you download and listen to later, there is no time for sophisticated digital error correction and high quality. The music is fed to the player in a form called 'streaming audio'. The quality can therefore be pretty poor if you are using a standard modem Internet connection.

When newer, faster Internet connections become common (see Chapter 4) it will be possible to get good-quality radio feeds, but it remains to be seen whether the Internet can cope well with this type of digital traffic. Streaming video for an Internet TV station would also be possible, but again it would be very demanding on the network.

In the USA a dedicated Internet radio receiver, called a Kerbango,* is being marketed. It comes with several thousand worldwide Internet radio stations already programmed in. There are plans to market this in the UK later in 2001.

A glimpse into the future: video on demand (VOD)

The Internet in its current form would not seem to be a sensible route to download whole films. But digital cable and other wide-band telephone line systems are. It is possible to download a requested film in broadcast quality in digital form. Video on demand (VOD) companies could have a whole library of titles for us to choose from, much better than the limited choice we get from digital TV or even the local video library.

This type of system is already being tried in the London area. A company called HomeChoice* has a growing number of films in its library which you obtain on a pay-per-view basis. It also has a library of classic sporting events and classic TV comedy shows (you could download the entire first series of *Friends*, for example), music videos and concerts, etc. HomeChoice claims to have over 850 films, 1,000 hours of television programmes and 1,000 hours of music videos.

When you use the Home Choice system, the videos and films are continually fed down a high-speed telephone line to your TV. However, you can still pause, rewind and fast forward the film. Home Choice costs from £6 per month to subscribe to; the exact amount will depend on the number of extra packages you opt for. Films cost from £2 to £3.50 each for 24 hours. In order to get Home Choice, you need to have a BT phone line that can be upgraded to the asynchronous digital subscriber line (ADSL) high-speed digital system and this costs £40 to install. This same digital telephone connection can also be used to bring fast Internet access at the same time, for an extra monthly cost.

Such a system could mean that future generations will never 'own' a video, DVD or music CD. All their entertainment will be 'on tap'. This implies a big shake-up of our traditional supply chains. We will no longer require discs to be manufactured nor distribution and retail chains to sell them.

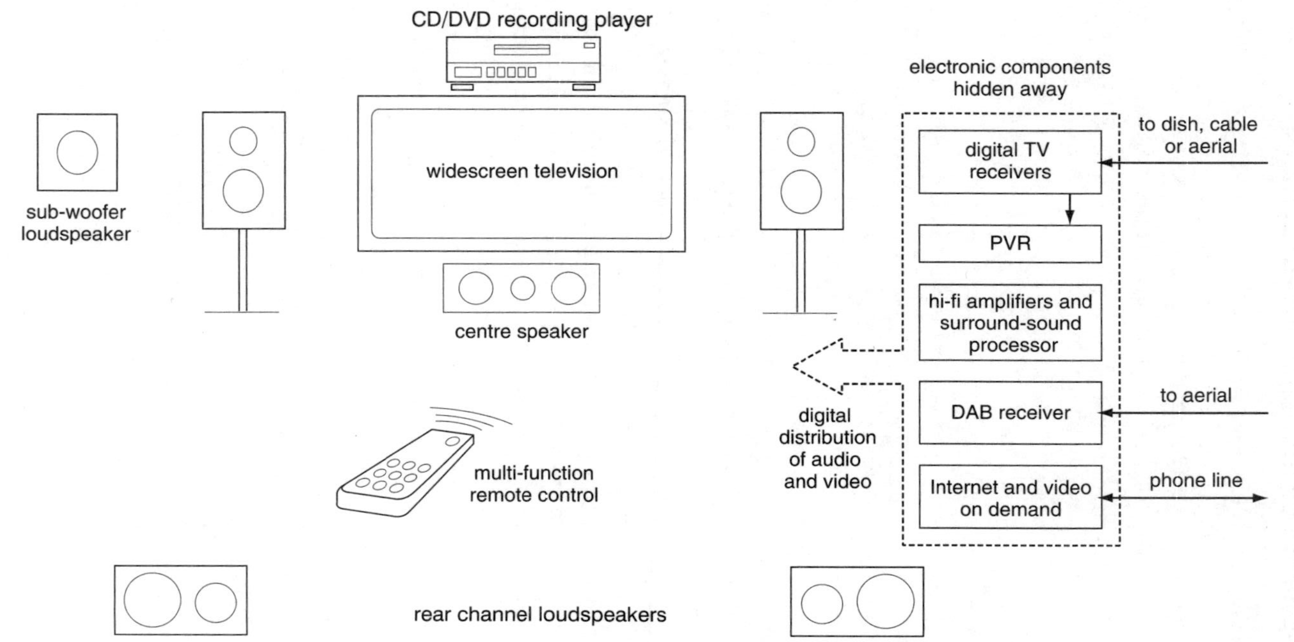

Diagram of a complete digital entertainment home

Convergence of digital entertainment systems

This chapter has shown how our audio and video entertainment systems have progressively gone digital. Moreover, they have begun to come together, or converge. For example, DVD players and AC3 home-cinema systems have brought the hi-fi and TV together. It is now possible to listen to digital radio on one's computer, and the Internet and telephone lines are poised to deliver forms of entertainment.

Chapter 2

Sources of information

The ability to convert the written word, pictures and sound into digital data has revolutionised the way we gather information. This applies not only to industry, government and commerce, but in the home too. We no longer have to spend days tracking down information in libraries and archives. We do not have to trawl through vast tomes or printed encyclopaedias to find the nugget of knowledge we are looking for. We do not have to wait for the next day's newspaper or even the next news broadcast to keep up with the latest news. A computer can do all this for us – or can it?

This chapter looks at how we can gather information in our homes, whether to keep up with a hobby, help with school or university assignments, or stay up to date with the news. The main options are the computer and the Internet, and teletext.

Teletext

It would be easy to dismiss teletext as an old-fashioned system – after all, it was introduced back in 1973. However, teletext was possibly the first digital system to enter the home and is capable of providing us with up-to-the-minute news and information.

Teletext is a very successful system and many people use it regularly to find out about the weather, TV and radio programmes, news, travel, business and entertainment. It is fairly slow – you have to wait for up to a minute for the next screen of text to appear – and the amount of information that can be stored is limited, so it tends to be used for up-to-date information rather than as an archive of knowledge. As in a newspaper or TV broadcast, the information is fed to us under editorial control: we cannot 'request' information.

Viewdata

While teletext was being developed by TV broadcasters in the 1970s, the Post Office was working on a similar system, called Viewdata. In it, digitised text characters were transmitted over the telephone line. Various companies could have pages of information stored by the Post Office for users to access. Indeed, *Which?* magazine had Viewdata pages for a short while. Users had to buy a modem that could be connected to a standard TV. The modem speed was 1.2Kbits per second – extremely slow compared with today's modems, which operate at 56Kbits per second. The system was in many ways similar to the Internet, but it was on a much smaller scale and was controlled by the Post Office.

Viewdata never caught on, possibly because it was ahead of its time and also because consumers were not accustomed to having to pay for information – as well as paying for their telephone line, they were charged for each page they accessed. However, several companies used 'private Viewdata' systems within their workplaces, a forerunner of today's intranets in organisations. In France a similar system called Minitel was set up by the government and this proved to be a great success, probably because the government ensured that it was cheap to use and that Minitel terminals and public kiosks were plentiful. The system is still in operation and its presence is partly responsible for the slow take-up of the Internet there.

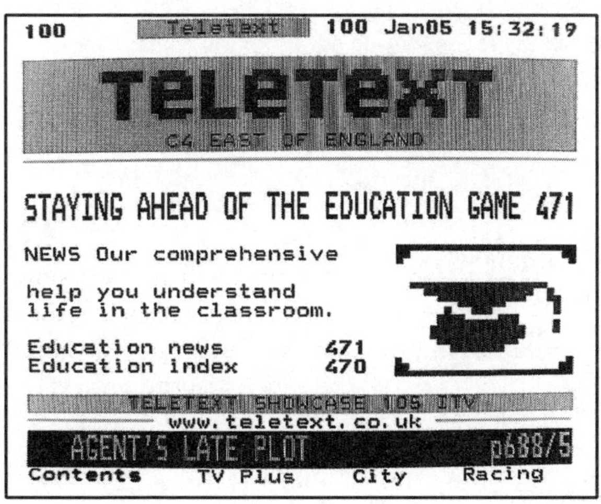

Traditional teletext

How does teletext work?

Teletext data consists of text characters (A–Z, a–z and 0–9) and some very simple graphics elements (blocks and lines). These characters are individually converted into digital data using an 8-bit code called ASCII. The same code is still used for text characters in modern computers. The result is a relatively low-resolution system that can be transmitted without the need for the high-speed data links that we use for the Internet now.

This ASCII code is transmitted by being 'piggy-backed' on to a standard analogue TV picture. In fact, it is sent as part of the TV picture at the top of the screen that you do not normally see. Although in theory a TV picture consists of 625 lines, this is not quite true because 25 or so of these lines at the top of the picture are not used. Teletext information is transmitted on some of these lines. In fact, if you have a TV which has a picture that is not properly adjusted, you may be able to see these lines in the form of little dots jumping around at the top of the screen. That is the raw digital teletext data. Of course, TVs have to be fitted with a teletext decoder in order for the text to be read.

If you are familiar with a teletext display you will realise that, although it has low-resolution characters, the characters themselves are very clear and bold on the screen compared with text characters (film credits, captions, etc.) transmitted on a TV picture. This is because teletext is digital and the characters are re-generated within the TV, so they do not suffer the quality degradation of the analogue TV picture.

The arrival of digital TV (see Chapter 1 for details) has allowed the teletext service to be further developed. No longer constrained by ASCII, it can now display improved graphics, and its own audio and video clips within each page. You still have to wait a while for each page to arrive, but you can scroll down the pages, so viewing sub-pages does not involve any waiting. This new teletext service is being introduced gradually so digital satellite TV and digital cable TV may still carry the old teletext signals as well. New teletext can allow you to continue monitoring the TV programme you are watching in a small window while browsing teletext pages.

Examples of new-style digital TV teletext

Digital terrestrial TV is currently the most advanced in this respect, having several channels dedicated to new teletext. Digital satellite TV introduced Sky teletext at the beginning of 2001.

New teletext can also be used to give more information about programmes you are watching. For example, on digital terrestrial TV the BBC Knowledge channel gives contact details, a programme synopsis and scheduling details of the current programme and future programmes. On digital satellite, the new teletext is used by Sky News Channel to give news, scrolling headlines and short video clips of news items, weather etc.

These services are likely to be developed further and will ultimately replace the old teletext service. If so, teletext is likely to remain one of the quickest and most immediate sources of up-to-the-minute information in the home.

Computers

In 1998, 34 per cent of households in the UK had a computer and by the end of 2000 the figure had increased to 40 per cent. This is impressive, but it is still a long way behind ownership of televisions (98 per cent), video-cassette recorders (85 per cent) or even the compact disc player (70 per cent).

In physical (or 'hardware') terms, a computer consists of three parts: a box of electronics (comprising the main circuit board or motherboard, a temporary memory area or RAM, disk drives, and graphics and soundcards), a keyboard and a monitor (or 'screen'). The computer's job is to run programs (or 'software') . Programs are simply special tasks that give a computer a set of instructions. A word-processing package is one program that many are familiar with, but there are programs that could enable you to edit photographs, draw, use a spreadsheet to produce a large table of figures and do mathematical calculations … the list is endless. Whatever task you want to perform, you ask the computer to load the appropriate program. Modern computers are versatile – they can run several programs at the same time (or 'multi-task').

When you have produced some work (perhaps a simple letter or a work of art) on your computer, you can print it out on paper using a printer attached to the computer and, more importantly, save that piece of work in electronic form inside the machine. When you save such a document, it is stored on a magnetic disk and is referred to as a data file, or simply a file. In fact, with all the program files and data files on your computer, your internal magnetic storage disk becomes your filing cabinet.

In addition to individual programs, a computer has another program called the 'operating system' (OS), which is loaded every time the computer is started up. Its job is to 'manage' your computer. It provides a pictorial interface (graphical user interface, or GUI) so you can easily instruct the computer what to do. The OS knows where all your programs and files are stored and what to do when you ask for something to be printed or saved. The most commonly used OS is Windows; Apple computers use their own 'MAC OS' operating system.

CD-ROM players

Even without an Internet connection, your computer can be used as the basis of an information source, thanks to compact disc read-only memories (CD-ROMs) and more recently the higher-capacity digital versatile disks (DVD-ROMs). Pretty well all modern home computers have a CD-ROM player built in, and the most recent ones may even have a DVD-ROM player, which will play both CD-ROMs and DVD-ROMs. (A CD-ROM player will not play DVD-ROMs.)

If you have an old computer without one of these players, it is usually possible to add one, either internally, if you are confident about opening up your computer, or externally. However, as most of the best CD-ROM software requires at least Windows 95, a soundcard and a fast graphics card, it might be time to think about buying a new computer.

If you have a computer with just a CD-ROM player, you can fit a DVD-ROM player to it either replacing the CD-ROM player or in addition to it.

Tip

If your computer has a soundcard and speakers, you can use the CD-ROM player to listen to standard audio CDs, and work on your computer at the same time.

Similarly, a DVD-ROM player can be used to play back DVD video discs if you have the correct video decoder card or equivalent software installed in the computer (look in the 'Programs' menu to see if you do).

CD-ROMs

A computer is an excellent tool for accessing information. The best medium for holding vast quantities of material is the ROM (read-only memory) – in particular, the CD-ROM, which is an optical storage disc. In fact, a CD-ROM looks identical to a compact disc that contains music. A newer entrant to the field of storage devices is the higher-capacity DVD-ROM which, as its name implies, uses the same optical system as DVD videos.

Other storage devices

CD- and DVD-ROMs hold pre-recorded information such as reference material and facts and figures, but users of computers need to be able to store their own data files. To do this, a variety of recordable and re-recordable storage systems is available:

- magnetic disks, such as the internal hard disk or floppy disks
- removable disk devices, such as Zip and HIFD, which are similar to floppy disks but have a much greater capacity
- optical storage discs, such as CD-R, which can be recorded on to once only, or CD-RW which, like the magnetic disks, can be used many times. These discs are in all other respects just like CD-ROMs.

A standard-sized CD-ROM can store 650Mb of data, which is about enough to store the entire print version of the *Encyclopaedia Britannica*, including the pictures but no multimedia elements. More recently, the DVD-ROM has been introduced which can store 4.7Gb, seven times the capacity of the CD-ROM. On such a disc, it is possible to store the *Encyclopaedia Britannica* plus several hours of sound and video clips and still have room to spare.

In addition to storing information, CD-ROMs are also used as the means of supplying computer programs. If you have bought a program (or game) on a CD-ROM, you have to install the program on to your hard drive and run it direct from the computer. The CD-ROM is then not needed (unless something goes wrong and you have to re-install the program). Sometimes, using a combination of storage devices is efficient: say, when you are using a program that needs to be supported by a library of data. For example, a desktop publishing program could be supplied on a CD-ROM which includes a library of ready-made pictures (called 'clip art'). You would have to install the program on your PC's hard drive, but still call upon the CD when you wanted to search for some artwork. Storing all the artwork on your hard drive is possible, but it would use up a lot of valuable hard-disk space.

Using your PC effectively

Not all home computers are used to their full potential. Most are used simply as word processors, while others have just games played on them. However, computers can be a valuable source of information in today's world, and as such have an important role to play in a digital home.

Computers as sources of information

One of the most important printed sources of information, the encyclopaedia, has been impressively transformed into CD-ROMs. In 1995 Microsoft launched the first edition of *Encarta*, its multimedia (sound, video and text) encyclopaedia, on CD-ROM, and in 1997 the text of the entire 32-volume *Encyclopaedia Britannica* came out on one CD-ROM. Although many other encyclopaedias have been published on CD-ROM, these two have consistently been the best to buy. *Encarta* has expanded and improved its content since it first appeared, while *Britannica* has added multimedia elements. As *Britannica* feels more authoritative, offering more 'depth' to its entries, it is probably preferable for serious research or study; *Encarta*, being more enjoyable and easier to use, is better suited for general family use and school homework. Both products are now available on multiple CD-ROMs (because of the added multimedia elements – sound and video clips take up a lot of disk space) or more conveniently on a single DVD.

CD-based encyclopaedias have several advantages over printed encyclopaedias, apart from the obvious one that they take up less space. They are able to use animated graphics and video to explain complicated subjects. They can use audio clips to demonstrate sounds. Using a system called hypertext links (see box) they can directly link you to other, related entries or maps within the encyclopaedia. This hyperlink facility is a real time-saver for looking up cross-references.

If your computer is connected to the Internet, your CD-based encyclopaedia can be kept up to date by downloading monthly updates. Also, if you want more information on a particular subject you will find Internet links with the articles.

Hypertext links

Hypertext links (or hyperlinks) allow you to jump from one document to another, or from one part of a document to another. Virtually any piece of text displayed on a computer can support such links, but they are most commonly found on Internet pages and CD-ROM documents.

Hypertext links are programmed in by the author of the document where a cross- reference is appropriate. They are easily identified: the word(s) identifying the link are in a different colour from the main text and are underlined. If you hover your mouse cursor over the link, the cursor will change, usually from an arrow-head to a pointing finger. Clicking your mouse on the link will take you to the cross-referenced document.

As well as general encyclopaedias, specialist reference works covering more specific subjects such as art, science and history are available, as are many educational CD-ROMs, some of which are targeted at specific age groups and educational curricula.

CD-ROM directories are also popular. You can get directories of films, popular and classical music releases, and so on. Some of these are just huge databases while others contain multimedia content

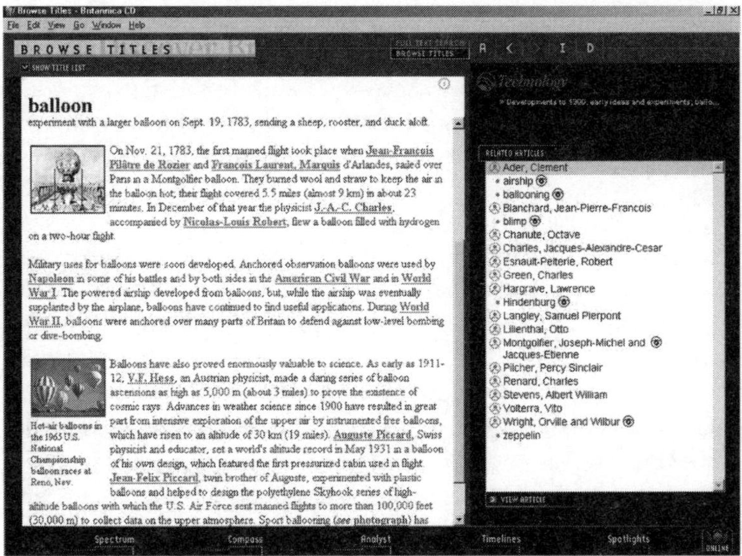

Typical encyclopaedia page

and reviews. However, some of these CD-ROMs have been superseded by data available on the Internet, often for free (see 'Information from the Internet', below).

The quality of content of these CD-ROMs is variable: some are clearly produced in a hurry while others are exceptionally good with useful multimedia content and interactive links. The only way to be sure of buying something satisfactory is to read reviews.

Other tasks that computers can perform

Here are just a few examples of computer software that can help you with hobbies or tasks.

Desktop publishing

If you want to produce a newsletter, perhaps for a local society or club, or just for the family, a desktop-publishing (DTP) package will be a useful tool. It is rather like a word processor but it helps you with positioning text and pictures on the page to make the document look like a newspaper or magazine, with the text in columns and flowing around diagrams or photographs. A good desktop-publishing software package suitable for domestic use can cost between £50 and £100. Most such packages come with an electronic library of ready-made pictures (called 'clip art') to liven up your work.

However, if you already have a reasonably satisfactory word-processing package and your publishing requirements are not too ambitious, you can use it to produce a newsletter with pictures and photos.

Route planners

A route-planning software package can replace the traditional road map and even improve on it. A good package will have a full road map of Britain on one CD, right down to street level. If you want to plan a driving route from A to B it will produce a road map and detailed directions for you to print out. It will also give an estimate of the time the journey will take. However, although route planners have every road and street, even cul-de-sacs, listed, they often ignore one-way streets or footpaths.

Photograph and video editing

With the right software, you can enhance or edit your photographs or produce professional-quality video films. See Chapter 7.

Office suite

An office suite consists of several programmes such as a word processor, spreadsheet, diary, address book and database. Buying them all in one suite can make it easier for you to link them together. For example, you could link addresses in your address book to a letter you wanted to send to several people. You can buy a good office suite for about £85, which should cover all home requirements. If you are working from home, and need something more professional, the software could set you back £200–£300 (see Chapter 8). A basic office suite is supplied with many new computers.

House and garden designers

These very specialised programs allow you to see the effects of decorating your house before you even start re-arranging the furniture or putting up wallpaper. You can do the whole thing visually on the screen. First you have to 'build' the room (or whole house) by telling the computer the dimensions. Then you can start putting in furniture, carpets and decorating the walls. You then have a pseudo 3-D view of the room, which you can move about so you can get a real feel of what the room will look like. The big drawback with these programmes is the time it takes to get the final results, and you need a lot of patience.

A good package will come with a library of furniture and decorations. Some US versions even have libraries of items supplied by retailers, reflecting their range of merchandise.

Similar products are available for garden design. These come with a library of plants and shrubs with details of their suitability for your requirements.

Games

Games have the biggest share of the computer software market, accounting for 57 per cent of sales. First impressions would suggest that the most popular games are of the 'shoot 'em up' variety, but in fact the more addictive adventure and strategy games account for nearly one-quarter of games sales. There are plenty of non-violent games on the market, including:

- **strategy games**, such as *SIM City*, in which you have to develop and run a city

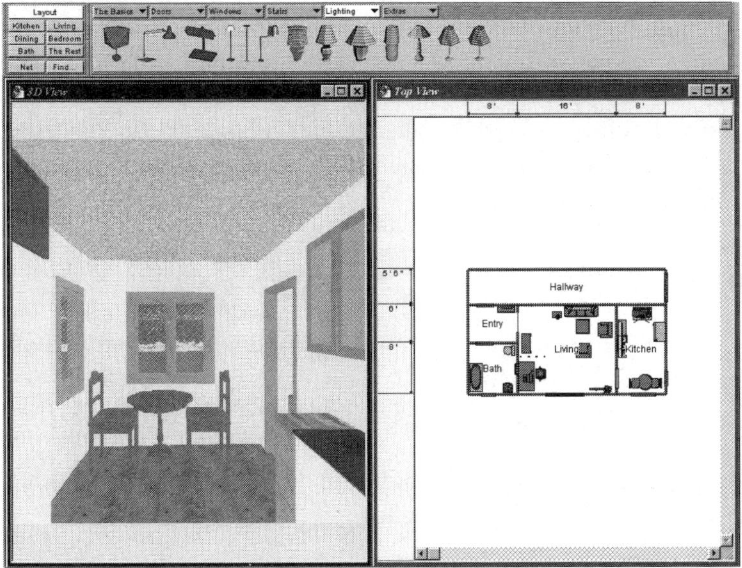

Room-design software

- **puzzle-solving games**, like *Lemmings*, in which you have to work out a safe route home
- **sports games**, such as golf
- **simulation games**, such as *Flight Simulator*, in which you get to control an aircraft, or *F1 Racing Championship*, in which you simulate being a Formula One racing driver
- **educational games** for children which combine playing and learning.

Genealogy software

Tracing one's family tree is a popular hobby, and several software products are available to help do this. A good package will contain not only the necessary display tools to see your final tree, but also large databases of births and deaths and other historical census information. This often requires several CD-ROMs. Make sure you get a package with UK data on it, as many contain US information. These products save you all the effort of hunting down old public and church records and reading gravestones. But perhaps the software takes away all the fun or sense of achievement.

Finance packages

These take care of all your home finances and even establish a link to your 'online' bank account. The two most popular products for home accounting are *Quicken* and *Microsoft Money*. The 'basic' versions of either of these should take care of all your needs. If you have to fill in an annual tax return, the Consumers' Association's *Taxcalc* is a useful package.

The Internet

Connect your computer to the Internet and you open up a whole new world of information.

The term Internet really refers just to the telecommunications infrastructure used to transfer electronic data. However, it is now more commonly used as a cover-all for several specific applications that use the Internet, such as email, Usenet newsgroups, the World Wide Web (the 'Web'), Internet chat and file transfer protocol (FTP). This section concentrates on three of them – FTP, the Web and newsgroups – that can be used to find information or to help you with specific hobbies or pastimes.

What is the Internet?

In a conventional telephone system connections are made largely on a fixed 'point to point' basis. This is adequate for person-to-person voice calls, but is quite a wasteful system for sharing information with everybody. For transferring Internet data the data is broken down into small chunks (or packets) and sent using fast electronic switches (called routers) on the telecommunications network over a path that can be constantly varied. This makes much more efficient use of the telecommunications network.

Different packets of data from different users can be interwoven and unscrambled en-route, as they make their way to their destination. When you request some data from the Internet, for example, a web page, these unscrambled data packets might even arrive in the wrong order. However, because each packet has its own name and address, it can be all sorted out by your computer and displayed on the screen. This system does mean that there is always an unpredictable time delay involved in sending and receiving data, and at certain times of the day, when the Internet is busy, this can be quite a problem. The delay can be reduced by improving the speed and capacity of all the interconnections en route, including your link to the ISP (see 'What you need to get connected to the Internet', below), but ultimately the speed is limited by the slowest link in the chain and this could be as distant as the site you are trying to access.

Sources of information using the Internet

File transfer protocol

Before the World Wide Web developed on the Internet, to obtain information over the Internet you had to transfer data files directly from a remote computer to yours. The system for doing this was called file transfer protocol.

Many FTP sites were set up on the Internet from which you could obtain (or 'download') these files. Some of these sites were for private use only (you needed a password to access them), but many were open to the public, and were known as 'anonymous

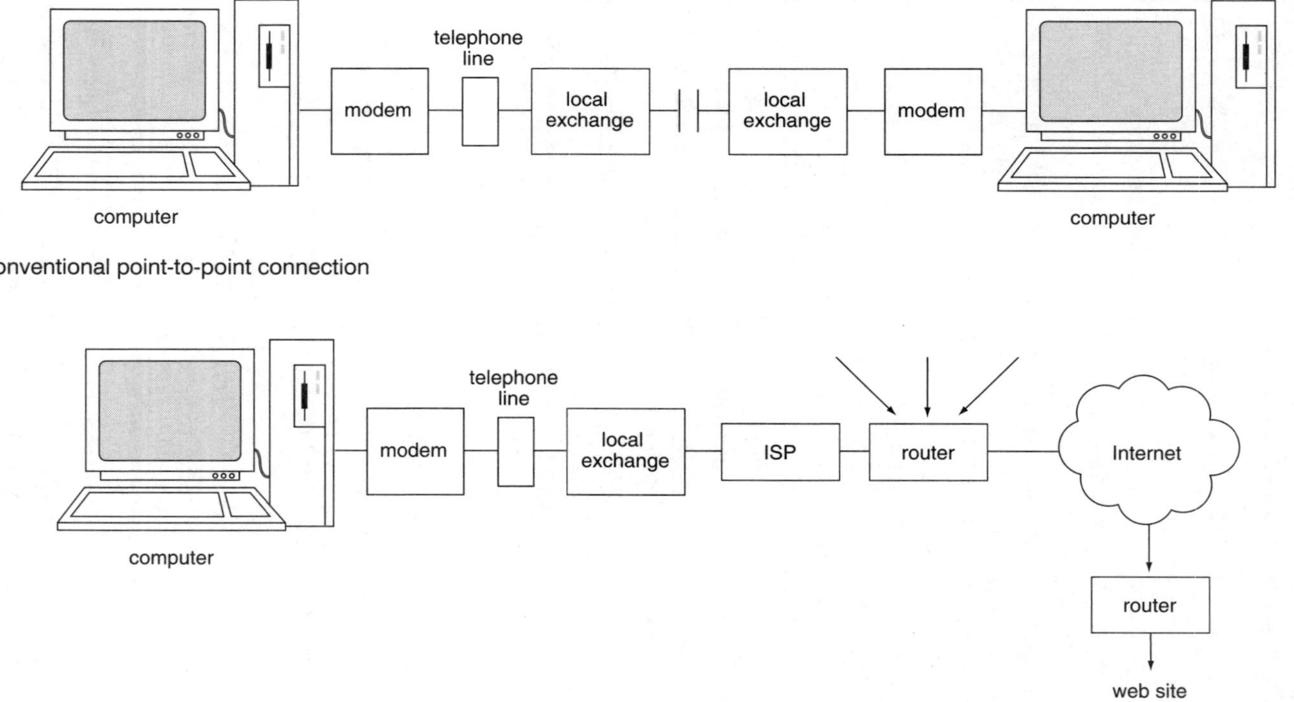

Conventional point-to-point connection

Web connection

FTP sites'. Typical anonymous FTP sites were those set up by academic institutions, museums and governments. Once you had connected (logged on) to an FTP site you could search through the files on its computers. These were arranged in directories, just like the files on your computer. When you had found the file you wanted you could download it on to your computer. The files were mainly text documents that you could read using a word processor or simple text reader on your computer.

Two examples of FTP sites still in use are:

ftp://ftp.stanford.edu/pub/clubs/homebrew/beer/
ftp://ftp.microsoft.com/

If you access these sites using your Internet browser, you will find the stored directories and files listed in the same way as your own directories and files are listed on your own computer.

Many more sites are available, and search engines can be used to find lists of FTP sites. There is a similar system, called Gopher, which is also still in use. One of the best-known Gopher sites is:

gopher://gopher.tc.umn.edu.

Although FTP technology is still used to download files, the process of searching through FTP and Gopher sites is dying out as it is not a particularly convenient method of finding information, unless you know exactly what you are looking for. The Web has superseded these systems.

The Web

The introduction of the Web in 1992 is what really made the Internet a practical tool for everyone. A typical web site is simply a collection of pages that you can display on your computer screen. Each page in a site can be accessed directly, if you happen to know its address (or uniform resource locator, URL). However, if you needed to know lots of addresses the system would be no better than the old FTP system described above. In fact, it is enough to know the address of the site's home page (see page 87). After that, all other pages are linked to each other, rather like a spider's web, hence the use of the term 'web'. Using special 'links' on each page, you can jump from page to page on the site, by clicking on your mouse. In many cases, a web site will contain links to other sites.

What you need to get connected to the Internet

The most common way to connect to the Internet is by computer. (You can now access it through television and mobile phone; see 'Accessing the Internet without a computer, pages 96–8.) For connection using a computer you will need the following:

- a **modem**, which is a device attached to your computer, either internally or externally
- a piece of **software** on your computer called a 'browser', which acts as your window to the Internet and gives you all the tools needed to surf the web. Microsoft's Internet Explorer and Netscape's Navigator are the two most popular browsers. Both are available free of charge
- an account with an **Internet service provider**. The ISP usually provides a CD-ROM which you use to set up an account with it and to configure your modem and computer to access the Internet. This CD will also contain the browser software mentioned above. Many ISPs no longer charge a monthly membership fee for domestic users and some have 'unmetered' telephone charges – you pay a fixed fee for unlimited use of the phone line.

Connecting to the Internet is very easy to do and is no longer the exclusive preserve of the computer enthusiast.

Using these links (known as hypertext links) you can skip from site to site on the web without having to know any specific addresses – hence the expression 'surfing' the web.

How a web address is constructed

Each web page has a unique address called a URL. The components of a URL are shown on page 87.

How do you find a site's home page?

There are several methods of finding web sites. For a start, you can simply guess it. The home page of the vast majority of sites belonging to well-known companies are in a standardised form. Hence, if you want to find the site for a newspaper, say, *The Guardian*, you may

http://www.therecordcorner.co.uk

http:// Used in most web pages, http:// means a 'hypertext' protocol. With modern web browsers you do not normally have to type in http://, it assumes this for you.

www This tells the browser that the hypertext document is on the World Wide Web. Variations such as www2 are sometimes used.

.therecordcorner This is the part of the domain name. In this example 'therecordcorner' is a company.

.co.uk The last part of the name tells us that the site is a UK-based company.

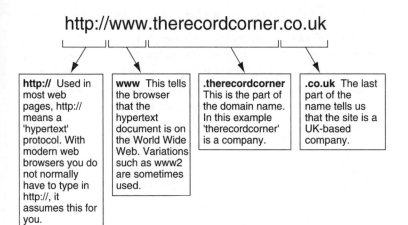

The above example of a URL is for a 'home page' (i.e. the main entry point or index to a web site). As you go into the site, accessing different pages, you will see the URL grow as the 'file path' is added to the URL. For example:

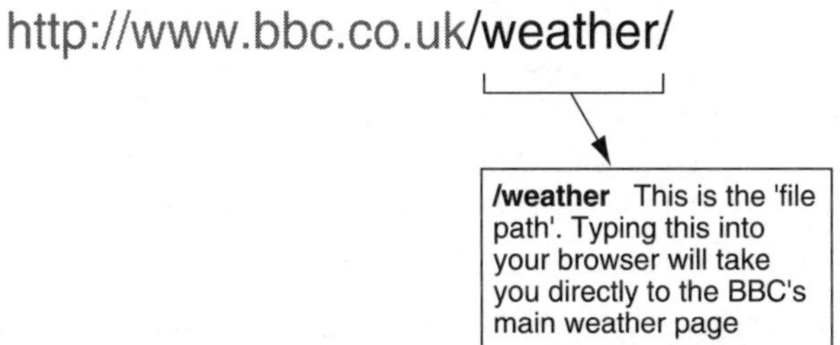

http://www.bbc.co.uk/weather/worldweather/index.shtml

takes you further into the world weather pages. On some very large sites, the file paths can become very long. You would not normally be expected to type it all in (although you could) – you would simply go to the home page and follow the links, or, better still, 'bookmark' the page under 'Favorites'.

How a web address is constructed

guess that its address is www.theguardian.com, so you type this into the address window of your browser. As it happens, this address does not work, so the guess was incorrect. With a bit of trial and error, you figure out the address you want is www.guardian.co.uk The ending part of the address has a particular meaning: .co.uk means a UK-based company whereas .com usually means an international or US company (see box above). As there are no fixed rules governing the use of these endings, you cannot always predict which one a particular company has registered for its use – some register both.

Happy endings

The last few characters of a web-site (and email) address are significant in that they indicate the type of organisation the site belongs to and often (but not always) the country it is based in. The USA is unusual in that web sites originating in it do not normally have a country code at the end. The following are some of the more common endings.

Some country codes

.au	Australia	.ie	Ireland
.ca	Canada	.jp	Japan
.de	Germany	.uk	UK
.fr	France		

Organisational codes

.co.uk	a UK-based company
.com	a company, usually US-based
.net	an organisation or company that provides Internet access
.org	a non-commercial organisation, such as a charity
.gov	a government site
.edu	a US-based academic site
.ac.uk	a UK-based academic site

At the time of writing there are plans to extend these codes to include .museum, .shop and several others. The current state of play regarding these and other new possible codes is available at www.icann.org.

A word of warning, however: while a wrong guess might simply take you to a site of an organisation or company with the same name as the one you are looking for, it might in some cases take you to a socially unacceptable site (see 'Is the Internet safe?', below).

Another way to find what you want is to use a 'search engine'. As the name suggests, these are sites that search the Web for you. You specify the keywords to look for, and the search engines returns suggested web sites or pages. There are many such search engines: some of the most popular ones are www.google.co.uk, www.yahoo.co.uk, www.lycos.com, www.askjeeves.co.uk and www.altavista.co.uk.

Alternatively, you can sometimes find useful web addresses in articles in newspapers or magazines. Whole books of web sites are also available.

Information on web sites

The amount of information on the Net is large and varied. The following three pages show just a few examples of what you can find out.

Anyone can set up a web site. Sites can be commercial, academic, governmental or private. They contain written text and pictures, and are easy to compose and publish.

As a consequence, the quality of information they contain is extremely variable. Some of it is supplied for commercial reasons, some for purely altruistic reasons; some of it is accurate and reliable, some distinctly unreliable and some even of a malicious nature.

Newsgroups

Another useful information-gathering system on the Internet, very similar to email (see Chapter 4), are the Usenet newsgroups – worldwide electronic discussion groups. There are tens of thousands of newsgroups, covering nearly every topic imaginable. By keying in messages you can join in and converse with like-minded people, share information and perhaps help solve problems. Your ISP will provide a connection to the newsgroups and your web-browser software will have a newsgroup reader built in. The first time you connect to the newsgroups it can take about ten minutes to download the complete list of available newsgroups. From this list you can select the newsgroups you are interested in and join them. Thereafter, you can go straight to the newsgroups you have joined to read the latest messages.

It is recommended that you browse some newsgroup messages before you participate in them. That way you will learn the unofficial rules, or 'netiquette'. When you are chatting to people via a keyboard it is all too easy to make blunders. What you think is a joke might come across as an insult to the readers.

Remember also that when you 'post' a message in a newsgroup, it is being read by everyone in that group, possibly around the world. Moreover, in doing so you are publicising your email address, so you could end up receiving junk mail. See Chapter 4 for more information on newsgroups.

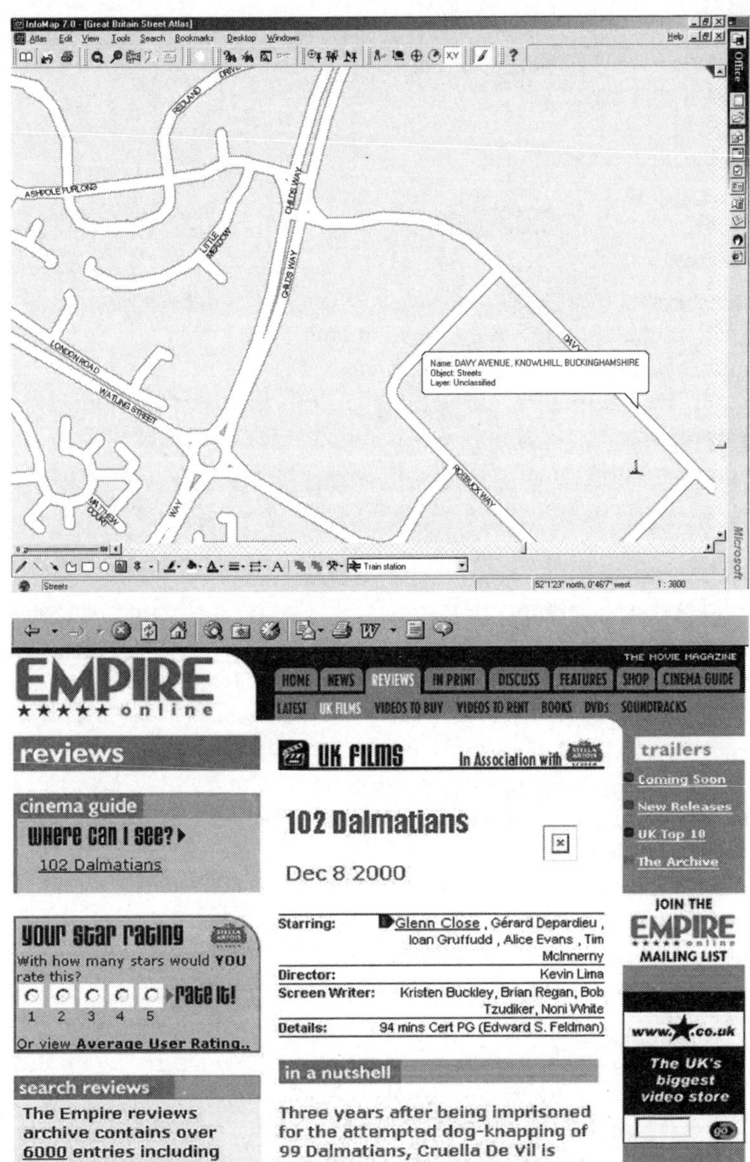

Typical web pages. Top: a local map; bottom: a film review

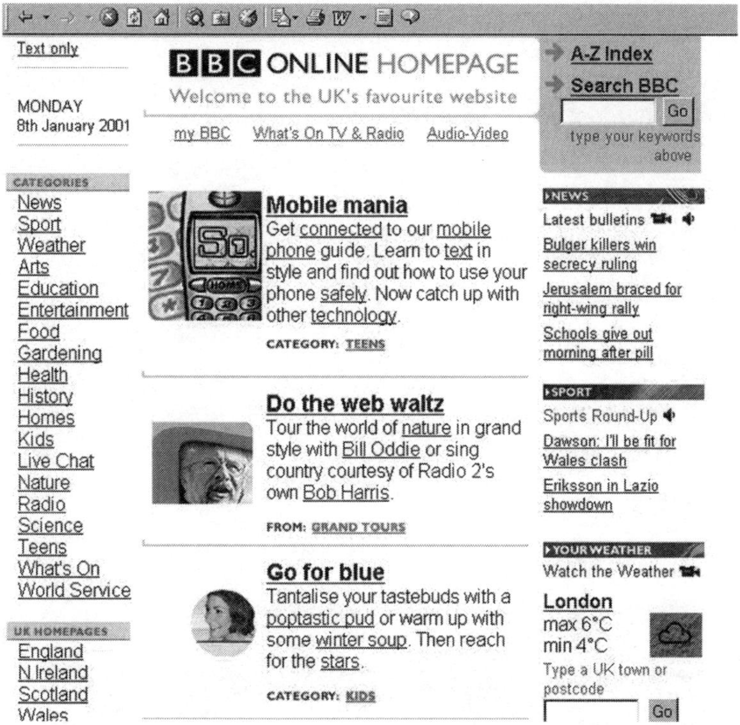

Text only
BBC ONLINE HOMEPAGE
Welcome to the UK's favourite website
A-Z Index
Search BBC
Go
type your keywords above
MONDAY 8th January 2001
my BBC
What's On TV & Radio
Audio-Video
CATEGORIES
News
Sport
Weather
Arts
Education
Entertainment
Food
Gardening
Health
History
Homes
Kids
Live Chat
Nature
Radio
Science
Teens
What's On
World Service
UK HOMEPAGES
England
N Ireland
Scotland
Wales
Mobile mania
Get connected to our mobile phone guide. Learn to text in style and find out how to use your phone safely. Now catch up with other technology.
CATEGORY: TEENS
Do the web waltz
Tour the world of nature in grand style with Bill Oddie or sing country courtesy of Radio 2's own Bob Harris.
FROM: GRAND TOURS
Go for blue
Tantalise your tastebuds with a poptastic pud or warm up with some winter soup. Then reach for the stars.
CATEGORY: KIDS
NEWS
Latest bulletins
Bulger killers win secrecy ruling
Jerusalem braced for right-wing rally
Schools give out morning after pill
SPORT
Sports Round-Up
Dawson: I'll be fit for Wales clash
Eriksson in Lazio showdown
YOUR WEATHER
Watch the Weather
London
max 6°C
min 4°C
Type a UK town or postcode
Go

RAILTRACK
travel
travel
search
site map
central menu
timetable
travel news
major stations
regeneration programme
Thameslink 2000
feedback
IMPORTANT NOTICE
The timetables on this site include all known changes at the time of issue. Please ensure that you phone 08457 48 49 50 to verify details of your journey. Click on this panel to reach more information including latest news from Train Operators.
From | To | Changes | Date | Depart | Arrive | Duration
London Euston | Milton Keynes Central | 0 | 8.01.01 | 16:20 | 17:14 | 0:54
London Euston | Milton Keynes Central | 0 | 8.01.01 | 16:43 | 17:24 | 0:41
London Euston | Milton Keynes Central | 0 | 8.01.01 | 16:58 | 17:33 | 0:35
details
earlier journey
later journey
return journey
new journey
Please ensure you confirm your journey details by calling National Rail enquiries on 08457 48

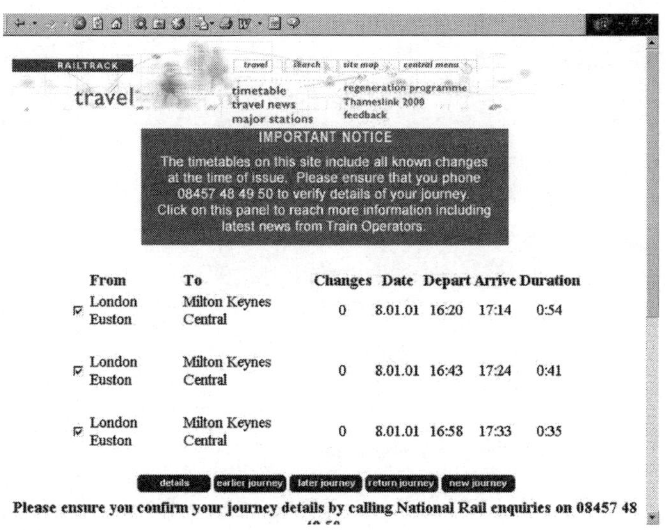

Top: The BBC's home page; bottom: Railtrack's railway timetable information

MUSEUM OF LONDON **Admission**

Museum and Shop opening times

Monday to Saturday 10.00am to 5.50pm

Sunday 12.00 noon to 5.50pm

Last admission 5.30pm

Café opening times

Monday to Saturday 10.00am to 5.00pm

Sunday 11.30am to 5.00pm

Map/ How to find us/ Opening times/ Admission charges/ Special needs

Map
How to find us
Opening times
Admission charges
Special needs

BBC HOMEPAGE | WORLD SERVICE | EDUCATION low graphics version | feedback | help

BBC NEWS

You are in: Business

Front Page
World
UK
UK Politics
Business
Market Data
Economy
Companies
E-Commerce
Your Money
Business Basics
Sci/Tech
Health
Education
Entertainment
Talking Point
In Depth
AudioVideo

BBC SPORT>>

Sunday, 7 January, 2001, 10:30 GMT

Gates unveils Playstation rival

Pro-wrestling's The Rock testified to Xbox's graphic ability

Microsoft Chairman Bill Gates has unveiled a video games system that is expected to pitch the Seattle company into a head-to-head battle with Sony, which dominates the $20bn-a-year console market.

The Xbox system - due on the market later this year -

We're getting to know the gaming community and we're

Search BBC News Online

GO

Advanced search options

Launch console for latest audio/video

BBC ONE TV NEWS
WORLD NEWS SUMMARY
BBC NEWS 24 BULLETIN
PROGRAMMES GUIDE

Games Wars

News and analysis

- Storming Europe
- US takes off
- Mania in Japan
- Playing to win
- Marketing hype

Rivals

- Nintendo's GameCube
- Microsoft's X-Box
- Sega's console dream

Analysis

Top: museum opening times; bottom: a BBC news page

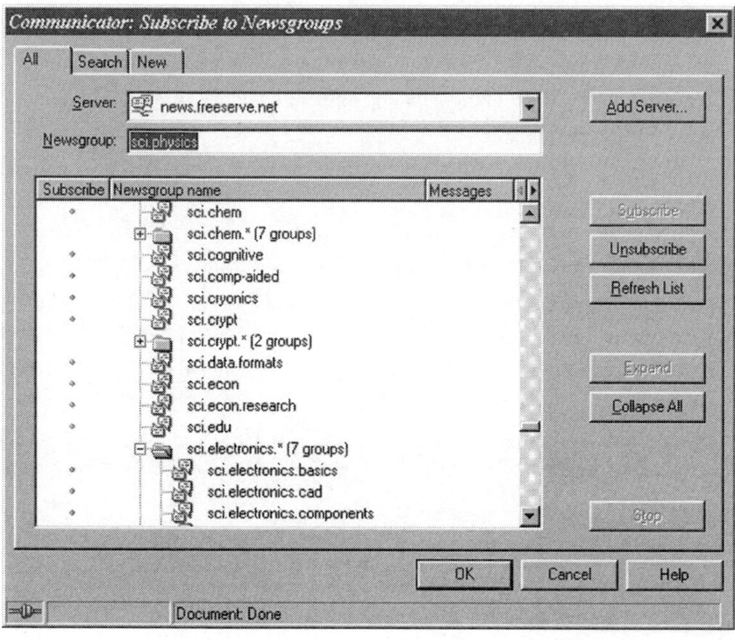

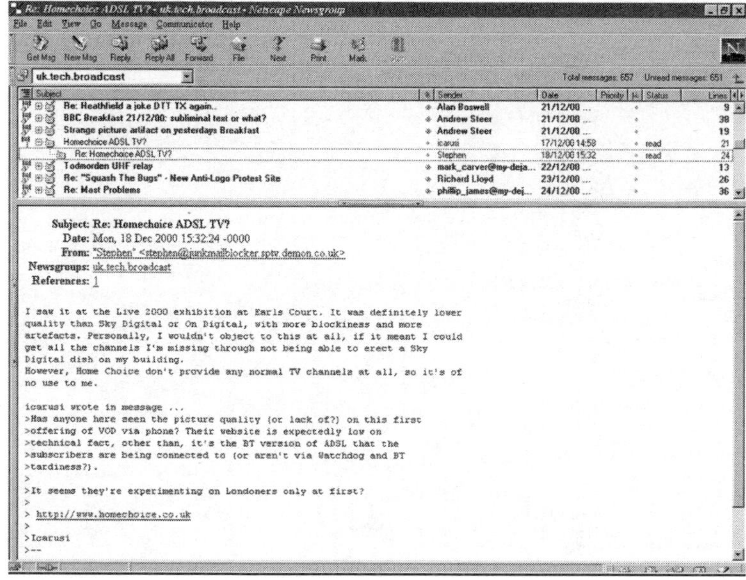

Top: part of a list of newsgroups; bottom: a typical newsgroup message

Is the Internet safe?

The expression 'safety on the Internet' refers to the danger of being offended or corrupted by material you may come across on the Net. In addition to pornography, which is the issue most people are concerned about, violence and social intolerance are also to be found on the Net. Arguably, part of the success of the Internet is that it is unregulated and so provides varied content and access for all. The unfortunate side-effect of this is that some of the material on it is offensive.

Some tools are available to help you avoid this material, but none is perfect. The browser software you use (typically Internet Explorer or Netscape Navigator) has a system called Recreational

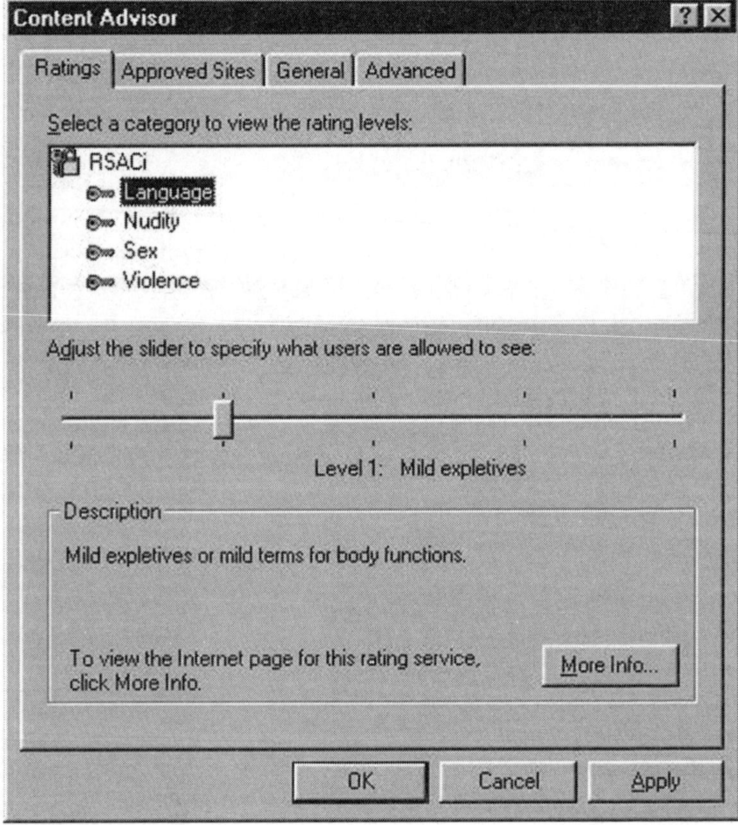

On-screen display for adjusting RSACi settings to control what web pages you can access

Software Advisory Council (RSACi), which can be found in the 'Settings' menu. You can use it to tailor the type of content allowed through on your computer. RSACi has settings for sex, nudity, language and violence, and each of them can be set to different levels of severity. The system works because those who publish material on the Web are meant to 'tag' their pages with the appropriate category, which allows the browser to filter out those pages whose ratings do not meet the criteria you have set. However, although it provides a first line of defence, the system is not foolproof because very few people who put material on the Web bother to categorise (or 'rate') their pages. Moreover, the system certainly would not work against those who maliciously publish offensive material. If you set the system to reject all unrated pages, you would end up cutting out most of the Internet, but this might be a useful procedure for families with very young children as they could still access children's sites, most of which are rated.

Alternative systems and filters

The RSACi system has not been universally adopted, but similar ones, provided by the Internet Content Rating Association (ICRA)* and Safesurf,* both containing more categories than the four used by RASCi, are being introduced. ICRA can be downloaded from the ICRA web site and Safesurf is supported by the latest version of Microsoft's web browser, Internet Explorer.

Software filters are more helpful as a defence against unwanted material. Products such as Net Nanny and Cyber-sitter check every page and suppress it if its address matches those in its 'bad list' or it detects certain words or phrases in the text. These products also work on newsgroups, whereas RASCi does not. The best filter systems also have the facility for blocking specified data – say, your address or credit-card number – from being *sent* from the keyboard. Some ISPs provide software filters as part of their service. AOL,* for example, provides quite a sophisticated version that can be tailored for different ages.

When you set up one of these systems on your computer, you have to supply a password; this enables you to disable it when you want to. The 'bad list' has to be kept up to date, and you usually have to pay a subscription fee to download the updates from the Internet.

Software filters are not perfect: they may inadvertently allow some unwanted pages through; block pages which are innocent; and can be bypassed by the more computer-savvy children.

The most effective type of filter, designed for the very young user, is one that allows access only to a 'good list' of web pages – that is, a large selection of pages that has been vetted and found to be satisfactory. Clearly, this would be too restrictive for older children and adults. Such a service is provided by AOL and Kidznet,* an ISP specifically designed for children.

Some search engines can be configured to filter out unwelcome words, so they will name only 'safe' sites in response to your search query. Altavista* has this option. Other search engines, such as Yahoo* with its 'Yahooligans' option, use a 'bad list' to block unwanted sites. Again, they are quite effective but not 100 per cent perfect.

Accessing the Internet without a computer

Accessing the Internet via a television set would seem to be an obvious alternative to using a computer, because the screen would double up as the monitor, and digital and cable TV usually mean that the TV is already connected to a telephone line.

Differences between TV screens and computer monitors

The inside surface of TV and computer screens are covered with tiny red, green and blue phosphor dots, referred to as pixels. They are illuminated by a very fast scanning electron beam, which varies the brightness and colour mix of the pixels to produce the picture. In a TV screen, these dots are placed 0.7 microns apart and the scanning beam updates the picture 50 times a second. This produces satisfactory quality for moving pictures viewed at a distance of about 2 metres. Most people are not seriously worried by the limited resolution or the 50-times-a-second flicker, but things are different on a computer. The still text and graphics generally viewed on a computer need to be viewed close up and need higher resolution. With a still image the flicker is also much more noticeable. So a modern computer monitor typically has a dot spacing of 0.25 microns and the picture is scanned at 60 to 70 times a second or more. A computer monitor screen is therefore more expensive than a TV screen.

Previous efforts to bring the Internet on to TV, such as Netstation back in 1997, have not caught on. Currently there are three options:

- the Sega Dreamcast games console, which connects to a TV, and offers Internet access as a bonus
- the TV manufacturer Bush, which offers an all-in-one widescreen analogue Internet TV giving full Internet access and email, but as yet, does not come with a digital TV tuner
- the digital TV operator ONdigital, which supplies a special modem that connects to the digital set-top box giving Internet access.

In all three cases it is necessary to connect the equipment to your phone line.

One disadvantage of accessing the Net via TV is that normal Internet pages often look awful on a TV. Televisions were designed to be viewed at a comfortable distance from the screen, not for sitting close to and reading text from, so while the resolution of the TV screen is satisfactory for the former purpose, it is not for the latter.

Some measures can be taken to solve this problem, and the service provided by the Bush TV and ONdigital (see Chapters 1 and 4) uses them. First, the size of the textual part of Internet pages can be increased and this is done electronically inside the Internet TV receiver. This makes them easier to read. (Of course, the whole page could be enlarged to overcome the lower resolution, but this is not really practical, as it would mean that less of the page would be visible, thus entailing more scrolling, up and down and left to right, to see the whole page.) The disadvantages of enlarging the text part of the page are that the positions of the text and images on the page have to be rearranged, thus spoiling the page designers' efforts. Moreover, text that is part of an image is not affected, making it less easy to read.

The other approach to this problem that ONnet uses is to get companies to design the web pages to look good on a TV screen – with less detail, larger text and simpler pictures.

One advantage of the ONnet system is that it allows you to view a small TV picture in the corner of the screen while you are using the Internet.

However, neither of these systems overcomes the 50-times-a-second picture flicker on the TV. More expensive 100Hz TVs (which use digital electronics to double the refresh rate artificially) do not suffer from this drawback.

Another problem with the early Internet TV projects is that, because neither the TV nor the set-top box has any significant memory or computing power, they cannot deal with some of the more advanced Internet features or send or receive files to and from other users.

Accessing the Internet via a mobile phone is another possibility, and it is explored in Chapter 5. One obvious drawback of this is that very little information can be shown on the small LCD screen.

Information-gathering in the future

The future of information-gathering is tied up with that of the Internet, as no other system gives us access to so much information, so quickly. However, the Internet is not without problems, which need to be solved if it is to become our principal source of information.

Problems with the Internet

The Internet can be slow The speed with which data can be sent or received over the Internet depends on various factors:

- the hardware and software your PC uses
- the nature of the pages you are trying to access
- the number of simultaneous users worldwide – hence, the time of day you are using the Net.

For access at home, one of the limitations is the standard telephone line and dial-up modem. Using current technology, the V90 modem is about the fastest possible, although the V92 offers a slight improvement. Faster telephone line systems that are available include special integrated services digital network (ISDN) telephone lines, and the newer asynchronous digital subscriber line (ADSL) system, which uses conventional telephone lines and offers a service that allows you to be connected to the Internet all the time – you do not need to keep on making a phone call to get connected.

Internet speeds

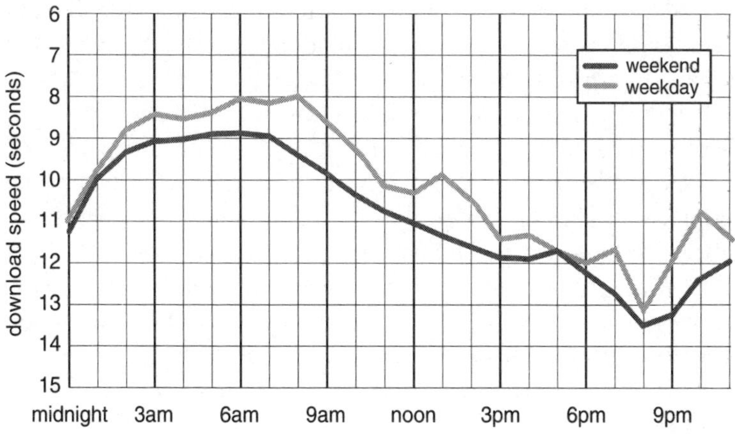

Internet access: time vs speed
Source: *Which?* magazine, May 1999

These systems have been adopted mainly by businesses, but as they become more affordable for home use they are likely to grow rapidly. If you live in an area where certain cable TV services are available, you may be able to subscribe to their broadband cable modem Internet services which are slowly being introduced. See Chapter 4 for details.

The satellite broadcaster BSkyB will also be offering a fast Internet via its satellite. With this system, data can be received at a fast rate but data sent from your terminal will still have to go via a telephone line at a slower rate.

In addition to constraints posed by technology, the design of web sites could also determine speed of access – generally, the more graphics a site has, the slower it is to access. Here, consumer pressure could force changes to be made – if a site is notoriously slow to view, its designers will have to improve it if they want as many visitors or customers as a rival site that is faster to access.

Meanwhile, new technology is being used to look at ways of globally speeding up the Internet with projects such as Internet2 and the Super-Internet being developed. However, they are still in their infancy, and it is impossible to say when such developments will become widely available.

It is difficult to find what you want on the Internet Using search engines to find something particular on the Net can be a bit hit-and-miss, but that is largely because the way the Internet is organised (or not organised) makes it difficult to catalogue it. One solution to this is the development of smaller networks on the Net where we can find most of the things we want. Some of these 'walled garden' networks are already operational. Many Internet service providers have what they call a 'portal site', which operates like a contents page and links you to other sites it recommends (or advertises). In addition, search engines themselves are improving all the time and some allow you to ask questions in plain English rather than use keywords and logical operators.

Computers are notoriously unreliable and generally awkward Access to the Internet will have to be made simpler and generally more convenient if it is to be used by everyone. Making the Net accessible via a TV is one solution, but, as we have seen, the quality is limited. Developing special 'TV-friendly' walled garden sites might be another answer, but as this decreases the versatility of a web site, Internet via a TV screen may be restricted to the more mundane uses. A more likely scenario is one where each house has a general-purpose communications and entertainment box instead of the digital TV set-top box. This box or 'multimedia home platform' would act as an all-purpose information and entertainment centre, and could be connected to whatever display system (TV, computer monitor, or hand-held screen) the user thinks appropriate.

Access wherever you are

The Internet is a two-way system. We can supply information as well as receive it, which is why it is useful for purposes such as banking and local and national government services. It is likely that in the not-too-distant future the more routine official and administrative tasks – such as voting in elections, filing census forms and applying for car and TV licences – are done via the Internet. (Tax returns can already be filed over the Internet.) So, connecting to the Internet may become a necessity, not an option. We may see a growth in information terminals or kiosks in the high street, where we can access the Internet or selected services on it. Such terminals are already available at major airports and railway stations, but these are commercially sponsored terminals for general Internet access and email.

If the Internet becomes a more efficient information source it could conceivably replace other information sources such as teletext and CD-ROMs – all the information we want will be literally at our fingertips.

Chapter 3

E-commerce

'E-commerce' (electronic commerce) usually means using the Internet as a method of buying goods. The European Union's definition of the term is 'any form of business transaction in which the parties interact electronically rather than by physical exchanges or direct physical contact'.

This chapter looks at shopping on the Internet, the interactive services offered by digital TV, and possible future methods of payment that could make banknotes and coins things of the past.

Shopping on the Internet

When the Internet was first developed; it was seen primarily as an efficient means for people and organisations to share information, in particular scientific and other research material. This was when the Internet was used simply to store and share data documents and computer programs, before the World Wide Web (WWW) came into being.

The development of the Web opened the Internet up to a wider audience and made it much easier for people to find information. Web sites, consisting of 'pages', were set up, so users could view the information they wanted directly on their computers. The pages could be linked together, so users could skip from one page to another, even if the pages did not belong to the same site. 'Surfing' the Internet became possible because at the click of a mouse button you could jump from one part of the world to another.

Telecommunications companies then saw the benefit of providing access to the Internet to private individuals, which gave rise to the internet service provider (ISP) industry. In the early days of the Internet, there was very little 'commercial' activity on it. However, as more and more people became connected to the Net, the concept of using it for commercial ends emerged. Nowadays, the Internet is regarded as both an information source and an important element in many types of commerce. Businesses have become increasingly interested in the Internet, much to the concern of many traditionalists, who see the Net as just a means of sharing information. The original anarchic nature of the Internet and the requirements of these new e-commerce users are not always compatible.

So-called dotcom companies are opening up all the time, selling directly to consumers over the Net. More than three million adults in the UK now claim to shop regularly online.

How e-commerce works

The procedure for buying something over the Internet (or 'online') is generally the same irrespective of the site – you access the shop's web site using your computer or TV Internet service, browse its products or search for specific items by entering some key words, then place your order. The goods are delivered to you by ordinary mail or a courier service, unless you are buying computer software or multimedia files, as these can be sent to you directly over the Internet at the time of purchase.

A good Internet shop has descriptions and photographs of all its items. If you want to buy an item you add it to your virtual 'shopping basket', usually by clicking on it and a button saying 'add to the shopping basket' . When you are ready to complete the order, you go to the 'check-out' page, where you are asked for your account details. If it is your first visit to the shop you have to spend a little time entering your credit-card details, address and email address. This information is usually sent over a 'secure link' (see box on page 106) to reduce any risk of unauthorised access to the details. If you have used the shop before, you should not have to enter this information again – you just have to enter your name and password.

The check-out page should show a list of the items ordered with their costs and any shipping costs. You can still cancel or modify the order at this stage. Check the final total. If you are happy to go ahead, you simply select the 'place order' option and your order will be sent. You should then receive an automatic email confirmation that the order has been received.

When *Which?* magazine tested Internet shopping services in 2000, it found that the system generally worked well but that occasionally there were problems, mainly with delivery. If delivery happens when people are at work, goods cannot be taken in.

It is a good idea to check the web site to see what delivery options are available and if necessary have the items delivered to your place of work.

Which? also found that most retailers had a good 'returns' policy and that returning the goods and getting a refund was generally unproblematic.

Consumer rights for online shoppers

Surveys of people who shop online show that a sizeable proportion of them feel they are taking a risk in supplying their credit-card details over the Net. However, these fears are generally unfounded – more credit-card frauds are perpetrated in the 'real world' than over the Internet. Indeed, it is quite difficult for fraudsters to download details of credit cards from the Net. Moreover, if you were to suffer fraud, you are well protected as a consumer.

When you buy online using your credit card you get the same protection under UK law as you do when shopping in the high street. The Consumer Credit Act already gives you greater protection if you pay by credit card rather than by debit card, for purchases over £100 and below £30,000. This act makes the credit-card issuer and suppliers jointly liable if there is a problem with the goods or services. However, this protection may not apply if you are buying from an overseas site. Now, under new Distance Selling Regulations, you get extra protection. These regulations cover transactions where customers and supplier do not meet face to face, and applies to credit and other types of card. You are entitled to claim back, from the retailer, any money paid out without your authority. Furthermore, you are also entitled to a 'cooling-off' period of seven working days, during which you can change your mind and cancel the goods or services you ordered. In addition, orders must be confirmed in writing, or by fax or email, and must be fulfilled within 30 days. The only exceptions to this are goods made to your personal specification; perishable goods such as fresh food or flowers; and sealed audio, video or computer-software products you have opened.

It is vital that companies trading online store their customer information securely so it cannot be accessed by people visiting or exploring the site. However, in the rush to get online, some organisations have not given security a high priority: a survey by the Department of Trade and Industry revealed that only one in seven companies trading online had a formal security policy. Some of the most high-profile security breaches reported in the newspapers have been because information has not been held securely enough by the companies concerned. If you plan to deal with an online company, check whether it has got a security policy, a privacy policy and clear terms and conditions. They are not always easy to find on the site but a with a little perseverance they can usually be found tucked away somewhere. It is also a good idea to print them off.

Where Internet shopping comes into its own

Shopping on the Internet has several advantages over traditional shopping. For one thing, the range of products available is extremely large and you can do it all with the minimum of physical effort. Tracking down obscure and unusual items no longer means walking miles in search of them. Moreover, you can exploit the 24-hour availability of the sites, and can do all your ordering when you have the time. Geographical boundaries are also irrelevant when it comes to Internet shopping. However, you will have to pay delivery charges.

Not everyone is convinced that Internet shopping is a good thing. It could be argued that there is little point in buying items such as clothing, fresh food or furniture over the Internet because you cannot see or try the products out in a way you can if you visited a shop. On the other hand, for many types of goods and services the Internet can provide a better service than a shop. Here are a few examples of how Internet shopping can offer value-added service.

Buying goods from overseas

Some of the more successful virtual shops have been the ones that sell worldwide. Products that are available in the USA or elsewhere are usually easy to import once you have tracked them down. Items such as books, DVDs and CDs are among the most popular Internet purchases, as they are cheap and easy to mail, and comparatively inexpensive in themselves. Overseas Internet shopping is also used by enthusiasts or collectors to obtain specialist products for their hobbies. Internet search engines are a useful tool for tracking down such items.

How the Internet is made secure

Because of the universality of access to the Internet, the Net is a rather insecure medium and in theory anyone could 'tap' into the data and decode information you are sending. In practice, you would need a fair amount of technical expertise or inside information to do so. To make the Internet secure for sending sensitive information such as your credit-card details it is possible to set up a temporary secure connection. The most common system, supported by most computer- and TV-based web browsers, is called secure socket layer (SSL). SSL disguises data by means of mathematical encryption.

The system uses two mathematical 'keys' – one public and the other private. Everyone who uses a computer has both types of key. The private key is hidden inside the machine, while the public key is available to the outside world. The latter can be used to encrypt messages but only the former can decipher them. Therefore, if you wanted to send someone some secret information, you would encrypt the information using that person's public key (you do not actually do it yourself – your computer or Internet terminal would do it for you). This information could then be deciphered only with the person's private key.

When you are sending information in this way, your Internet system should inform you that a secure link has been established. On computers, the web browsers Internet Explorer and Netscape Navigator show that a secure link has been established by displaying a closed padlock icon at the bottom corner of the screen. If you hold your mouse pointer over these icons, or press the right-hand mouse button on them, you should see a number. This tells you how strong the encryption is: 128-bit encryption is the level normally used by online banks; lower levels such as 40-bit are often used by retail sites. Web sites will not encrypt all the pages on their site, only those where personal information is being input.

This system works well for transactions carried out by individuals (business to consumer transactions), but more secure systems are available for more complex business and financial transactions. These can involve an independent 'trusted' third party, such as a bank.

Buying books

A good bookselling site, such as www.amazon.co.uk, has a much larger selection of books than the average bricks-and-mortar shop and, in most cases, can supply what you order within a few days. You do not need to know exactly what you want – once you have accessed the web site, you can 'search' for a book knowing only part of the title or author, or you can look for books on specific topics. One useful aspect of buying books online is that many of the sites have comments or 'reviews' by previous buyers which may help you decide whether the books are worth buying. You too can contribute reviews. You can use the site as a catalogue in the same way that you might spend an hour or so browsing in a large bookshop.

An even better example of how the Internet can help you buy a book is the Net-based book-search service, www.bibliofind.com, which offers a service that links hundreds of real second-hand bookshops around the world. All you have to do is to enter as much detail as you can about the book that you want, and the site will report back with details of shops that can supply it. More often than not you will be provided with the names of several shops that have the book and you will be able to choose the cheapest, a first edition or the one in best condition. Prices are given in the currency of the country where the shop is located, but the site provides a currency converter so you can see what a book costs in sterling. If no shop has the book, the details can be kept on file until a copy turns up. The system seems to work well. When *Which?* tested the service, it was able to obtain immediately an out-of-print novel, from a shop in Australia, and after a nine-month wait a very obscure book on the history of London, from the USA.

Buying groceries

For many, traipsing round a supermarket is a real chore. Many of the supermarket chains – and a number of specialist food suppliers – in the UK offer online shopping for groceries. Typically, they have a different approach from other retailers on the Net in that rather than having all their products listed on a web site, they provide it to customers on a CD-ROM. This means you can 'browse' through the store and select products, without spending time on line. However, you do need to connect to the relevant web site to download new prices, products and offers. The goods are delivered to your home at a time selected by you a day or two after you place the order.

You may find that you prefer to visit the shop to select fresh food personally, and buy the more routine household goods over the Internet.

Buying music

Shops on the Net selling CDs are able to offer a level of service that it is difficult for any real shop to compete with. As with bookshops on the Net, you can search the stock for items you want and then read reviews from other customers or professional reviewers.

If your computer is equipped with a sound card and speakers, you can even hear short clips from selected music tracks on each album so you can be sure that the music is what you want.

A step-by-step guide to buying a CD from www.cdnow.com is shown on page 109.

Online auctions

One of the more unusual applications of e-commerce is an on-line auction. Several sites are dedicated to auctions in which you can buy or sell just about anything, from a single CD to a valuable antique.

To take part in an auction you first have to register with the site, which may mean supplying your credit-card details and email address. Registration can be a fairly lengthy process but once you have done it you are ready to buy or sell.

The web site in effect acts as an automated auction house. A vendor posts an item for sale by providing a description of the goods, with perhaps a photograph, a closing date or time for the auction and a reserve price. The item is then listed under the appropriate category for that particular product: video film, theatre tickets, computer accessories, and so on. Vendors can be private individuals, professional retailers or even the auction house itself.

A prospective buyer can then bid for the item. Unlike in a real auction, you do not have to keep increasing the price you are willing to pay to outbid other customers because this process is done automatically by the auction. You simply state the highest price you are prepared to go to. The automated auction will start your bid off at a price lower than that and go up in regular increments till it reaches the limit you have set should others be bidding against you. You can monitor this process online daily to check your progress or the auction house can email you if you have been outbid. You can then choose to raise your limit.

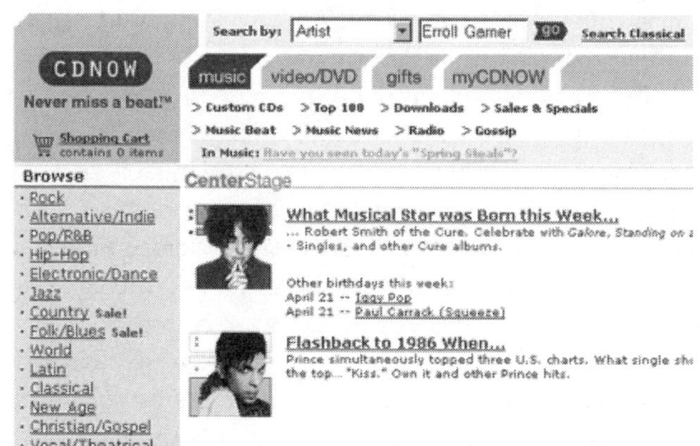

STEP 1 Opening page of a shop. You search for a CD by entering details (top) or you browse through the music types (left). Special offers or new releases are shown centre.

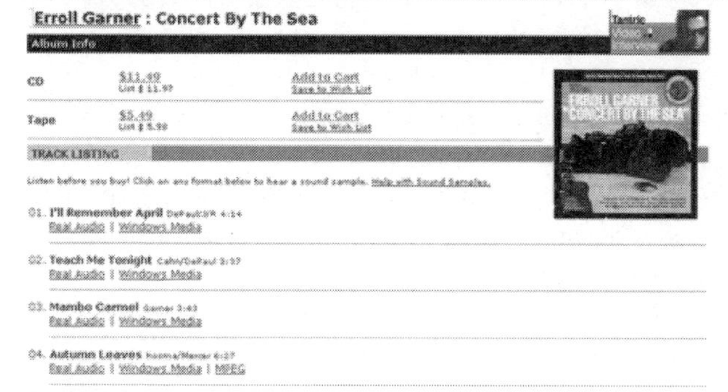

STEP 2 Details of selected item are shown, with prices (top) and track listings (bottom).

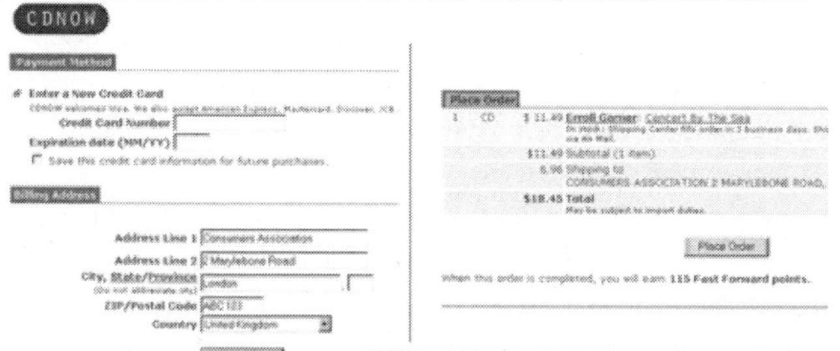

STEP 3 If this is your first visit to the shop you have to enter your details.

STEP 4 Total cost of your purchases are shown before you finally place the order.

At the end of the auction, typically a week or so, the successful bidder will be notified by email. The vendor and the successful bidder then have to contact each other by email to arrange the transaction. The obvious problem with this system is that because the two parties do not know each other the risk of fraud is high. To help overcome this, the auction site keeps its clients' details on file and encourages all those who use the site to post messages detailing how successful or otherwise their transactions were. This allows you to read reports on regular users of the system so you can find out if a particular buyer or seller has a good track record.

It can be fun just browsing auction sites to see what is on offer. You soon realise that there is a mix of professional sellers and private individuals who are buying and selling on a regular basis. The system could be described as being a cross between a car boot sale and a well-established auction house. When *Which?* magazine tested these sites in 2000, researchers bought and sold theatre tickets, digital cameras and DVD films without any problems but the savings were small.

Before you are tempted to take part you must read carefully the online help or tutorials provided so you know the rules and general etiquette involved. You should also read the terms and conditions so you understand what liability the auction house accepts in the case of a failed transaction.

Despite the safeguards provided by some of the sites, *Which?* did find some instances where people have been ripped off. A common problem is the unreliability of the clients' details mentioned above. One way to overcome this is to is to use an 'escrow' – a type of transaction in which a third party acts as an intermediary between the buyer and seller. The auction houses themselves can provide this service but they charge for doing it, so it is not worth doing it for low-cost items. Which? Web Trader (see box) does not cover any auction sites.

Buying tickets

Buying travel, theatre or cinema tickets is relatively unproblematic – most people already do this over the telephone in any case. The Internet is an alternative that, because it is interactive, gives you the opportunity to search for what you want and consider other options at your own pace.

For example, if you want to buy a train ticket, you would start by visiting the Railtrack web site.* This site does not sell tickets, but is a good place for planning your route. Choose the 'Timetable' option and enter the start station, the destination and the date and time of travel and it comes up with a selection of trains and connections. Armed with this information you can then visit a site such as www.thetrainline.com to buy the ticket. You pay by credit card and the ticket can be sent to you or be picked up at the station before you leave.

Theatre and cinema tickets can also be bought online, saving time spent on the telephone to get through to the box office.

Buying airline tickets online can also be advantageous, as it is much simpler to shop around for the cheapest offers and check for suitable connections. You can buy online direct from an airline or through a travel agent.

Which? Web Trader

Consumers' Association (CA) has drawn up a code of practice for online traders to encourage the highest possible standards and make sure that consumers are treated fairly. Companies which agree to follow the code can display the Which? Web Trader logo on their web site, which is an indication to shoppers that the site is reliable and they can use it with confidence.

When a UK company applies to CA for permission to display the mark, CA carries out checks to make sure it is genuine and meets the required standards. Once the company is accepted, CA carries out random checks to make sure it is sticking to the code.

If CA receives reports that a trader is not following the code, it will investigate and, if it finds the allegation to be true, it will ask the trader to put things right or remove it from the scheme. This threat is not an idle one – it has been used.

The logo does not imply that *Which?* recommends the actual goods or services offered or the customer service provided by the trader outside the areas covered by the code.

Full details of the Web Trader scheme can be found on the Which? web site.* The scheme is supported by the government's TrustUK* scheme and the European Union and has been adopted by several other consumer organisations in Europe.

Which? Web Trader and TrustUK symbols

Ten tips for shopping on the Internet

Here are some hints on how to shop safely on the Internet.

- Shop around. Using the Internet makes it much quicker and much simpler to compare prices than visiting lots of different shops, telephoning, or studying mail-order catalogues.
- Pay by credit card, rather than by debit or charge card. The vast majority of e-shopping sites use credit cards as the preferred payment method. Generally the site and the credit-card company offer you some protection should things go wrong. The Consumer Credit Act protects you if the company hosting the site goes bust, provided you have spent over £100 and under £30,000. The new Distance Selling Directive is a safeguard against fraud, while the card's insurance should protect you against faulty goods. Check with your credit-card company for the exact details of its commitment.
- When giving your card details and address over the Internet, make sure that a 'secure link' has been established – if it has, a 'closed padlock' symbol or an unbroken key symbol will appear on a toolbar at the top of the screen or on the status bar at the bottom.
- Before you place the final order, check availability. Many sites list items that they may not have in stock. A good e-shop will give an idea of delivery time.
- Before completing the purchase check whether VAT is included in the price and what the delivery charges are.

- If you are importing from another country, be aware that you may have to pay extra import duty or VAT on delivery.
- Check how the item will be delivered. If the company uses a courier service or sends goods by post, will you be at home during the day? If not, will it deliver to an alternative daytime address if this is different from the address on your credit card?
- If buying electrical goods from overseas, be aware of different voltages, licensing agreements and TV standards that may make your purchase unusable.
- Make sure that the site you use will send you an email confirming your order. Keep a copy of this email in case of problems. It is also a good idea to print out the order as it appears on the screen.
- Check the retailer's returns policy. Details of how to return faulty goods should be given on the site. Many e-shops also accept returns of 'unwanted' purchases.

Shopping via your TV

Since the introduction of analogue satellite TV, viewers have been able to buy products while sitting in front of the TV, via shopping channels such as QVC. When you see a product being promoted on TV and want to buy it, all you have to do is phone in to order it, quoting your credit-card number.

Shopping channels are really just multimedia mail-order catalogues. Their customer base consists largely of shoppers who tune in regularly, credit card at the ready. Most of the products on offer are either luxury goods, gadgets and other non-essential items.

Alongside the introduction of the new digital TV channels (see Chapter 1), a new type of interactive shopping is on offer from digital and cable companies. The system is quite simple: your digital TV or set-top box is connected to your phone line. In the case of digital satellite TV, this connection will have been made at the time it was installed as a part of your contract and is why the company gives you the set-top box for free. Even if you are not subscribing to the company's channels, you are still supposed to keep your box connected to the phone line, because the company hopes that perhaps one day you will use the shopping service. In the case of cable boxes, these are permanently connected to the cable phone line.

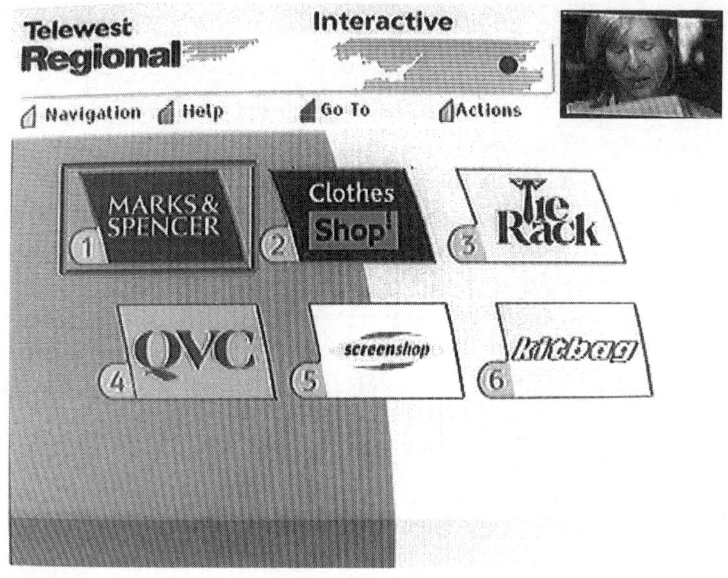

Interactive shopping menu page from Telewest

When you press the 'interactive' services option on your remote control you are taken to a menu of options. Typically, this could include shopping, information, financial services, email, games, and so on.

Selecting 'shopping' will take you to another menu where you have to choose the type of item you are interested in (such as electrical goods, food or toys). You will then see a display of a number of specialist retailers for you to choose from. These will typically be well-known high street retailers such as Woolworth, Argos and Marks & Spencer. By selecting one of these shops you can browse the items it has on offer.

What is immediately obvious is that this is not as versatile as shopping on the Internet. You have only a limited number of retailers to choose from (typically about 50) and each of these retailers offers only a few hundred items. For example, the shops selling CDs or DVDs offer only a limited range – say, a 'top 10' for each format.

When you have selected the item or items you want to buy, your order is sent automatically to the retailer using the cable connection, or in the case of OPEN, the telephone line.

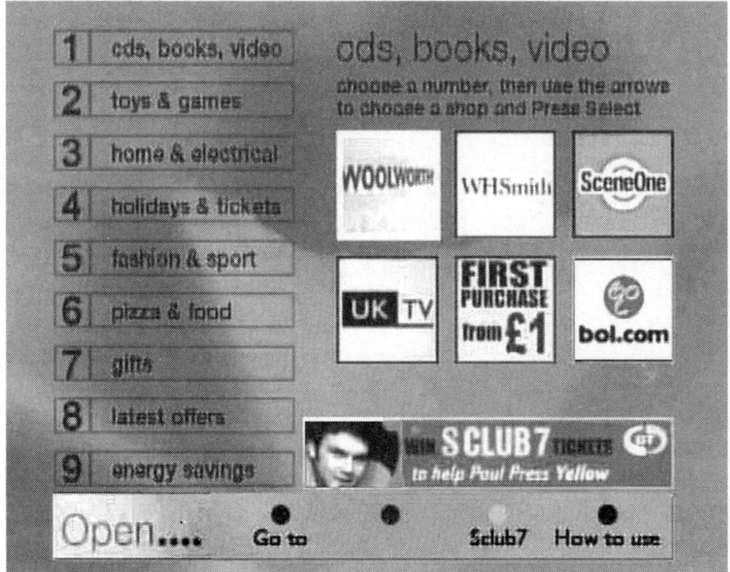

Interactive shopping menu page from OPEN

Customers have much more control over what they buy in this manner than they do when they buy from the shopping channels, but the overall impression is still that of ordering from a mail-order catalogue. Using the Internet, on the other hand, allows you to browse complete shops. In late 2000 the items available via digital cable and satellite channels were largely restricted to non-essential goods such as CDs, videos, toys, chocolates and electrical goods.

Whether or not shopping via your TV is simple is questionable. For example, if you were to order a pizza in this manner, you might find that with certain services you had a very small range of toppings and only one size to choose from. The process itself is rather slow and awkward, too. You have to keep waiting for the next screen to appear, and 'navigate' the menus using your keyboard. While this is probably no worse than navigating the Internet, the fact that you have a very limited choice and cannot ask or search for what you want is likely to make you less patient when it comes to waiting for a screen to appear. The chances are that you could place your order for a pizza over the telephone in less than half the time you would take via your TV.

However, if you need a last-minute gift or feel the urge to buy a digital camera after all the shops have closed, then digital TV shopping could be the answer. Generally, delivery of the goods is satisfactory, and the prices are similar to the shop prices, plus the cost of delivery.

As well as shops, the interactive TV menu offers a few additional services such as a local film and restaurant guide, news and weather and arcade-style games. They are not there for altruistic reasons – you may be charged for these services via your phone bill, or they may be commercially sponsored and therefore not independent. Interactive TV also offers financial and banking services, which are discussed later in this chapter (see 'TV banking').

The service offered by the cable companies is generally better than that offered by digital satellite's OPEN – they have more shops to choose from, they are generally easier to navigate and you can continue watching and listening to your TV programme while using them (you can retain a small TV picture in a top corner of the screen). With the digital satellite service, you lose the TV picture completely and have to endure continuous background music and advertising. Advertising promotions also litter most of the pages on OPEN.

Shopping via digital terrestrial TV

ONdigital, the digital terrestrial TV service, does not have the capacity (frequency bandwidth) to implement an interactive shopping service in the manner of digital satellite and cable companies. Instead, it can supply a special Internet modem to connect to your telephone line and to the ONdigital set-top box. This is called ONnet, and it gives full access to the Internet, displaying the web pages on your TV. You can also retain the TV picture in one corner of the screen, so you can continue watching TV while surfing the Internet. There is a subscription charge for this service of (currently) £5 per month, which is more expensive than the rate charged by the average ISP, but reasonable for households without a computer.

The ONnet box uses special electronic software inside it to reformat Internet web pages so that they look acceptable on the lower-resolution screen of a TV. This works fairly well although some graphics and icons are difficult to read. ONnet is also signing up some shops to produce web sites especially for it, which will look fine on the TV screen. So, with ONnet, it is possible to carry out true Internet shopping via your TV, which is ultimately more versatile than the services currently offered by the other digital TV systems.

Digital banking

Whether you are fed up with visiting your local bank or are unhappy with its limited opening hours – or, worse still, find that your branch has been closed down – home banking may be the answer. You can do home banking via the phone or, more appropriately for the digital age, via your computer or even digital TV.

With home banking it is possible to do most of the things you can do at a high street bank – transfer funds, check your balance, set up a standing order and operate multiple accounts (savings, current and credit card). Not all banks offer all these services and flexibility varies from bank to bank. With the best ones, you can do everything you want except paying in cheques and drawing out cash.

Telephone banking

There are two types of telephone banking: automated systems and operator systems. With the former, you first have to go through a security check and then choose the service you want from a recorded menu. You enter your choices and information using the phone's keypad. This type of banking has fewer options than other types of home banking, but with some of them you can transfer to an operator-based service for other transactions. Operator-based systems generally put you straight through to a human being who performs a security check and carries out your requests. This system tends to offer the widest range of services of all home banking systems.

Banking online with your computer

You can do your banking from home using a computer in one of two ways – using a direct link to the bank from your computer and modem or via the Internet. Both ways allow you to view your account on-screen and carry out a range of transactions including checking your balance, viewing pending transactions, paying bills and transferring funds between accounts.

For the first type of banking (the direct-link variety), you need a computer and modem. Special connecting software will be provided by the bank which allows you to dial directly into the bank's computer. You have to pass through security checks before you can access your account. One drawback of this system is that you can access your account only via the computer on to which you have loaded the software, although some banks may allow you to load the software on to a second machine (say, at work).

For Internet banking, you will need to have an account with an ISP. You access your bank account through the bank's web site, passing through the security checks by entering numbers and passwords. As described in the previous section on Internet shopping, you will notice that the 'padlock' icon at the bottom of your web browser will be in the locked position, denoting a secure link. One advantage Internet banking has over the direct-link computer banking is that you can do it from any computer with Internet access.

TV banking

You do not have to have a computer to take part in online banking – several banks are beginning to offer banking via the interactive services on your digital TV. A potential disadvantage of this form of screen banking, one of the newest, is that while your bank may have teamed up exclusively with, say, a digital cable company, you may be a digital satellite subscriber, which would make it impossible for you to make use of it.

How universal this system is likely to be is yet to be seen. The banks expect to be able to offer a range of services similar to the computer-based services, but you will not be able to print out your statement until special printers are marketed to attach to your TV or set-top box.

Digital terrestrial TV would appear to be at a disadvantage here as it does not have the frequency bandwidth to transmit interactive services in the way that the other digital TV companies do. However, the digital terrestrial TV operator ONdigital offers Internet banking via its ONnet service.

Mobile banking

For those who like to be constantly in touch with their finances, mobile-phone banking could be the answer. This is now possible using a digital wireless application protocol (WAP) mobile phone (see Chapter 4). WAP offers good security, owing to its encryption systems. A few banks now offer this option and you can pay bills, transfer funds and see your balance. However, currently, WAP services on mobile phones leave a lot to be desired and cannot display much information. The next generation of mobile-phone systems (see Chapter 4) will be able to provide faster and more versatile WAP services, which would enable mobile banking to take off in the future.

Testing the services

Which? magazine asked some of its members to test home-banking systems. Of those using computer-based banking, about half experienced technical difficulties at least once during the two-month trial period. Some of the users also thought that the system was slow. However, on the plus side, they liked the fact that computer-based banking allows you to display a complete statement on-screen and to print it out. Moreover, some computer-based systems also let you download your data into accounting software packages such as Microsoft Money and Intuit Quicken. So computer banking is probably better suited to carrying out many tasks or for checking multiple accounts.

The *Which?* testers found little to choose between Internet computer banking and direct-connection computer banking. One advantage of the latter was that using the software supplied by the bank it was possible to set up the transactions you want to carry out before connecting to the bank, thus cutting down on the amount of time spent online and hence the phone bill. With Internet banking, how long you spend online may depend on how fast your modem and ISP are. Because banks use security check software, downloading information could take time, so a good, fast connection is desirable.

The experiences of the testers for *Which?* magazine suggest that for common transactions such as checking balances, transfers, paying bills and checking recent transactions, simple phone-based banking is faster and easier than the computer-based systems.

Things may improve for the Internet-based systems in the future as Internet access becomes faster.

New methods of payment

In future, online retailers are likely to use digital signatures to check that customers are who they say they are. This will be done by the use of 'smart cards', which are similar to credit cards. Instead of a magnetic stripe, however, they will have a microchip on them, just like cards used in digital TV set-top boxes. Each chip will hold a unique security identity – or digital signature. Smart cards will also be used in high-street shops. Instead of signing a receipt with a pen, you will be asked to enter a PIN into a keyboard. This way, the smart card does not leave your possession at all. Moreover, the retailer or other customers cannot see what you type into the keypad. This system is already in use in some continental European countries.

Another method of payment being proposed is the electronic purse. This is a smart card that you keep 'topped up' with cash. You could use such a card for buying small items that you would normally pay for with cash – the advantage being that you would not have to carry money around with you. Such cash transactions are called 'micro-payments' – transactions that are too small for them to be worth processing by the banks as credit-card payments.

A method of making micro-payments that is already available is a mobile phone. Each time you make a call, you are charged a relatively small amount of money for it. As this system is already in place it is being proposed that it can be modified and used for buying other items. Experiments are being conducted to see if a person with a mobile phone can buy a can of drink from a vending machine and charge it to his or her phone bill – in other words, he or she has to 'call up' the vending machine in order to make the purchase.

Chapter 4

Communications

The digital revolution has had a huge impact on our ability to communicate with each other. In particular, mobile phones and email have led to changes in the way domestic and business users keep in touch with friends, family and colleagues.

Interestingly, it has also created a big difference of opinion among consumers. Many have embraced the technology with enthusiasm while others regard it as a nuisance, or at best a waste of time and money. This chapter will explain how these digital communication tools work, and help you decide which, if any, suit your needs.

For years, the Post Office (now re-named Consignia) was the chief instrument of our communications, operating both the domestic telephone system and the postal service.

The first big digital change in the telephone system occurred outside the home. During the 1970s and 1980s telephone exchanges and trunk lines in the UK were fully digitised. Together with improvements made possible by satellite links and fibre optics users were able to make more calls, of better quality and reliability. This was just the beginning – digital technology was about to bring with it new services as well.

Fax machines

The affordable fax (facsimile) machine was the first piece of communications equipment to offer serious competition to the letter and the telephone call. The fax machine is not a true digital device – it is a hybrid of analogue and digital technology. It allows you to send pictures and text just as you can in a letter, but without the delay inherent in a system that relies on physical transportation.

Unfortunately, the fax machine was not quite as versatile as it first appeared. It could not transmit colour and was a very low-resolution system so the image that reached the recipient could be of fairly poor quality. The early thermal printers had to use special paper that tended to fade with age. In addition, because the fax machine is an electro-mechanical device, the mechanical part of it was prone to paper jamming. Users also had problems with the fax machine, telephone and telephone answering machine all sharing the same line, particularly when all three tried to answer an incoming call.

Modern, plain-paper fax machines have solved most of these problems, but they are still bulky pieces of equipment and expensive to run for non-business use. Combination machines can be connected to a computer, offering faxing, scanning and printing of documents.

If you have a computer with an Internet connection, you have an alternative to a fax machine – most modern modems can also send and receive faxes. They can answer a call, detect that it is a fax and record it digitally. You can then display the result on your monitor or print it out. The latest modems can record faxes even if the computer is not switched on. You can also send faxes by this method,

How fax machines work

Fax machines are a combination of three systems: a low-resolution scanner, a modem and a thermal or inkjet printer.

When you place a document in a fax machine, the scanner records it by detecting the brightness of a light beam reflected from its surface. This output from the light-sensitive detector is converted to a digital signal. By modern computer standards, the scanner is of low resolution.

The digital signal is sent down the telephone line by the modem at a speed of about 9.6Kbps, which is about a quarter of the speed of a modern computer modem. If the telephone line has interference or noise on it, this speed is reduced even further.

At the receiving end, the modem on the fax machine answers the call and decodes the signal, converting it back to its digital form. It applies some digital error correction to replace the odd 'digit' lost en route. This is sent to the printer, which prints out the final result. The printer could be a modern inkjet type (that is used with computers) or a thermal printer, in which a tiny heated element is scanned over temperature-sensitive paper to form the printed characters.

but only of documents stored in the computer. However, if you have a computer and modem, more convenient methods of communication, such as email (see below), are available to you. Fax machines are useful because they allow you to communicate with people or businesses that do not own computers.

Telephones

The advent of the digital telephone exchange and the introduction of electronics to telephones themselves have improved quality and reliability and reduced costs. New technology has also led to the development of several new telephone services: you can, for example, discover the telephone number of the last caller to your phone, be alerted to the fact that someone is trying to call you when you are on the phone, or set up a service to ring you when a number you have been trying to call becomes free.

Probably the biggest innovation in telephone technology has been the cordless phone. You can now wander about while chatting on the phone. Early analogue cordless phones were disappointing – they were noisy and had a poor range. Modern analogue cordless phones are an improvement on them, but the new digitally enhanced cordless telecommunications (DECT) phones are even

Typical DECT phone with base station

better. Both the latest analogue phones and DECT phones work well in all the rooms of a typical house and garden. The DECT phones offer more facilities than their analogue counterparts. For example, you can have up to five handsets operating from the one base station and you can make calls from one handset to another. The digital models also offer better privacy than the analogue phones, as it is not possible to 'eavesdrop' into the transmissions.

DECT: the versatile cordless phone

DECT phones work using similar technology to digital mobile phones. This means that it is possible to have a dual-mode phone that functions as a DECT phone in the home but seamlessly changes to a mobile phone when the user is on the move. Products of this nature are available in the UK but they have not caught on, possibly because they are expensive.

DECT has other applications too. Users in a local neighbourhood, typically served by a telephone company's wired local loop, can be connected instead by a cordless phone that exchanges signals with a neighbourhood aerial. These systems are not generally used in the UK but they have been set up in some other European countries.

Answering machines

An answering machine is a device that can take a message from a caller if you are unable (or unwilling) to take the call. An early model of one, made in the 1960s, used 'open reel' tape and was bigger than a video-cassette recorder. Modern analogue answering machines are tiny by comparison and use a single micro-cassette tape. This tape has your announcement message recorded at the beginning and the incoming messages are recorded in sequence on the remainder of the tape. The only problem is that as the machine starts to fill up with messages the tape has to fast-wind from the announcement to the next bit of blank tape while the caller holds on.

Once again, digital technology has led to an improvement in the quality of these machines. By using solid state memory chips and digital compression, it is possible to store the announcement, and up to 15 minutes of messages, electronically. A digital voice also announces the time and date of each message. Digital answering machines can be made even smaller than analogue models and they work instantly and efficiently. Unfortunately, however, most of them have pretty poor sound quality. The very severe digital compression applied to the recorded voice signal, plus the fact that they use very small loudspeakers, can, in extreme cases, make them unintelligible – and sometimes worse than analogue answering machines.

However, all is not lost for the digital answering machine. The digital answering service provided by the telephone exchange, such as BT's 'call-minder' service, and equivalent services from cable companies work very well. They operate just like a regular answering machine but your announcement and incoming messages are stored as digital recordings at the telephone exchange. Another advantage of these systems is that people calling in can leave you a message even if your phone is engaged, which is something a regular answering machine cannot do. When you pick up the receiver, a special dialling tone tells you whether you have messages waiting, which you can access using a password. Also, as with regular answering machines, you can retrieve your messages from any other phone.

Social alarms

Social alarms are telephone-based devices that allow elderly, infirm or disabled people to call for assistance by simply pressing a button on a small pendant that they wear round their neck or on their wrist. The pendant sends a high-frequency radio signal to the 'base station'. On receiving this signal, the base station automatically dials a local 'control centre'. When contact has been made with the control centre the base station first sends a coded signal down the line so the person at the control centre immediately knows where the call is coming from and any other relevant data. It can even tell the control centre the condition of the battery in the radio pendant device. The control centre can then open up an intercom-style speech link with the caller or can arrange for the appropriate medical or emergency services to visit.

Because of the medical and safety considerations in using and operating these services, it has been advisable to use local authority or other professional control centres, which can respond quickly and operate 24 hours a day. More recently, BT has introduced a similar system that can be used by friends or relatives who are acting as carers. The 'BT In Touch 2000' service has several safeguards built in to allow for situations where the carer is not in, or is already on the phone. The system also uses digitally recorded voice announcements to inform and reassure the user and carer.

For this type of use, the method used to send the information and other instructions down the telephone line is surprisingly simple. The data is coded using dual-tone, multi-frequency (DTMF) tones, which are the musical tones used by the phone to dial numbers. The term 'dual-tone, multi- frequency' arises because each keypress consists of a different combination of two, very precise, musical tones. This means that the chances of any combination being generated accidentally, say, by an ordinary sound (such as your voice) being sent down the telephone line, is almost nil.

Most people who phone large companies are faced with automated messages asking them to press specific numbers (which translate into DTMF tones) on their phones so their call can be directed to the appropriate department. With a social alarm these tones are used to great advantage. Instead of a single tone being sent, whole groups of tones are sent automatically. Each tone represents a particular piece of information – the user's identification, status of backup batteries, which radio trigger was pressed, etc. There is even a special 'handshake' tone sequence, which the control centre has to send to the alarm to identify itself, so the alarm knows it has not reached a wrong number.

These DTMF tones are analogue tones but are being used as a very simple digital code. They cannot signal fast enough to be used to digitally convert analogue signals such as picture or sound, or to navigate the Internet, but they can be used, very effectively, to send and receive very simple information.

As the number of elderly people, many of them living alone, continues to rise, the social alarm seems likely to become increasingly important. Alarm manufacturers are already looking at newer digital systems such as the DECT digital cordless phone standard and possibly using permanent Internet connections to control centres or emergency services. Given our ability to send large amounts of data digitally and very fast, it is likely that a complete remote social and medical monitoring system could be developed and used for all of us in the not-too-distant future. Not surprisingly, companies that produce social alarms also supply home burglar-alarm systems. Many such systems automatically dial out to an emergency centre, or to the police, when an alarm has been triggered. The development of these home-monitoring systems in the digital age is discussed in detail in Chapter 6.

Mobile phones

The growth in the popularity of mobile phones during and since the 1990s has been phenomenal. It is estimated that more than half the population in the UK now owns one.

The original mobile phone network in the UK was established in the early 1980s and operated by two companies, Cellnet and Vodafone. This was an analogue service – that is, the radio signal was sent using technology similar to that used for FM radios, even though it was at a higher frequency.

The analogue network in the UK is due to be switched off in mid-2001 because the mobile-phone system has moved over to using a digital system. The analogue network was not without problems. There was nothing to stop someone listening in on an analogue mobile-phone call, using a scanner that cost under £200. It was also possible to capture a handset's details off-air, and make a 'clone' of it, enabling a person to make calls that could be charged to someone else's account.

As the size and the price of the phones shrank, they became steadily more popular, until the network was in danger of becoming congested.

The switch to digital services in 1992 helped to solve or reduce these problems. Extra frequencies were made available for digital and thus the capacity was significantly increased. Also, the digital system operated by Cellnet and Vodafone, called GSM (global system for mobile communications), was the standard used across continental Europe, so British mobile phones became usable in more countries. Two more networks, Orange and Mercury One2One, started up in the UK. Confusingly, they are incompatible with the Cellnet and Vodafone services because they use a system called PCN (personal communications network); although the type of digital processing used is the same as that used in GSM they operate in a higher frequency band (about 1,800MHz). This system is also referred to as GSM1800. In the USA there are several different mobile networks, one of which is a GSM network. Unfortunately, it works on yet another frequency range, so unless you buy a dual- or triple-band GSM phone, you will not be able to use it there.

In theory, the use of digital signals instead of analogue signals should improve the quality of transmission and provide immunity from interference. In practice, it is not quite as simple as that. The final quality is influenced by other factors such as the amount of 'digital compression' that is applied to the signal in order to maximise the capacity of the network. Moreover, because of the time delay introduced by the digital processing, users occasionally hear echoes on the line. Another problem with digital mobile (and DECT) phones is that because the transmissions send the digital data in bursts of radio frequency, they cause interference to hearing aids.

How digital mobile phones work

Mobile phones do not work like traditional walkie-talkies or citizens' band (CB) radios, which are essentially 'point-to-point' radio links with limited range and dialling capability. A true public mobile-phone system needs to be integrated into the conventional telephone network and has to be accessible over a large area, ideally the whole of the country.

So the analogue and the current digital mobile-phone networks operate by means of a 'cellular network'. In a cellular network, coverage throughout the country is divided into a number of small areas called cells. Each cell has its own base station radio transmitter and receiver. This is often depicted diagramatically as a honeycomb, but in reality the cells are not quite so regular in shape and overlap. This is because, at the high frequencies being used, local terrain and buildings alter the radio reception.

When you switch on your mobile phone, it sends a very short transmission signal to identify itself. This is picked up by the local cell's base station, to register your location with the network. If someone phones your number from either a normal telephone or another mobile, the central processing centre knows where to route the signal. If you move into another cell, your phone will tell the new cell of your new location.

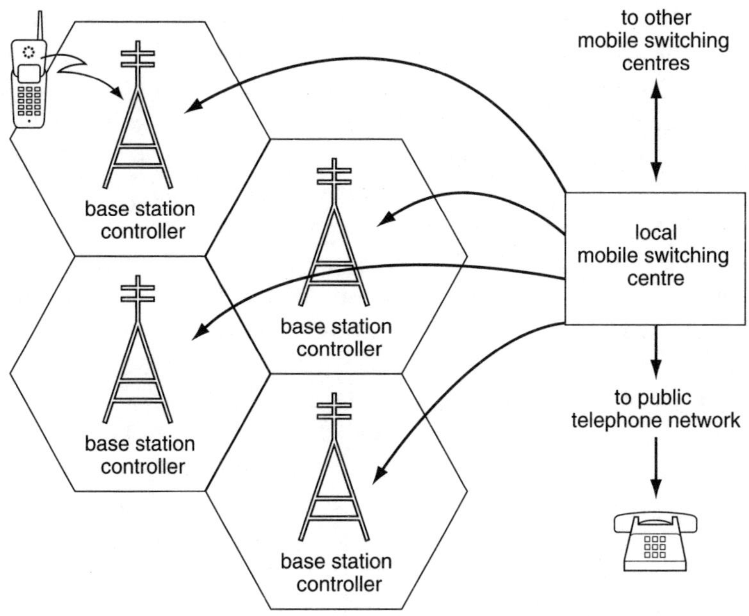

Schematic diagram of cellular network

Each cell can handle a limited number of calls at any one time. The 'network planners' will have estimated the appropriate capacity of the cell depending on how populated the area is, so instances of overload (when you cannot get a connection) should in theory be rare. When planning a cellular network, the phone companies use a computer program that has a built-in map and topological detail. It can predict the likely coverage and help the phone companies choose the best site and power for their masts.

Today's digital mobile phones can be used for more than just talking. For example, they have 'mailboxes' which use digital voice recording to store messages from callers should your phone be switched off, out of range, or if you simply do not want to answer. The phone will indicate that messages are waiting. This facility is basically the same as a normal telephone-answering system, such as BT's 'call minder', but the mobile phone companies call it a 'mailbox'.

You can also send short text messages over the digital mobile network using a service called SMS (short message service). You can send these text messages from one mobile phone to another and they are read using the small display on the phone. To type in the message, you have to use the numeric keypad on the phone. Each numeric key represents 3 or more letters of the alphabet, so key '1' is used for A, B or C. If you want to type an 'A' you tap the key once, to get a 'B' you tap it twice, etc. Clearly this is a tedious process but it does not seem to have stopped the service catching on, and after a bit of practice users are able to type messages quite quickly. One advantage of SMS is that it is cheaper than making a phone call because you compose the message before you dial the number. Moreover, sending a message means that you do not disturb the recipient, who can read it in his or her own time.

Mobile phones are clearly here to stay and the network is being enhanced to handle more calls and provide more services. Chapter 5 looks more in detail at some of the developments in this area.

Email

As its name suggests, email ('electronic mail') is the process of sending text messages from one person to another in electronic form, and can also refer to the actual message(s). In this respect, email is nothing new. As far back as 1924 there were systems that could send text messages using digitally coded alphabetical characters – they were based on what were generically called teleprinters or 'Teletype' machines. The systems caught on slowly, and between the 1960s and the 1980s the Post Office ran a 'Telex' service which was used only by business and industry. The Telex system became less popular as fax machines became affordable.

Email as we know it today has become available to everyone thanks to the coming-together of the computer, the telephone-line modem and the Internet.

If the idea of having email at home, for business use or just to keep in touch with family and friends, appeals to you but you do not want the inconvenience or cost of installing a computer, you can avail yourself of one of the non-computer-based email services discussed later in this chapter.

Computer-based email

For a simple computer-based email system, you need a computer, a modem and a telephone line. You then have to open an account

Digital failures

Not all innovative communications ideas have been successful – here are a couple of expensive failures.

The CT2 story

In 1989, when mobile phones were still mainly analogue and very expensive, some telephone companies came up with a novel alternative. This was the digital CT2 phone (CT1 phones being the old analogue domestic cordless phones). The CT2 phone was basically a digital cordless phone with handset and base station but it could also be used outdoors like a mobile. The snag was that it could not be used anywhere you wanted – you could use it only in the vicinity of a small radio receiver-transmitter box. These boxes were typically to be found at railway stations, in high streets, and so on. Initially there were several incompatible rival systems, and although later one system called 'Rabbit' evolved, it never really caught on and was shut down in 1994.

Iridium

Iridium was a satellite telephone system set up by Motorola. The company planned to launch 77 satellites to circle the earth, so wherever you were in the world you would be in range of at least one of these satellites and could use it to make phone calls. (The name derives from the fact that 77 is the atomic number of Iridium.) Your call would be passed along the satellite chain and then beamed down to the recipient. In the event, Motorola launched more than 88 satellites, but of these only 74 were operational. Unfortunately by the time the system was up and running, the handsets were bulky and expensive by present-day standards and the system did not have the capacity or speed to deal with the large amount of data today's businesses require.

The only people who found the system useful were those who lived or worked in remote parts of the world but there were not enough of this type of subscriber to make the system financially viable and so the system was switched off in 2000, leaving Motorola with about 90 unwanted satellites.

with an ISP and install its software, usually supplied on a CD-ROM. The installation is straightforward on most computers. You can obtain the software directly from the ISP, or major high-street retailers or from one of the CD-ROMs given away as cover mounts on computing magazines. If you do not have a CD-ROM player on your computer you will have to contact the ISP to obtain the installation program on a floppy disk (not all ISPs can supply these). Similarly, if you have an Apple computer you may have to contact the ISP directly.

Part of the software the ISP provides includes an email program, which allows you to compose, read and save your mail. With most systems you connect to the Internet only to send and receive your mail – you do not have to be connected while you are reading your mail or writing new messages. So the system can be quite cheap in terms of the phone bill.

Nowadays, most ISPs aimed at the domestic user do not charge for their service although some, such as CompuServe,* AOL* and Which? Online,* charge a small monthly fee to cover additional exclusive information content (for example, Which? Online is a 'content provider', offering access to current and back issues of all Which? magazines and to other services which are not available to non-subscribers).

An account with an ISP provides you not only with access to email but also to other Internet facilities such as the World Wide Web (see Chapter 2).

The advantages of email

Many people are natural letter-writers, deriving great satisfaction from writing to friends and relatives. For those who regard letter-writing as a chore, email has made it easier to keep in touch with contacts near and far – keying in a short message every now and then is not as time-consuming or cumbersome as writing and posting a letter. The most attractive feature of an email, of course, is the instant delivery of the message – for a fraction of the cost of a long telephone call or even a postage stamp. Furthermore, with the right computer software, emailers can send 'attachments' such as photographs, home-designed cards or even short sound clips with their messages.

One disadvantage with emails is that it is sometimes hard to convey a message in the tone you mean to: if you are not careful, what you may have intended to be a short, jokey comment could be perceived by the reader as an insult because he or she does not have the tone of your voice to go by. So before you press the 'send' button, read through the message you have composed to make sure it will be received in the way it was intended. Many emailers use emoticons or symbols to denote the mood of an email. For example, **:-)** means 'I am happy' or 'it's a joke', while **:-(** means 'sad'. The web site http://paul.merton.ox.ac.uk/ascii.smileys.html lists all the commonly used emoticons.

Emails should be kept fairly short. If you want to send a lengthy document, send it as a word-processed attachment. You can use acronyms to keep messages short. For example, TVM means 'thanks very much' and IMHO means 'in my humble opinion'. For a list of email acronyms, see www.apc.net/ia/scrmaim.htm.

Multiple emails and spam

One advantage of email is that you can set up email groups, allowing you to send one message to all members of your family or a club. Similarly, you can join an email group that sends regular newsletter-style mailouts – fan clubs and other special-interest groups often offer this facility.

However, this 'advantage' is used to great effect by businesses to send unsolicited marketing emails. This can be useful if the marketing information is of interest to you. For example, you may have bought an item from a web retail site and the e-tailer may then send you monthly mailshots to inform you of other similar products. More often than not, this type of mail simply clutters up your mailbox and takes time to sort out. This problem is easily resolved as most legitimate marketing companies have an automatic 'unsubscribe' option, details of which are usually to be found at the end of the message.

The more annoying type of junk mail is the mass mailouts sent by organisations or individuals – these are not messages that are targeted at particular users, but are sent to various possible combinations of usernames, in the hope that someone will actually read and act on them. Often, the messages are of an offensive nature. These nuisance emails, sent in a quick-fire, repetitious process, are referred to as spam (the name derives from a Monty Python sketch). It is possible to control the problem of receiving junk email. Some ISPs claim to be able to detect and filter out spam. Alternatively, you can obtain software to do this yourself. Some spam email may seem to offer an 'un-subscribe' option but beware, this may just be a ruse to 'collect' your email address.

Another solution, which is probably more effective, is to get two email addresses from different ISPs, and use one for personal email, buying from safe sites, etc., and the other for less safe activities such as posting messages in newsgroups, Internet chat and online auctions, where your email address can become more public. This way your first – and more important – email address does not get circulated, therefore you do not receive junk mail; as for the second account, you can just ignore anything that comes into it because it will not be from anyone who matters to you. Moreover, if you choose your main email ISP carefully and avoid the large international ones, you are less likely to be targeted.

Viruses

Another drawback of email is the risk of receiving a computer virus – a program designed to cause annoyance or damage if run on your machine. Some viruses are fairly harmless, simply displaying a message on your screen, say, while others can be quite harmful, erasing data or causing your hard disk to require reformatting.

The term 'computer virus' is quite wide ranging in meaning. The two main categories of viruses are self-replicating viruses and Trojans (malicious code).

The most common types of self-replicating viruses are associated with applications such as Microsoft Word and many popular email packages. Using a special type of programming language, these 'macro' viruses try to attach themselves to emails or documents so that they can spread.

Trojans are less common and are named after the Trojan horse of Greek mythology because they are programs that are disguised in an attempt to fool users into allowing them on to their systems. In the late 1990s, e.g., a program purporting to 'analyse your personality' was available for download from a number of adult-orientated newsgroups on the Internet. Once installed on an individual's PC, the software tried to erase the hard disk. These types of Trojans are rare but still crop up, especially in the form of DOS programs which can circumvent some Windows-based anti-virus software.

Viruses are a threat to even the most prepared. In the summer of 1999, an outbreak of a new type of virus called Melissa even forced Microsoft to shut down its mail services for several hours while the infection was treated. In May 2000 the so-called Love Bug virus wreaked havoc on computer systems across the world.

The best protection against viruses is to have virus-protection software installed on your computer. However, it is not 100 per cent effective. The various brands of anti-virus software are similar in terms of price and performance and are available from most computer stores or via the Internet.

You can also protect yourself to some degree (for free) by following these simple steps.

- Avoid downloading EXE files from web sites you are not familiar with or if the manufacturer of the software is unknown. Trojan programs often have no documentation with them and require you to perform unusual tasks (such as booting from a clean disk) before installation.
- The most common types of viruses use a simple programming language also used to write macros. If you do not use macros within applications such as Word or Excel, turn this feature off from within the program's options to prevent macro viruses.
- Be cautious of unsolicited email which come with either EXE or DOC files as these can contain viruses. If you receive such an email, check with the sender that he or she has sent it intentionally before you open up the attachment. Infected computers can often send out mail with the user knowing.
- Be cautious of software that is not on original disks or comes without boxes or manuals. This suggests that the software is pirated (illegal) and could contain viruses.
- Never leave a floppy disk in the drive when you power the system down. Viruses can live in the boot sector of the disk and can infect your system when it is next started up. This method of infection often leaves anti-virus systems powerless as the virus is already in memory before the anti-virus software has a chance to load up.

Email without a computer

If email sounds as if it could be a useful tool for you but you do not want the bother of using a computer, or having to buy one for the purpose, you could use alternatives. These tend to be less versatile than a computer but work well for simple messages.

Email via a digital TV

All three of the digital TV options, cable, terrestrial and satellite (see Chapter 1), offer subscribers an email service. For this to work your digital receiver has to be connected to a phone line. You also need a keyboard on which to type your messages. (Although this is optional with some services, typing using the digital TV's remote control is so fiddly that most people soon give up.) The keyboard sends the signals to the digital TV receiver using an infra-red link so there are no awkward cables. It is early days for this type of service and currently it is not easy to print out the emails but this facility should be available in the future. For satellite and cable digital TV your emails can be stored only at the service provider's server, so you have to dial up even to read old mail. The email service from ONdigital, the terrestrial digital TV service, called ONmail, allows some mail to be stored in the set-top box. Another limitation of TV email is that it cannot handle attachments such as word-processed documents or pictures, although ONmail does allow you to send pictures captured off the TV screen.

Another possible drawback of accessing email via your TV is that other members of the family may not be too pleased if you are using the facility when they want to watch TV. Moreover, you will have little or no privacy in reading your mail – it will be displayed for all to see on the TV.

The electronics company Bush sells a portable 14-inch analogue television with email facility. It comes complete with a built-in telephone modem and keyboard, but like its digital TV counterparts it has limited facilities.

Email phones

Amstrad and BT both market a very futuristic-looking 'emailer phone', which is a standard phone with a keyboard and screen attached and costs about £80. It is very easy to use, but you cannot send or receive attachments. It currently costs 12p to send each email, which makes it more expensive to use than other email systems.

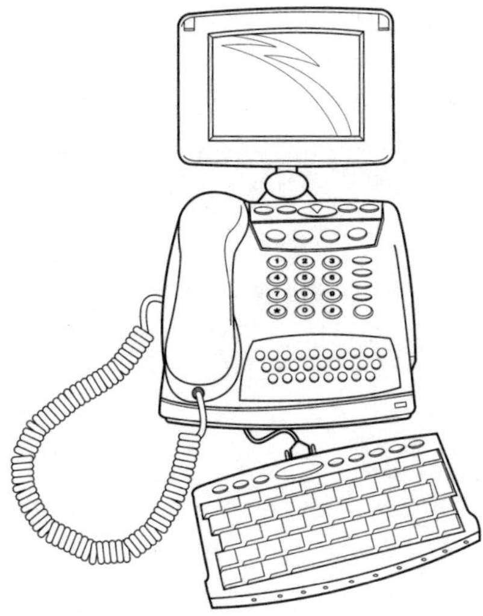

An emailer phone

Newsgroups

Newsgroups, forums or conferences are email-type discussion groups in which the emails, instead of being delivered to an individual recipient, are held on a public Internet server and can be downloaded by any member of the newsgroup (see also Chapter 2). This allows people from all over the world to have discussions with each other. The largest system, Usenet newsgroups, has tens of thousands of international discussion groups. You do not have to pay to take part in them. ISPs generally provide access (newsfeed) to a few thousand newsgroups, not necessarily all (because there are so many of them).

The software needed to participate in Usenet newsgroups is usually the same as the software you use to read and send email (*Outlook Express* in the case of Microsoft's Internet Explorer web browser and *Netscape Communicator* in the case of Netscape's Navigator browser), and should be provided by your ISP.

Before you can start reading messages in newsgroups you need to download the complete list of newsgroups available to you. This is quite straightforward to do (click on the 'Help' button in your email or web browser menu for advice) but it takes several minutes. Once you have downloaded and stored the names of the available newsgroups, you should not have to do this again, except to update the list with new newsgroups. It is generally wise to join only one or two groups initially, otherwise you may find you have taken on more than you can handle.

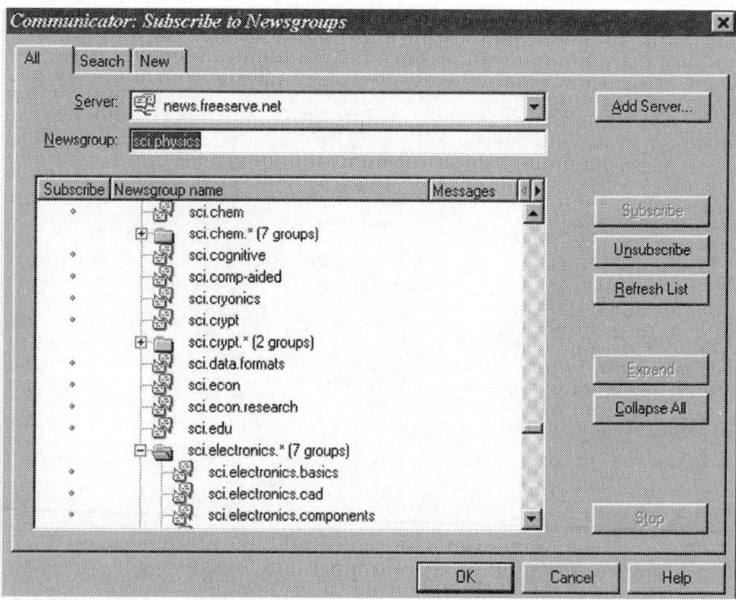

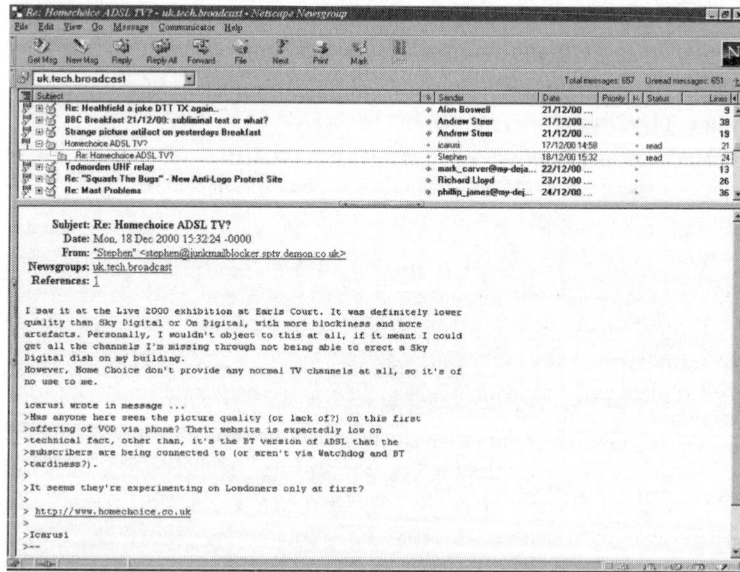

Top: part of a newsgroup list; bottom: a typical message (or 'posting')

Newsgroups have a two- or three-part structure to their names to identify their subject matter. The first group of letters gives the broadest category, the next group defines a narrower category within the hierarchy, and so on. This makes it easy for you to home in on newsgroups that appeal to you. For example, if you are interested in star-gazing you could choose 'sci.astronomy'; if it is gardening you want to communicate with people about, you could join 'uk.rec.gardening'. The main categories you will come across are:

- comp – computer-related groups
- rec – recreational
- sci – science
- soc – social issues
- biz – business and commercial
- uk – newsgroups mainly for UK users or topics.

But there are many more, including the very large 'alt' (or alternative) category, which covers the less organised, more anarchic newsgroups. Within this section you may find alternative versions of the more organised groups, for example, 'alt.sci.astronomy'.

Unfortunately, in the 'alt' category and in other more obscure categories are to be found a number of socially unacceptable discussions which have given Usenet newsgroups a bad name. This is a shame because the more organised newsgroups host a wealth of interesting discussions and provide access to other people who are ready to help you solve your problems or answer questions. If this type of activity interests you, but you are worried about your children accessing unsuitable newsgroups, ask your ISP if it can supply a 'filtered' or 'family friendly' newsfeed. Some ISPs, aimed at family use, automatically supply a filtered feed.

If you decide to try out these discussion groups, do not jump in feet-first. Read the 'postings' and get a feel for how the messages and replies are threaded together. Familiarise yourself with the tone of the discussion group – is it very serious or is it laid-back and jokey? Some discussion groups have an associated 'frequently asked questions' (FAQ) section. It is wise to locate and read this before asking any questions.

One feature of Usenet newsgroups is the fact that, in the main, they are worldwide forums. This means that popular newsgroups get hundreds of messages each week, but few of them deal with regional issues. Moreover, the system is largely uncontrolled and although many groups have someone monitoring them (called a 'moderator', and usually the person who set the group up), little can be done if people in the group try to disrupt its activities.

Forums and conferences

If you are interested in taking part in group discussions on the Net but are wary of unregulated newsgroups, you could consider joining in the newsgroups (or forums) run by UK-based ISPs. For example, Which? Online has a number of forums in which members can discuss a wide range of topics of consumer Interest and can call on expert advice. The ISP Compuserve also has many forums, mainly of interest to business and other professional users. Another alternative is provided by CIX,* an independent ISP. Before surfing the Web became a popular pastime, CIX set up an online conferencing service. This is still thriving and you can subscribe just to this service (which also provides email) without having to sign up for its Internet access. CIX runs hundreds of conferences, all of which are moderated. They cover a wide range of subjects but most tend to have a technical or enthusiast bias.

Live communications

Although both email and newsgroups are an effective and quick way of contacting people, it is not 'live communication'. If you want to talk, or communicate by typed messages, to another person or group of people live on the Internet, you need a fair amount of computer skill and some patience. Below we list some of the possible forms of communication.

With a computer, you can set up a live link to another person and simply type messages to each other. This is known as chat. If you have a soundcard in your computer with a microphone and speaker attached, you can actually talk to another person. Sound quality can be quite poor and the delay of a few seconds caused by the processing of the digital data on the Internet can make communicating quite awkward. The main reason people use this system is that it saves money – you can phone overseas for the price of the call to your ISP, which is likely to be at local rate or free. The most popular service that allows you to communicate like this is Microsoft's

Net Meeting. This is in effect the Internet equivalent of CB radio: both parties need to be connected to the Net at the same time before the link can be established. If you have a small video camera (called a webcam) attached to your computer you can also send moving pictures to each other. Picture quality is rather limited and the motion is quite jerky.

Internet phones

Some companies (for example, Net2phone,* Mediaring* and Deltathree*) offer an Internet phone service which takes advantage of the fact that you pay only local call rates to access the Net. By using a microphone and soundcard on your computer to digitise your voice, you can send it over the Net rather than via normal telephone exchanges. This makes international phone calls very cheap.

All you need to do to avail yourself of such a service is to install special software on your computer. You can then use the system to phone anyone anywhere in the world on his or her conventional phone. Your call is routed to one of the many Internet gateways the

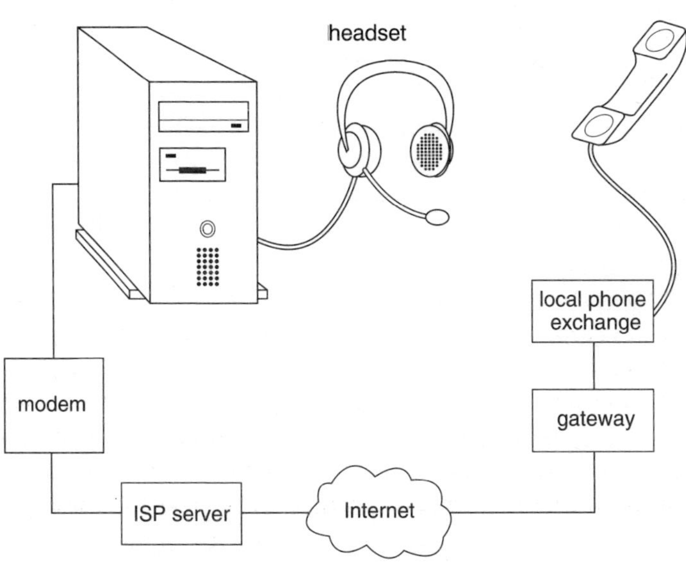

The Internet phone system

companies which operate this service have located around the world. This will then connect to the local 'land line' phone system in the area of the person you are calling and make his or her phone ring, thus connecting the call. All you pay is the cost of your local call (if any) and a small amount to the service operator which is paid for in advance in the form of a 'virtual' phone card. You pay for this by credit card over the Internet and 'top it up' as and when required.

Tests done for *Which?* magazine showed that some of these phone services are fairly complicated to set up and the sound quality (in particular the delay of a few seconds in sending and receiving the sound) is quite poor. Therefore, the system has had limited appeal in the UK so far. However, if you make a lot of international calls, you can save money and, in the future, when Internet connections improve with high-speed, digital phone lines, this system is likely to improve.

Faster communications

The traditional telephone line was not designed to carry anything other than voice communications. Even by audio standards, it was considered pretty poor because of its narrow frequency range. Measured in hertz (or cycles per second), the frequencies it could cope with ranged from 300Hz to 3,300Hz – enough for speech but not for deep bass or very high notes or musical harmonics. The frequency range for a normal human ear or a hi-fi system goes from 20Hz (lowest note) to 20,000Hz (highest note).

Nowadays we want to send more down a telephone line than mere speech – we want it to transmit digital data too. Unfortunately, the narrow frequency range (or bandwidth) that limits the quality of our speech transmission also constrains the speed at which data can be sent. The faster we want to send data the more bandwidth we need. Fax machines and teletext-style information systems, such as the now-defunct Viewdata, are examples of early data systems that used telephone lines. They had speeds of about 1.2Kbps.

Rather like a radio transmission uses different methods of putting the programmes on to the radio wave (amplitude modulation, AM, and frequency modulation, FM), the data being sent down the telephone line is 'modulated' on to a wave, in this case an audio wave signal. In order for you to be able to send and receive these modulated data signals, you need to have a 'modem' ('**mo**dulator and **dem**odulator'). The modem sits between your computer and your phone line.

Over the years, telecommunications engineers have developed methods to enable more and more digital bits to be squeezed into the telephone bandwidth. These improvements have taken place gradually and have had to be standardised so that, say, you and your ISP have modems of the same standard. These international standards are designated by using numbers prefixed by the letter V (for example, V32 and V34). The current, most commonly used domestic standard, is called V90 and has a speed of 56Kbps for receiving data and 33.6Kbps for sending data. A more recent development, V92, claims to offer a slight improvement to this, boasting 56Kbps in both directions. These domestic modems are often referred to as 'dial-up' modems simply because they dial up to the Internet only when needed. This saves you money, makes sure your telephone line is not always engaged and also ensures that the whole telephone system does not grind to a halt because too many connections to the Internet are being made simultaneously.

When you initiate a connection to your ISP, your modem performs an electronic 'handshake' with the modem at the other end. Between them they establish which 'V' standard they conform to and if necessary one may have to step down to a lower standard so they are both operating at the same level. They also establish how good your telephone line is. If it is a noisy line, or in some other way deteriorates the signal, the modems will select a slower data speed. V32 and V34 modems normally achieve their stated maximum data rates, but V90 modems rarely, if ever, achieve the rate of 56Kbps over the domestic telephone network (a speed of about 44Kbps is typical). Although a speed of 56Kbps is pretty much the most we can expect of traditional telephone lines, Internet users still complain about how slow access to the Internet is. A speed of 56Kbps (or more typically 44Kbps) is not really satisfactory for receiving continuous audio and video signals, for downloading files and programs or for accessing modern web pages that contain a lot of pictures and complicated graphics.

Higher-speed Internet access is possible and commonly used by businesses. Until recently, systems that offer it have been considered too expensive for home use. However, prices are dropping and consumer desire for higher speed has increased, so we are beginning to see high-speed (or broadband) domestic data connections. These will be mainly used for Internet access but they can provide other services such as video on demand (see Chapter 1) and facilitate teleworking (see Chapter 8).

Different high-speed systems are available, but in practice your choice will be restricted by where you live.

ISDN

Integrated services digital network (ISDN) has been available to businesses for several years. In the consumer market, it is better known as 'BT Home Highway'. To use ISDN you need to have a special phone cable run to your house. The cable provides two 64Kbps connections. You can use them in different combinations (for example, one for the Internet and one for voice calls) or you can combine them to provide a faster (128Kbps) Internet connection, so long as your ISP supports this speed. If you do the latter, you will be charged for two phone calls, but you will get a reasonably fast connection, which is useful when you want to transfer large files. Even the single 64Kbps rate is a useful improvement over the typical connection speed from a standard V90 modem.

ADSL

The asymmetric digital subscriber line (ADSL)* service was introduced at the end of 2000 to a very limited area of the UK. Using the very latest communications technology, ADSL has made it possible to achieve very fast data rates over an existing BT telephone line. Unfortunately, this works only if you live close to an ADSL-equipped exchange (within 3km, in fact). When this book went to press, only a few BT exchanges were capable of supporting ADSL. With ADSL, data rates of up to 512Kbps are possible.

There are two important differences between the ADSL system and ISDN or standard V90 modems. First, with ADSL you do not have to dial up to get connected to the Internet – you are connected all the time. This means you do not have to wait while the modem dials up, and also that you are notified of emails as soon as they arrive. You are not charged for the time you are connected; instead you pay a fixed monthly subscription or only for the data you receive.

Second, your ADSL connection may be shared with a number of other people living in the same area as you. The speed of your connection is affected by the number of other users who are receiving or transmitting data at the same time as you. The ADSL providers should be able to tell you the maximum number of other users you are sharing with. This number is called the contention ratio. A contention ratio of 10:1 would mean you would have a fast connection; one of 50:1 would be poorer. The ADSL system can achieve its maximum speed only when there is only one user and all the other users are dormant. Your actual connection speed will therefore be variable but for most of the time it should be a significant improvement over dial-up modems.

ADSL is available mainly from BT (its 'Openworld' service), but a number of other ISPs say they will also be providing ADSL connections in the future. To do so they need to have access to BT phone lines.

Broadband cable modems

These modems use the cable network provided by ntl* or Telewest* cable companies so they will be available only if you are in a cable area. The two cable companies are introducing the system gradually throughout their networks so you may have to wait before you can get a modem. Unlike ADSL and ISDN, with a cable modem you have to use the cable company's own ISP. Like ADSL it is an 'always on' connection to the Internet and your connection is shared with other users so the actual data rate achieved will vary depending how many others are using the system at the same time as you.

Security considerations

If you are connected to the Internet all the time, as is the case with ADSL and cable modems, you are more vulnerable to hackers because they would find it easy to gain access to your computer. To reduce the risk of this it is recommended that you install special software called a 'firewall', which restricts access to your system from outside. This software is extensively used in businesses which have a permanent, direct connection to the Internet. Low-cost versions of the software, such as Norton Personal Firewall (£30), are now available for home use. You could also try the free Zone Alarm for Windows at www.zonelabs.com .

High-speed phone line systems compared

	ISDN	ADSL	Cable
receiving data rates	64 or 128Kbps	up to 512Kbps	up to 512Kbps
sending data rates	64 or 128Kbps	up to 256Kbps	up to 128Kbps
dial-up or permanent	dial-up	permanent	permanent
suppliers	BT Home Highway	BT and some ISPs	ntl and Telewest
typical installation cost	£50 to £290[1]	£150	£150
typical running cost (per month)	£27	£40	£20
geographical availability	most of the UK	limited	limited to cable areas
use phone while surfing	yes (at 64Kbps data rate)	yes	yes

[1] Home Highway prices depend on whether you are already a BT customer and which tariff you choose.

The speed of mobile communications too will keep improving (see Chapter 5).

Chapter 5

On the move

Digital technology is transforming portable entertainment and communication systems as well as those we use at home (or at work). As well as broadening our horizons in terms of what we can do, this has brought about significant social change. We can now communicate with friends or work colleagues pretty much wherever we are, and can carry electronic sources of entertainment around with us.

This chapter looks at what is available for when we are travelling, for leisure, information access or keeping in touch, how it works, what is worth buying, and where the fast-developing technology is leading.

Entertainment in transit

Just as radios, cassette players and CD players for the car and personal stereos to 'wear' when travelling may have started as status symbols, some of the devices described below might seem non-essential except for those anxious to establish their 'street-cred'. Certainly they are about fun and fashion as well as convenience, and although the market is volatile some of these products are already well established.

Music

Even before the days of analogue electronics people wanted to be able to carry recorded music around with them. Perhaps the bulky wind-up gramophone of the early twentieth century could be regarded as the original 'Walkman'. There were even portable radios using valve circuits, running from high-voltage batteries, and car radios with valves. But it was the transistor radio in the 1960s that really gave impetus to portable music, in conjunction with the 'off-shore' radio stations of the day. Also in the mid-60s, Philips launched the portable compact cassette-tape player.

In 1979 Sony introduced the first Walkman (initially called the Stowaway in the UK) and henceforward portable entertainment became 'personal'. It was socially acceptable to walk around with headphones on.

Three years later, in 1982, personal entertainment became digital when Sony introduced the first personal CD player. Although it was somewhat bulky and used up batteries rather quickly, it was regarded as little short of a miracle.

One of the problems of this and other early portable CD players was that they tended to 'skip' the music as you walked, so you had to walk around very cautiously. The solution to this was ingenious: a digital 'buffer' or 'anti-jog circuit' which acted as a temporary store for the digits so they could be played back unhindered by any occasional jogs the laser and disc might experience.

Mini-disc – small is beautiful

While the personal CD player is well established and has the obvious advantage of being able to play your CD collection, it has two digital rivals: the personal mini-disc player and the MP3 player. Both these players are smaller and, without any doubt, far more fashionable.

The mini-disc format has been slow to catch on. It was first released by Sony* (again!) back in 1992, but only since the late 1990s has it become popular in the UK. Pre-recorded music mini-discs are

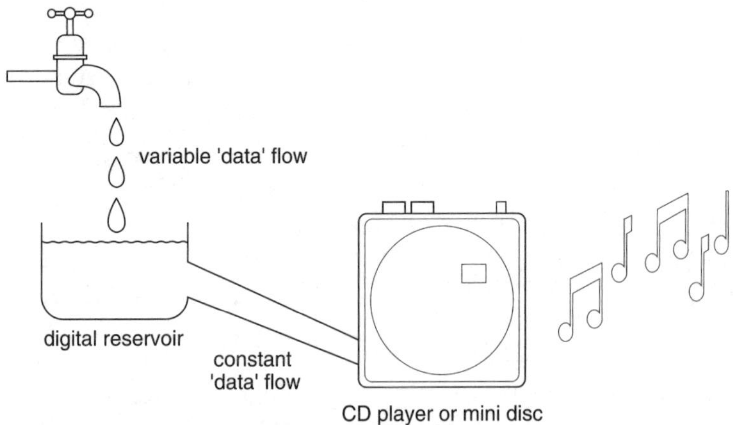

How a portable CD player's anti-jog system works

available, but there are relatively few of them, not many record shops stock them and the prices tend to be higher than for normal CDs. So the mini-disc is used mainly as a self-recording format, an alternative to the blank tape.

Sales of blank mini-discs, which sell at similar prices to blank cassette tapes, have now taken off and the format can safely be said to be established.

Mini-disc recorders can be connected to your hi-fi system in the conventional manner, using two pairs of phono leads to connect to one of the 'tape' in/out connections on your amplifier, so the mini-disc recorder can be used for recording and playing back. They can also be connected 'digitally' using a fibre optic connecting cable. This cable carries the actual digital signal in optical form, which means you can connect only in this manner, to another digital device such as a CD player, a DAB radio receiver or another mini-disc. Connecting in this way means that you are sure of getting the best possible quality when you record from the CD player, and if the CD has tracks this data will also be copied to the mini-disc.

Unfortunately there are two formats for connecting using a digital cable: optical, which is used by mini-discs; and coaxial, which is an electrical (wire) connection using a single phono lead. Most CD players and other digital equipment have both systems but some have coaxial only, which presents a problem when you want to connect to a mini-disc recorder.

As well as being under half the size of a personal CD player, personal mini-disc players are typically also, at only 150 grams, less than half the weight.

Most users of mini-discs make their own compilations from their CD collection for playback on their personal mini-disc player or car mini-disc player. To do this you will either have to buy a combined record/play personal mini-disc player or a home hi-fi mini-disc recorder and a play-only personal player.

Home recorders can be either a hi-fi separate or part of a complete mini hi-fi system. The separate home hi-fi recorder is by far the most convenient option as it can be permanently connected to record from your CD player (or from your radio); adding titles to the tracks or editing the tracks is much easier on a larger unit.

Portable mini-disc players all have the digital anti-jog circuit built into their playback circuits and are remarkably good at handling movement, so these are definitely what you should go for if you want music while you are out – er – jogging.

The other advantage of recording on mini-disc is that you can re-arrange or delete tracks, or parts of tracks, on the discs without leaving annoying blank spaces in the way you do with a cassette. The mini-disc is a 'random access' disc, more like a computer hard drive than a tape. Mini-disc players are not alone in having the advantages of anti-jog capability and track editing – MP3 players (see below) can be equally versatile.

Blank mini-discs are available with 74-minute and 80-minute recording times and cost £1–£2. On some recorders you can double the recording time if you record in mono. JVC has launched a portable mini-disc recorder that can give double or quadruple stereo recording times from a disc by using extra digital compression with only slight audio quality reduction.

MP3 players

The MP3 player is yet another personal music playback machine. However, it is fundamentally different from all that has gone before. Your music is stored in it only temporarily.

A personal MP3 player is currently useful only if you also have a computer fitted with a soundcard and ideally an Internet connection. MP3 is a system for digitally compressing digital audio signals – similar to that used by digital TV sound and digital audio broadcasting but slightly different from that used by mini-disc. (For details of how digital compression works see Chapter 1.)

With sufficient compression of an audio signal it becomes possible to fit an hour or more of music on to an integrated-circuit memory chip. Therefore, an MP3 player is nothing much more than an electronic memory, similar to the RAM memory in a computer, plus a battery, amplifier and headphones. In fact, there are no moving parts.

One convenient feature of the MP3 format is that you can select the amount of digital compression used when making your recordings – the more compression, the more you can fit into the memory, but the lower the sound quality. The 'best'-quality setting gives a sound quality that is often described as being 'near CD' quality: this is a fair description, because only if you listen to MP3 recordings through a high-quality hi-fi system can you tell the difference.

However, at anything other than this best setting, the sound quality is noticeably poorer and has an odd fuzzy quality to it.

Most MP3 players are supplied with a limited amount of built-in memory, typically 32Mb (enough for about one hour's music if set to the best quality). However, with most players the amount of memory can be expanded using plug-in memory cards of the type used in digital cameras. These expansion cards tend to be costly, but you can get them in sizes up to 128Mb (and even larger ones are being launched), giving you several hours of music at the best-quality setting. Unfortunately a 128Mb card is likely to cost well in excess of £200.

So how do you get the music into the player?

To convert your existing CDs into MP3 format you need some special software on your computer. This software is usually supplied with the player, or you can download it from Internet shareware sites, or find it on the 'free' CDs commonly found attached to the covers of computer magazines. This software will record your CD through the soundcard's analogue or digital input, convert it to an MP3 file and store it on your computer's hard disk drive. You can then play these tracks on your PC through the soundcard using the MP3 software or download them on to your personal MP3 player. You can store as many MP3 tracks on your hard drive as space permits, re-charging your MP3 player with new tracks whenever you like.

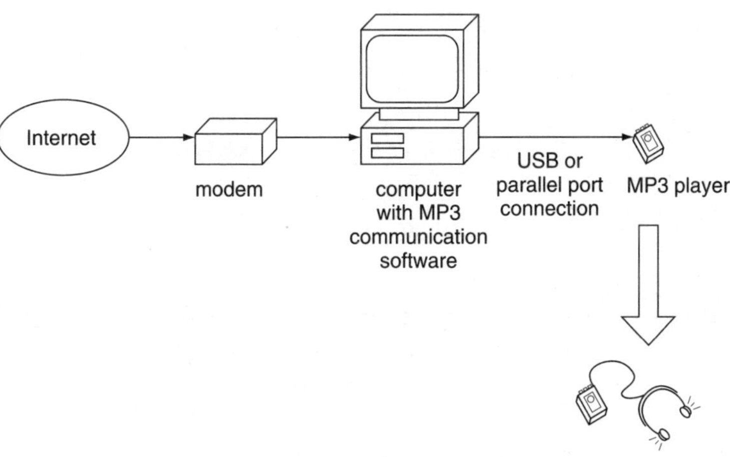

How MP3 files are downloaded and played

The more popular use for MP3 players is downloading music from the Internet. For this you have to locate web sites that offer MP3 tracks available for downloading direct to a computer. Once you have found a track or tracks you want, follow the web site's instructions to download the file. The process, using 'file transfer protocol' (FTP), is handled automatically by your web browser. Typically, with a standard 56Kbps (V90) modem, a 3-minute MP3 track will take 4 minutes to download and store itself on your hard drive, so clearly this is a time-consuming process. You can then play the music through your computer's soundcard using a software MP3 player or you can download it on to your personal MP3 player.

Thousands of web sites offer MP3 titles. Many of these are perfectly legitimate, offering copyright-free material from new pop bands or items specially recorded for the Internet; others may charge you (via your credit card) for the download. Other sites are not legitimate, offering tracks pirated from commercial CDs. The most popular MP3 site is www.mp3.com.

Napster

An MP3 music web site that has been in the news is www.napster.com. This site falls into a legal grey area, under challenge as we go to press. Napster operates as a free service enabling people on the Internet, worldwide, to swap their MP3 files. When you log on to Napster, you download their software that automatically searches your hard drive for your MP3 files, thus Napster can build up a huge database of MP3 files. The idea is that if there is a particular piece of music that you want, you search the Napster lists and then you can download it, not from Napster itself, but direct from the computer of the person who has the file – assuming they are on line at the time. Naturally, the music industry is not amused by this apparent loophole in the copyright law and has been trying to close Napster (and similar services) down; but some companies, more recently, have adopted the 'if you can't beat 'em' approach by trying to join forces with Napster instead. In early 2001 Napster was forced to modify its *modus operandi*: it will have to charge for its services and try to prevent users accessing copyright material. It is not clear whether Napster can survive this, but it has not stopped several other lower-profile web sites starting up similar services.

MP3 and the music industry

The music industry is not particularly keen on the MP3 format because the files are so easy to copy. Hence, piracy is impossible to control.

Alternative systems have emerged which allow you to download a music file that you have paid for but there is a digital code in the file that limits how the file can be copied or distributed. One such system, called secure digital media initiative (SDMI), is incorporated into the digital compression systems supported by the music industry. Unfortunately, the music industry has at least three different systems that use SDMI, Microsoft Windows Media Audio (WMA), the Advanced Audio Codec (AAC) and Sony's OpenMG/ATRAC3, which makes it far from straightforward to choose suitable computer software or personal audio players. It is difficult to see how the music industry's initiative can succeed when the MP3 format has already become so established.

Sony now produces a personal player that works with MP3 files and its ATRAC3 system, but it is expensive at £300.

Headphones

Whenever *Which?* magazine has tested personal audio it has found that in all but a few cases the sound quality can be improved by buying separate headphones for about £20–£30. There are two types of headphone to consider – the 'in-ear' type and the 'on-ear' type. Also worth considering are the large hi-fi headphones, designed to go over the ears, but these are not ideally suited to being worn in the street.

In-ear headphones tend to be of lower quality than the on-ear types and are less good at reproducing bass notes. Expect to pay as much as £25–£30 for a pair of these if you want to be sure of an improvement.

Many people find 'in-ear' phones uncomfortable; and if you do not have standard-shaped ears, you may find that they will not stay in place. Upgrading to some 'on-ear' models is usually worthwhile (buy from a shop that allows you to try before you buy).

Buying advice for music on the move

A personal CD player is still an attractive option as you can play your existing CDs on it. The disadvantages are that the players are relatively bulky and have a tendency to skip the music if jogged. If you are thinking of buying one it is worth spending about £100. This ensures reasonable-quality headphones of the type that fit in the ear. You should also look out for an anti-jog buffer circuit, rechargeable NiMH batteries and charger and a remote control in the headphone lead.

If you are after something smaller and a little more up to date, a mini-disc player is the best option. As it is difficult to find pre-recorded titles for this format in the shops you will also have to have a mini-disc recorder so you can make your own compilations. Expect to pay about £200 to ensure good sound quality and a remote control in the headphone lead.

MP3 players cannot be generally recommended unless you are really keen on tracking down new music and are prepared to spend time downloading it from the Internet. A basic MP3 player will cost about £100–£200 depending on the amount of memory it contains.

E-books

The day when electronic books overtake print-on-paper ones as the preferred medium of the majority may never come, but in the meantime various technology-led (rather than market-led) initiatives have given us a number of competing e-book formats to consider.

The RCA (Rocket) e-book was one of the first hand-held, portable electronic books, weighing in at just under £200.

There are three competing formats for e-books. Two of these – Microsoft Reader and Glassbook Reader – are simply computer programmes to run on your desktop or laptop computer. But the really interesting one is the Rocket e-book system because it uses a dedicated portable e-book machine. Originally called Rocket eBook, this product is now marketed under the RCA and Gemstar brand names.

The e-book reader has an 11.5 x 8 cm LCD screen, which produces an admirably clear image for text and illustrations. The font used enhances text legibility and a backlight is provided so that you can read in bed, in the dark. However, bright indoor light or sunlight can reflect on the screen and make the text difficult to see. Pages are 'turned' at the press of a button and to look up an individ-

The RCA Gemstar e-book

ual word in the pre-loaded dictionary you have only to touch it. The reader can store about ten books at once.

Books are downloaded from Internet bookshops via the computer and stored on your hard drive or inside the e-book reader. The web site http://ebooks.barnesandnoble.com is typical of e-book shops, and there are many more. The range of books includes everything from recent releases to great works of literature, with prices ranging from $1 (for, say, a classic such as Shakespeare's *Midsummer Night's Dream*) to about $20 for a top-selling biography or novel. Generally, the prices are below $10 and lower than they would be for a printed book

When you have paid for the e-book (over the Internet, using your credit card) it is emailed to you. It can take several minutes to download a typical book, so the cost of the phone call must be included in the overall price you pay.

In addition to this system are two other e-book formats, Microsoft Reader and Adobe eBook Reader. Neither of these has a dedicated portable eBook reading device. Instead you can read the book on your PC or even download it to a personal organiser such as a personal digital assistant (PDA). Unfortunately, PDAs are so small that reading long tracts of text can put a strain on the reader's eyes.

Buying advice

The portable e-book may well be the book of the future but to present any sort of competition to printed books it will have to become cheaper, lighter and run longer between battery charges when being used in a portable format. (It can, of course, be run direct from the mains too.)

Other portable digital devices

Portable DVD players are available from manufacturers such as Panasonic★ and Sharp.★ These are expensive at about £1,000 but the quality from the built-in 'widescreen' LCD display is impressive.

Portable digital video recorders are available from Sony. These use camcorder-sized digital video (DV) or digi-8 tapes and are very compact. Sony have models, with or without a built-in LCD screen, which cost £500–£1,000; blank tapes for these are readily available at about £5 each.

Several types of portable digital audio recorder are available. Some have a limited amount of internal memory and are suitable only for note-taking. Others have removable memory cards such as 'flash memory' or Sony's memory sticks. The sound is compressed

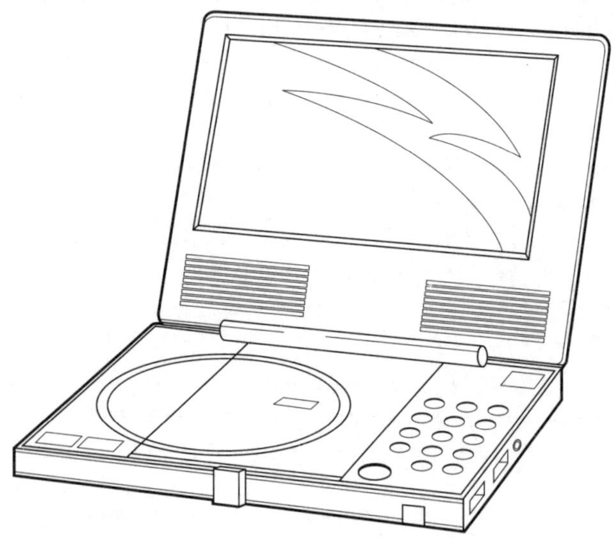

Portable DVD player

Sony Video Walkman

to achieve optimum recording time – several hours' worth – so these are highly suitable for voice recording. Such devices are popular with private detectives because they are small enough to be concealed about the person, record for several hours and operate silently. At home, you could use one to make audio messages which you can then load on to your PC and send to friends and relations as an email file attachment.

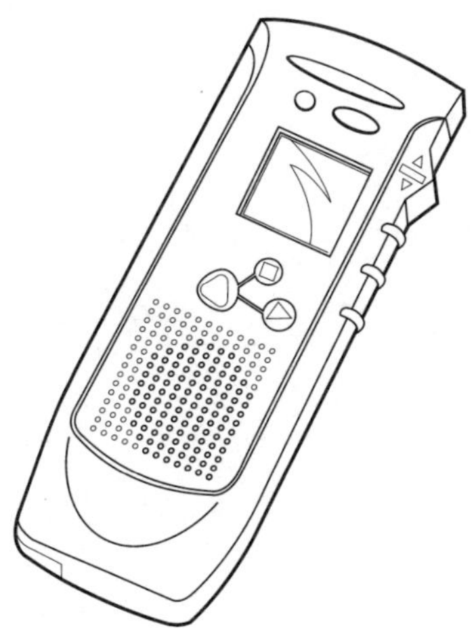

Digital voice recorder

Mobile entertainment – the future

A product recently tested by *Which?* magazine gives us a glimpse of what might be around the corner.

'Personal displays' such as the Olympus* Eye-Trek, costing approximately £500, consist of a pair of spectacles containing two small LCD displays and two earpieces that can be plugged into any standard audio/video source such as a TV, VCR or DVD player and were designed as companions to portable versions of these. While the Olympus device, specifically, is not compatible with computer display outputs, similar products do exist for this application which are ideal for games. As supplied, the spectacles are mains-powered via a mains adapter; they can also be used with an optional rechargeable battery pack. Although the spectacles work satisfactorily, the picture quality is of rather low resolution.

It is likely that more of this type of product will appear on the market and in due course the computer link should mean that a display can be achieved that is not just three- dimensional but so realistic that the user would become totally involved in the program – a so-called virtual reality display.

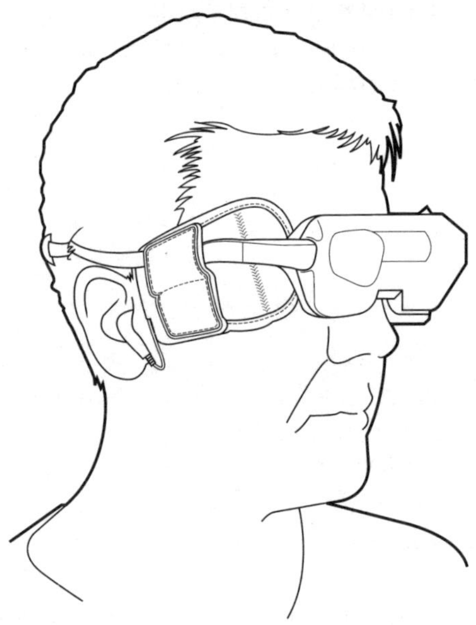

The Olympus Eye-Trek personal display

Virtual reality presentations can go beyond audio and video displays. Gloves and other clothing can be used to reproduce the effect of touching and feeling, for example. Until now, virtual reality environments have been used mainly for industrial training such as flight simulators but as the technology develops and becomes more affordable it is quite possible that it will be used in the domestic environment, not only for games but also for leisure (for example, you could have virtual tours of cities or buildings) or educational purposes.

The ultimate virtual reality display will be one that creates a true three-dimensional image and that pans the scene when you move your head – a trick that needs considerable processing power from a computer. In the meantime we may be offered 3-D effects from DVD players but these are likely to be little more than the 'stereoscopic' images we have seen before. These work by producing a limited degree of perspective by displaying two images taken from slightly different angles – fun, but not convincing.

Mobile communications

While Chapter 4 touched on mobile phones and the GSM digital systems currently in use in the UK, this section explores how, during the next few years, this network is going to expand. Will there be a major new development in communications that gives us access to more detailed information and services than is currently possible, wherever we are, thus changing the way we work and play? Or will the 'hype' exceed the reality?

WAP (wireless application protocol)

The digital mobile telephone systems in the UK are based on an international standard called GSM (global system for mobile communication), which transmits telephone calls at radio frequencies around 900 and 1,800 MHz in the radio spectrum. The audio (speech) signals are digitised. This digital signal contains too many digits to be transmitted efficiently over the network, so it is compressed by the rejection of parts of it that are redundant. In fact, for telephone use, quite a lot of information can be rejected as hi-fi quality is not needed. The digits are then transmitted as a series of short bursts of data, not as a continuous stream. This allows several phone calls to be interleaved in the same radio channel. At the receiving end, the data bursts are put together again and converted back to an analogue speech signal. The actual data rate available for any one phone call is only 9.6Kbps (9,600 bits per second), which is fine for digital speech but rather slow for something more ambitious – such as, for example, Internet connections.

For example, compared to the norm for computer Internet connection, a modem claiming 56Kbps (in practice, note that modems rarely achieve better than 44Kbps on a domestic phone line), this is clearly too slow by a factor of more than four. Nevertheless, as we have all heard, manufacturers have gone ahead and WAP-equipped mobile phones have been on the market for a while which are able to access special WAP pages on the Internet. WAP also lets you send and receive email from your phone. But how well does it work?

The answer is that if you want to surf the Internet using a WAP phone, you may find the waves a bit on the small side, and rather few and far between!

A major difference between the WAP net and the Internet is that the WAP is more like teletext on your phone rather than the Internet on your computer. Although the WAP net is growing all the time, it has nowhere near as many sites or as much information on it as the Internet.

Many mobile services already allow you to send and receive short text messages (SMS) to other mobile phones. WAP technology enables you to send and receive proper emails direct from your phone to other people's email accounts. However, it is also now possible to send and receive email from any mobile phone that is capable of sending text messages – via special 'mobile-email' services, such as www.bulletin.net. So do not assume that email on a WAP phone necessarily works better than it would with a conventional phone.

As with a standard mobile phone, when you turn on a WAP phone a menu is displayed. From this menu you choose what you want to do on your phone, such as making a phone call or using the WAP services. Once you have chosen the WAP services, you will be taken to the mobile phone network's portal. The portal links you to further sites on the (WAP) network. Each network has developed its own individual portal, providing direct links to a growing variety of sites that are being recommended or promoted. Most networks provide links from their portals to a news service, sports information and entertainment listings.

If you cannot find the information you are looking for on the portal, or there is a specific WAP site that you want to visit, you will need to get there by tapping in the address of the site that you want to visit, which is extremely tedious using a phone keypad. This takes you beyond the network's portal, through what is called a 'gateway' to the wider WAP net. The sites on the portal are selected by your ISP. You can make your own choice of sites easier to access by bookmarking them. Once you have logged on to a site by entering its address, you can then bookmark it from the menu options. This way you can compile a folder of favourite sites and will not have to retype the address every time you visit one of them.

Which? magazine recently tested the WAP service by giving WAP phones to a panel of volunteers. Each WAP service was tried out by six people, each of whom tried at least two services. The first surprise was to find that even after they had bought and registered the phones, there was more to do before they could get going. The phones do not come with ready-to-use WAP services so the testers had to get this set up. This was done by contacting the networks, which provided instructions (by telephone or email or by sending a signal to the phones to activate the WAP services).

Getting started was hindered firstly by the fact that little or no information was supplied with the phones explaining what needed to be done, or, once it was done, how to access and use the WAP services.

Ten of the twelve testers did not feel at all confident about giving their card details to buy goods or services on a WAP phone. Originally, WAP technology (WAP 1.1) did not enable information, such as credit-card details, to be sent in a secure manner. Upgraded technology now available (WAP 1.2 and beyond) means that information can be sent via WAP as safely as via a secure web site (by scrambling the information using encryption).

The WAP testers were asked whether they had found any sites or services themselves that were useful. The ones they mentioned included Currypages, an Indian restaurant guide, and the classified advert service from Loot, *wap.loot.com.* They had also used a WAP search engine, www.wap.google.com; and the email service www.jumbuck.com/wap/.

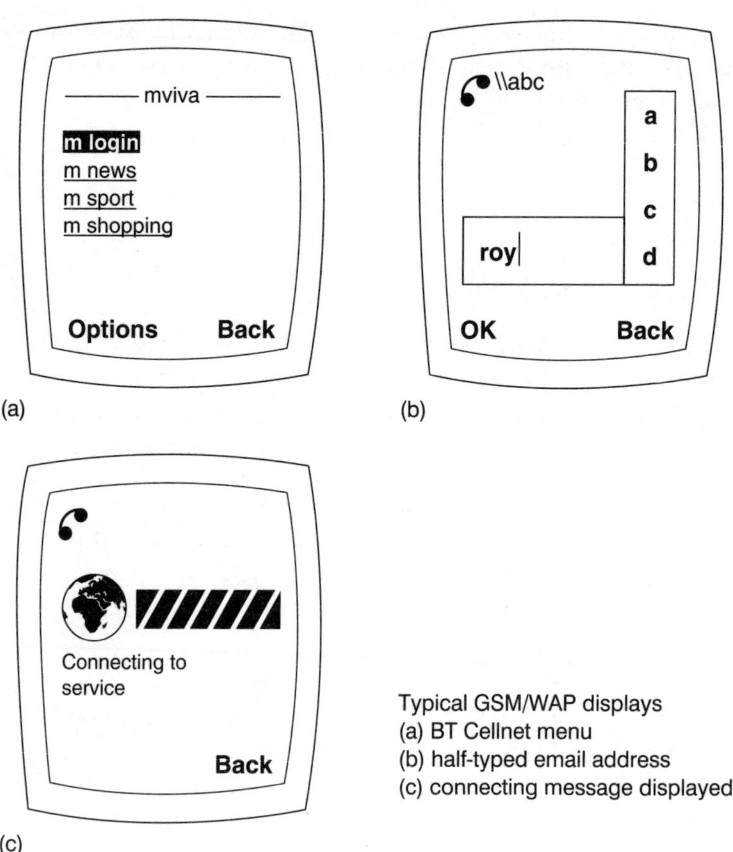

Typical GSM/WAP displays
(a) BT Cellnet menu
(b) half-typed email address
(c) connecting message displayed

The users found that the benefits of being able to send and receive proper emails to computer users were diluted by the fact that the process was fairly tedious and not as easy as using the regular short message service that is available on all digital mobile phones. The SMS system is intended for sending messages between mobile phones only, not to personal email accounts; however, as mentioned earlier, mobile-to-email services, such as www.bulletin.net, exist that automatically convert your SMS message into an email.

Buying advice

Despite all the hype, WAP is fairly basic technology. Surfing the WAP net can be a costly, time-consuming and unrewarding experience. Perhaps 'paddling', or even wading, would describe it better.

The people who tested WAP on behalf of *Which?* were generally disappointed with it, especially if they had had previous experience of using online services, and found it quite difficult to use.

Better services are on the horizon.

GPRS

A progression of mobile services, based on the GSM mobile phone, is planned. These are the main stepping stones:

GSM ⟶	WAP ⟶	GPRS ⟶	UMTS
Basic digital mobile phones	Simple text Internet	Faster, better Internet	Third-generation multimedia with Internet

Along the way you are likely to encounter such acronyms as EDGE (enhanced data rates for global evolution), itself an enhancement of GPRS, and HSCD (high-speed circuit-switched data), which is an alternative to GPRS and is being used by the Orange network (see below).

As ever, no marketing skill seems to have been employed in the naming of these services: the field of mobile communications seems destined to remain littered with awkward, instantly forgettable acronyms.

The next step will be GPRS (general packet radio service), launching in the latter part of 2001. This system makes more efficient use of the available radio channels, which in theory allows data to be received at a faster rate. Where there was one burst of data for GSM, GPRS allows users to receive up to four bursts of data – hence, higher data rates. These are likely to be about 64Kbps or higher in the UK. For sending data from the handset the speed will not be quite so good, though speeds of 30Kbps are said to be possible. This would make the data speed very close to that available from today's desktop computers with 'dial-up' modems.

However, some industry insiders have suggested that these speeds may not be achieved in practice; first-generation models, in particular, may achieve only half, at best, of the theoretical data rates. Whether GPRS can live up to the claims, made by some telecom companies, of delivering multimedia features such as video and audio, or whether it will just allow us to surf the web, remains to be seen.

GPRS brings a significant change to the way in which we connect to the digital world: using this service, we will not have to dial out to send or receive data, because GPRS is 'always on'. This means that we will see emails as soon as they arrive. Also, because the data channels for GPRS are shared with other users, the costs can be lower; users are charged for data they use rather than for the amount of time they are connected.

Meanwhile, the Orange network has launched a system called HSCD, which offers data speeds of 22.8Kbps. With the right interface software, you can connect this phone to a PDA and get quite acceptable web-browsing speeds. PDAs have rather limited screen resolution and size compared with a regular computer so some web sites and web portal sites are being designed specifically with them in mind.

UMTS

UMTS (universal mobile telecommunications system) is the so-called third-generation phone system. The British government netted £20 billion from the telecommunications companies when it sold licences for this system, which suggests that it is a serious proposition.

Data rates of up to 2Mbps (2,000Kbps) are being predicted, which would mean true multimedia performance and bring the mobile phone in line with what will be available on computers. This quoted data rate is an ideal – in reality, it will be somewhat slower than this, depending on factors such as signal strength and how many others are using the system. With UMTS mobile phone users or personal computer users will be constantly attached to the Internet as they travel, and the intention is that the system should eventually become a worldwide standard. Until this happens, UMTS phones will be multi-mode devices that can switch back to basic GSM where UMTS is not available.

With UMTS we can expect video-phones, video-conferencing and access to multimedia entertainment. We will also have access to our computers at home or our computer network at work. UMTS phones, linked to global positioning systems (GPS), will be able to give us localised information and maps.

How UMTS works

UMTS – third-generation or '3G' phones, or whatever they are finally called – have been allocated a higher band of frequencies than is used by GSM phones, in the range 1900–2100 MHz.

Technically, UMTS is based on the GSM and GPRS systems mentioned above and on the Internet-style 'packet-based' transmission system, which means the data (text, voice, video, etc.) is divided into small packets.

Today's GSM cellular telephones use a circuit-switched system, with connections always dependent on the availability of a circuit. Packet-switched connection, using Internet Protocol, means that a connection is always available to any other end point in the network. It will also make it possible to provide new services, such as alternative billing methods (pay-per-bit, pay-per-session, flat rate, etc.). The higher bandwidth of UMTS also promises new services, such as video-conferencing. UMTS could be used in conjunction with other technologies such as satellite connections and smart home technologies. Like GPRS it is an 'always-on' system (you do not have to dial into the system except for individual person-to-person phone calls).

The key to UMTS's improved versatility is how the data is transmitted. Instead of each phone selecting specific frequency channels in the allocated frequency band, the signal is effectively spread thinly across the entire band along with all the other data. This system is called wideband code division multiple access (W-CDMA). In traditional radio systems this would produce chaos but with the latest microprocessors it is possible to recover each signal at the receiver.

The net effect is much more efficient use of the available frequency band than is achievable with traditional systems that split the band into channels. This spread-spectrum technology should also mean less radio interference caused by mobile phones; in addition, it offers greater security.

The new devices are unlikely to look much like today's mobile phones. They will probably be bigger, looking more like a PDA (see below), with a large, thin screen and fold-away keyboard. They will become our mobile office and entertainment centre, replacing the personal organiser, phone, briefcase and personal stereo.

Mobile phones and safety

Since its universal adoption, the telephone has been regarded by many as a life-saving device, not a life-threatening appliance. The growth of mobile phone usage has both confirmed and altered this perception, because notwithstanding its usefulness in an emergency – for summoning help or alerting others to danger – mobile phone usage can also pose risks.

Making calls while driving a vehicle obviously puts the driver, other road users and pedestrians in danger.

Another potential risk, that of the radiation emitted by the mobile phone, has been the subject of international debate. Mobile phones emit non-ionising microwave radiation. 'Non-ionising' means that it does not harm or destroy the atomic structure of cell tissue, because the radiation is too low-frequency and too low-power to do this. X-rays, on the other hand, are an example of 'ionising' radiation. From this it would seem that the worst the radiation from your phone could do would be to heat you up, rather like a microwave oven, and this is exactly what a mobile phone does. However, the power being emitted by the phone is a fraction of what is emitted by a microwave oven and so the heating effect is going to be very small, typically less than 1 degree centigrade over a small area. In fact, the power emitted by a mobile phone and then absorbed by the user's head should be well below recommended national and international safety guidelines.

This does not mean we should be complacent. The recommended safety limits are just guidelines and no evidence exists to suggest that regular exposure to low-level microwave radiation is totally harmless. On the other hand, there is no hard evidence to suggest that it is harmful: the handful of scare stories that have appeared in the press, describing tests carried out on animals, do not necessarily indicate that the same effects would be experienced by humans.

Some researchers suggest that the 'heating effect' is not the issue: their worry is that the radiation can 'interfere' with the brain's processes, resulting in cognitive side effects, which may or may not be harmful. Large-scale research work being carried out by the World Health Organisation, and not due to be finished until 2003, is likely to shed more light on the issues. Until then, the government's recommendation, published in the Stewart Committee's Report (2000), is that while the balance of current research evidence does not suggest that mobile phones cause adverse health effects, as a precaution it would be wise to limit their use by children under 16 because their brains and nervous system are still developing and may be more vulnerable that those of adults.

A leaflet on this subject from the Department of Health★ is available from most mobile phone retailers; it can also be read on the Internet at www.doh.gov.uk/mobilephones.

Information on the move

As the pace of modern life becomes more frenetic and people want access to information wherever they are, it is not surprising that devices that can provide this service are being developed at a rapid rate. WAP phones (see 'WAP', above), PDAs and laptop computers are prime examples of such gadgets.

The personal digital assistant (PDA)

PDAs have been around since the mid-1980s. Probably the best-known brand is Psion, which launched its first Organiser in 1984. In its simplest form a PDA can be thought of as an electronic personal organiser (like a Filofax), but modern PDAs are interactive and can therefore do a lot more. PDAs are also often called palm computers. Names such as Organiser (Psion), Palmtop (Hewlett-Packard) and PalmPilot (3Com) are generally used to describe a PDA.

The techy shops and magazines are now full of PDAs, and they can look confusingly similar. They range in price from £99 to £700 and data storage capacity (memory) varies from 2Mb to 32Mb. Are they useful things to own or are they just executive toys?

What distinguishes a PDA from an electronic calculator or electronic address book is its computational ability. More than an electronic information store or simple adding machine, it can actually run programs and interface with other equipment such as a computer. What distinguishes it from a portable (laptop) computer is its small size and the fact that its internal software is different from that found in Windows or MAC computers. It is designed specifically to be a PDA.

These are typical features of a PDA:

- an address book that can automatically remind you of birthdays and anniversaries
- a diary that can warn you of forthcoming appointments and meetings
- diary and address book data can be shared with your home computer using cable that provides an infra-red connection
- a source of Information: a PDA can store street maps, restaurant guides, etc.
- a word processor: o.k. for typing short notes, but even this can be a trifle fiddly as the keyboards are very small; however, some PDAs have a keyboard on the screen, which you use by tapping the keys with a stylus
- a notepad/sketch pad. Some PDAs allow you to hand-write or sketch by hand on to the touch-sensitive screen. The most famous of these was the Apple Newton, launched in the early 1990s, which, with a great deal of practice, could learn to read your handwriting and convert it into typed text
- spreadsheets and databases. Many PDAs actually run cut-down versions of computer programs that can interface with your home computer
- e-book reader. Some PDAs can be used to store read e-books that you have downloaded on to your computer
- colour screens, which some modern PDAs have
- various optional accessories such as an optional mobile phone attachment; the Psion PalmPilot has a digital camera attachment. Built-in MP3 players are also common nowadays.

Soon you might be able simply to talk to your PDA rather than type into it. Voice-recognition software, currently being developed, will let you access stored email messages, addresses and phone numbers using voice commands. The PDA can 'read' the requested information back to you.

Beat the battery

When you have a portable organiser, the last thing you want to have to do is carry round a charging unit and extra cables in case the batteries let you down. Fortunately, some machines will last for two

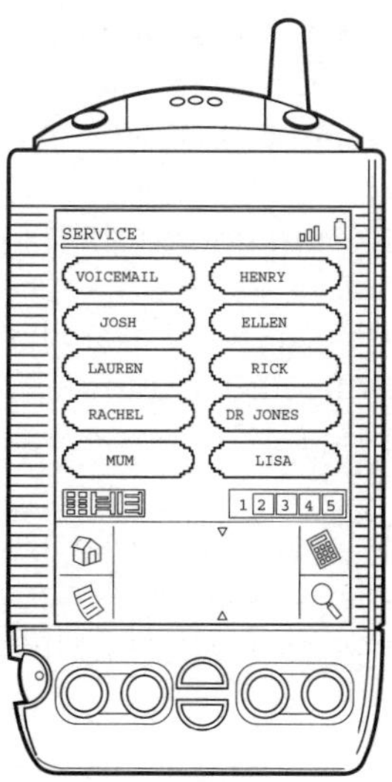

Handspring PDA with attachment

months without a battery change or recharge. Others – especially those with colour screens and lots of memory – might peter out after just a few hours. If you are taking your PDA to a desert island – or simply do not want the hassle of changing batteries or recharging – go for a black-and-white version with little memory, like the Palm m100. The versions that work with standard AA batteries can be good if you are likely to be stranded without your charger.

Buying advice

A versatile PDA is quite expensive, costing several hundred pounds, so it is worth thinking very carefully about whether you really need it or are just tempted by its gimmickry or status value. If you use and rely on a diary and address book while out of the office or away from home, analyse what advantage the PDA would give you over pen and paper, and whether, if you had a PDA, you would find the time to keep it up to date.

Things could change rapidly in the near future. It will become possible to connect your PDA to a mobile phone device – more dramatically, the two devices could converge into one gadget, such as the Mitsubishi 'trium' launched in April 2001 which works with the GPRS phone system. These developments will make PDAs more useful and, for some people, essential. Ultimately they could combine your MP3 player, web browser, video player and mobile phone.

If you decide you cannot live without one, make sure it is compatible with your home or work computer, and check how long the batteries last. Finally, try it out in the shop to make sure it is comfortable to use.

Portable/laptop computers

A wide range of portable (or laptop) computers is now on the market and their performance can compete with most desktop models, but you will pay at least half as much again for a laptop that can match a desktop computer. Modern laptops are less bulky than they used to be; some are only about 3cm thick and weigh in at under 2 kg. For the overall dimensions to be any smaller would compromise the usability of the keyboard.

Liquid crystal display (LCD) technology has improved so much in recent years that it is possible to play games and watch videos on a laptop. The main improvement has been the development of TFTs (thin film transistors), sometimes called active matrix displays. Computer displays are made up of thousands of coloured spots (pixels). On a desktop computer, these are made up of phosphor dots on a cathode-ray tube which produce a very bright and fast responsive display. On early laptops the pixels were made up from liquid crystal elements with coloured filters. Each pixel was activated by applying a voltage on a row of pixels and on a column of pixels. Where the row and column intersected, current flowed and this pixel was activated. An activated LCD pixel reflected more light than an inactivated pixel. In effect, the LCD displays relied on either 'incident' light (light shining on it) or light transmitted through it; the LCD pixels do not generate their own illumination as in a cathode-ray tube.

A display screen made with TFT technology has a transistor for each pixel, which means that the electric current that triggers each pixel's illumination can be smaller and can be switched on and off more quickly. So a TFT or active matrix display is more responsive to change. For example, when you move your mouse across the screen, a TFT display is fast enough to reflect the movement of the mouse cursor. With a passive matrix display, the cursor blurs or temporarily disappears until the display can 'catch up'. Hence, the TFT produces a much more useable display.

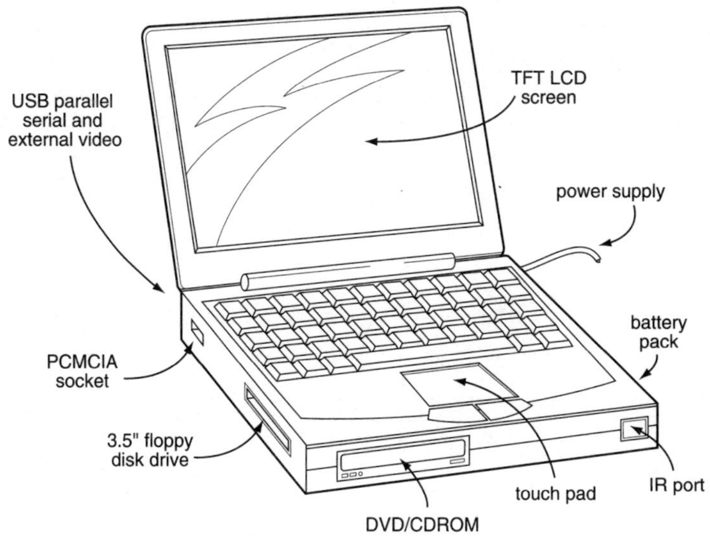

Anatomy of a laptop computer

Laptop computers demand their own range of small, slim-styled peripheral devices. The PCMCIA interface and the USB interface are ideal for these. For laptops, the touchpad is now accepted as being preferable to the mouse and most people find it easier to use than the 'rollerball' found on earlier laptops.

The future

The advanced PDA with built-in third-generation phone and Internet access would seem to be the ultimate mobile information and communication device. But for those who want more computing power the answer may lie in the merging of the PDA and laptop computer with some of the larger peripheral devices such as keyboards, magnetic or optical storage and larger screen; who knows, the whole works might be built into our clothing. Maybe we will be able to dispense with the hardware altogether, accessing our own personal information by radio and viewing and listening on a personal headset with the information projected in our field of vision – the so-called 'head-up' display.

On the other hand, with improved access to information and communications, why should we ever need mobile devices at all? We may never need to leave home.

Chapter 6

Smart homes

The automated home is a dream long entrenched in the human imagination. Back in the days of silent film comedies, audiences were marvelling at devices that tipped you out of bed and made your breakfast. Comparatively recent films such as *Back to the Future* and those featuring Wallace and Gromit have featured similar devices – contraptions which, like their antecedents of the early twentieth century, tended to rely on strings, pulleys and cogs for their technology. Films and TV series from Woody Allen's *Sleeper* to *Dr Who* have also given us a taste of what it might be like to have a labour-saving robot around the house.

While we may still be waiting for the robots to run our homes, they have been used in industry for the last two decades, especially by car manufacturers. These are rather large and expensive robots and although they can be 'programmed' to perform different tasks on a production line, taking care of varied household chores is likely to be a harder job.

Underlying the intent to use robots to entertain lay a genuine quest for automation. As long ago as 1951, visitors to the Festival of Britain were eager to witness the latest electrical innovations, including the first 'automatic' domestic appliances to reach the UK – for example, the Russell Hobbs coffee percolator that turned itself off without human intervention when the coffee was ready. Such products naturally lent credence to the idea of the fully automated home driven by electricity.

While automated appliances such as the Teasmaid and automated domestic facilities such as the thermostatically controlled central heating system have now been around for some time, these aids to modern living have traditionally relied on electro-mechanical switches and motors to control their functions. In particular, they used a device called a bi-metal strip, which bends as it gets hot, and can therefore be used as a temperature sensor that can operate an electrical switch. In recent years, electro-mechanical switches have been superseded by temperature-sensing transistors, which can be more accurate and reliable.

But to date *fully* automated systems for the home, in which everything electrical is automated, have been the domain of the technical enthusiast. The sorts of d-i-y systems developed so far have tended to concentrate on remote or automatic control of appliances. Few could claim to be 'intelligent' systems that can think for themselves, but such developments are not far off.

The ability of digital signals to transmit complex instructions, and the ability of digital electronics to carry out computations and make decisions, mean we can forget the strings and pulleys and the electro-mechanical switches. The digital, or 'smart', home will truly be an intelligent, thinking home.

From 'automated' to 'smart' is, in technological terms, a big step. It may help to think of the development in three stages.

'Home automation' is simply a system enabling household equipment or services to be automatically or remotely controlled. Normally, this means switched on or off. A basic timer- controlled central heating system might be one element of such a system.

The 'wired' or 'networked' home is likely to have electrical or electronic services running throughout the house, or at least through part of it. For example, the hi-fi might be piped to all the rooms, or computer data might be available in both the home office and the sitting room. Nowadays, even simple telephone sockets can be 'wired' throughout the house, if not transmitted by digital radio signals. Traditionally, the wired house has been thought of as one with metres of signal and data cables connecting all the rooms, but in the not-too-distant future we shall be using high-frequency radio signals to network our homes – the wire*less* home, in fact.

The 'intelligent' or 'smart' home is also not so far off. Thanks to a combination of mini-computers, home automation and lower cost signal distribution systems, cabled or wireless, we can create an environment where our various domestic appliances and services can communicate with each other and make 'electronic' decisions on our behalf – such as selecting TV programmes, suggesting what provisions to buy, monitoring and managing our energy consumption for optimum efficiency, controlling our environmental conditions and delivering news and information to us wherever we are and when we need it.

Smart-home technology

Smart homes use electronic networking technology to integrate the various devices and appliances found in almost all homes, plus building environment systems more common in factories and offices, to enable the entire domestic living space to be controlled centrally – on-site or remotely – as a single entity.

Smart Homes, a report produced in August 2000 by Consumers' Association for the Joseph Rowntree Foundation and the Chartered Institute of Housing, used the following description of the smart home concept which comes from *Digital Futures: Making Homes Smarter*, by David Gann *et al.*

> *Cars have central locking, electric windows, remote-controlled mirrors, CD auto-changers – and the rest. And factories, offices and shops are often highly automated, giving staff control over their environments, and making buildings more efficient. Automatic doors, blinds that close when the sun comes out, infra-red lighting controls – they are all becoming commonplace.*
>
> *But you do not find that sort of thing in people's homes much – or do you?*
>
> *We have remote controls for our TVs, we have smoke detectors and passive infra-red burglar alarms, we have timers on our central heating. But all these devices are separate entities. Each affects only one activity or aspect of the home.*
>
> *Smart homes are about something much more exciting. They are about using the latest information and communications technology to link all the mechanical and digital devices available today – and so create a truly interactive house.*

Although the truly smart home is not yet a reality, many potential components of it are. Some of the newer digital technology and gadgets that are already available are too expensive for mass consumption; others require technical or d-i-y skills. But all of them, in one way or another, point the way forward.

Today's clever appliances

Some digitally controlled, automatic and intelligent domestic appliances are already on the market. They include washing and drying machines, refrigerators and lawnmowers.

Washing appliances

In the field of washing machines, tumble driers and dishwashers, two principal innovations have been adopted. For many years now, the overall temperature controls, water controls and wash cycles have been controlled by electronics using a microprocessor – a customised computer with an integrated circuit programmed for a specific sequence of tasks.

In recent years this digital electronic control system has been enhanced by a software process called 'fuzzy logic'. Normally, digital logic circuits are thought of as having only two conditions, '1' or '0' ('true' or 'false' ; 'on' or off'; 'yes' or 'no', etc.). With fuzzy logic the digital circuit's end result can have intermediate states or 'degrees of truth'. This is achieved by looking at all possible true and false states in the system and using some computing power to determine the best overall intermediate state. It could be described as the computer equivalent of the calculated compromise.

In the case of a domestic appliance such as a washing machine, this process is used to improve efficiency and performance. With a conventional washing machine, you select the wash program you want and the machine then uses a selection of pre-determined cycle times, temperature and water quantities. In a fuzzy-logic machine, instead of the program relying on fixed values, it uses a range of sensors to 'interrogate' your wash before and during the washing. For example, it might weigh the wash. Then, by adding some water and sensing the resulting water level, it might measure how absorbent that particular load is. During the wash it could analyse the water optically, adjusting the amount of detergent or increasing the wash time if the water is dirty.

Armed with information of this type, the washing machine is able to modify its wash cycles. It could do this by using all the data it has collected in a mathematical formula which calculates the optimum wash parameters, or by checking all the data against some predetermined scenarios (a 'look-up table') held in its internal electronic memory. Clearly, the overall success of this type of system ultimately depends on how many parameters there are, the degree of relevance of all the parameters the system can measure, and how good the calculation or look-up tables are.

Tests at a *Which?* laboratory have found that these fuzzy-logic appliances do perform better than ordinary machines.

Robotic appliances

One of the first domestic robots on general sale has been developed to cut down routine work outside the home rather than in it. At about £400 the Robomow* lawnmower may be rather pricey, but if you have a large lawn, or simply want to impress the neighbours, it might be worth it.

Before you can use it you have to install a wire around the lawn's perimeter. Once this is done, you can leave the mower to its own devices. Once it has mowed the perimeter, it criss-crosses the whole lawn, perhaps covering it several times over. It systematically works its way around the whole lawn, avoiding obstacles. Whereas the Robomow is designed to be stowed away and recharged manually, a similar product, the Husqvarna* auto mower, will even park itself in its charging station. It then sits around until it judges that the lawn needs mowing again. *Gardening Which?* magazine recently tested the latest version of the Robomow and found that it worked reasonably well – it cut the grass clippings very finely and spread them as mulch over the lawn and seemed to cope well even if the grass was wet.

The idea of a robotic vacuum cleaner is not new, but again, it is only recently that one has become readily available on the consumer market. This time it is from the innovative manufacturer Dyson,* which already has a large share of the conventional vacuum-cleaner market. Its DC06 vacuums a room by navigating a spiral from the outer edges of the room into the centre. It can navigate around obstacles and will not tumble down the stairs. Unfortunately, neither will it climb the stairs by itself, a problem it shares with the early versions

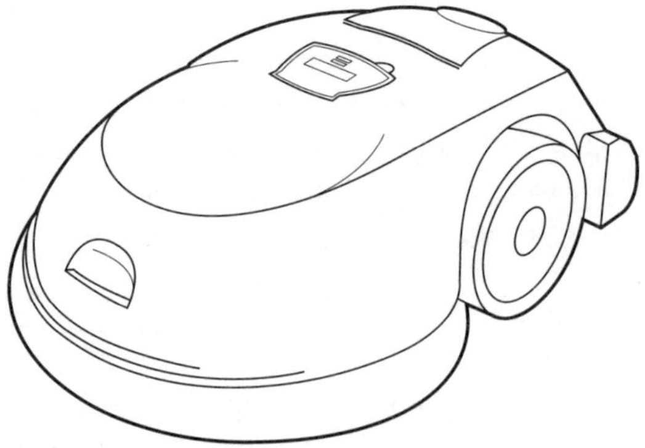

The Robomow

of Daleks. Another thing it appears to share with Daleks is its ability to recognise when it is under threat. According to the manufacturer's web site: 'A red glow appears if DC06 is feeling distressed or threatened, for example by a pet or child. The DC06 has fail-safe systems to detect potential problems and keep it out of trouble. If a dog attacks it, or a child jumps on it, DC06 has been designed to pause.'

This socially tolerant robot is in fact quite intelligent. According to Dyson: 'The knowledge DC06 builds of a room allows it to assess when it has finished' and it 'constantly adjusts to navigate the most efficient route.'

The cleaner derives its intelligence from using over 50 sensory devices to detect the environment around it and three on-board computers.

The communications kitchen

Fridge manufacturers seem to be very keen on entering the intelligent home market. Electrolux,* for example, is working in this area and has supplied equipment to those working with experimental smart homes. The Far Eastern electronics manufacturer LG* recently launched an 'Internet fridge' on the market, which is designed to do rather more than simply keeping food fresh. The

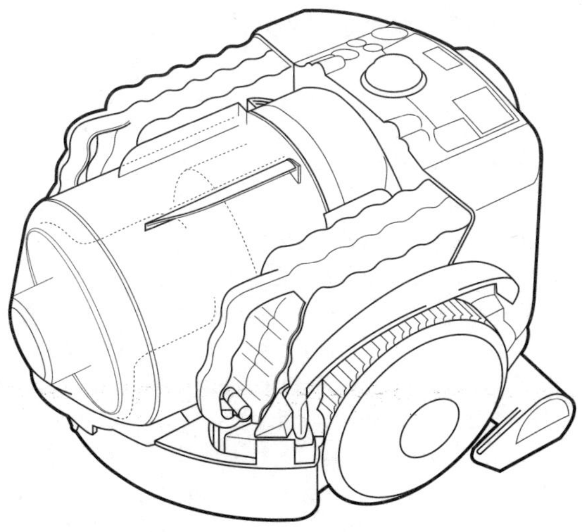

The Dyson DC06

appliance is a large, US-style refrigerator with an ice dispenser on the front and two doors side by side. The first special application is a video screen mounted on the front of the unit: connection via a telephone or cable socket which brings full Internet access and entertainment to the kitchen. You could, for instance, watch TV, search the Internet for a recipe or email friends, all from this single kitchen appliance.

The second application is more significant: the fridge incorporates a bar-code reader so it can read the code of an item as you put it into the fridge and thus monitor the contents. It can warn you if products are approaching their 'use-by' date and it can create a shopping list of items you have run out of. Moreover, it has the ability to connect to your supermarket to order the items for you. LG says that the fridge could suggest recipes based on what it knows to be stored in it. While it might find four cans of lager, a packet of fish fingers and a strawberry yoghurt rather a challenge, if the fridge were fully stocked for a large family, the suggestions could be quite practical.

The LG Internet fridge costs about £8,000, which suggests it is really a specialist product at the moment but it represents a significant example of the sort of intelligent appliance that could well be at the centre of the intelligent and automated home.

In the future other kitchen appliances could be linked to the Internet and to each other. For example, if you put an item in your microwave oven, the oven could ask the fridge what the item is and at what power and for how long it should be cooked. Or, your fuzzy-logic washing machine could call up the Internet to update its information if it detects that you have put in some type of material it does not recognise.

Another interesting development is the offer of a 'complete washing service' from the manufacturers of washing machines. Instead of selling you a washing machine and not having any dealings with you after that unless you call it to have a fault repaired, the manufacturer could supply you a machine at a subsidised price (or even free). When the machine is plumbed in, it would also be connected to your telephone, cable or whatever communications system you have installed. You then simply 'pay per wash' and are charged monthly via your phone bill or credit card. The provider of the service would be responsible for remotely monitoring your

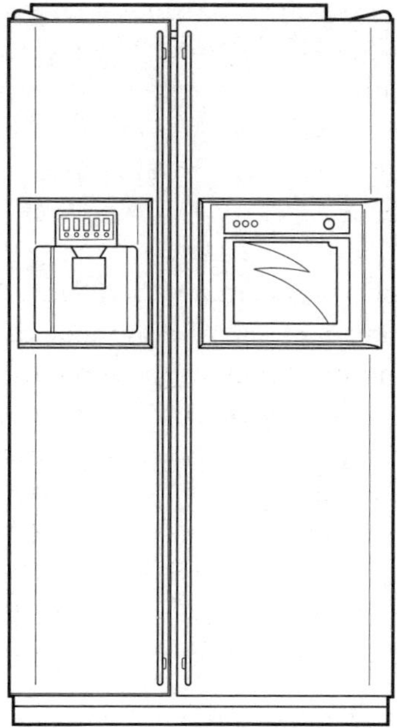

The LG Internet fridge

machine – with the appropriate diagnostic tools, it could even detect in advance if it is in need of servicing or replacing.

Networking

The key to an intelligent or smart home is the ability to distribute digital signals (both control signals and multimedia audio/video signals) around the house. This can be done with wire cables, fibre-optic cables or radio signals. A home computer would either be a part of such a system or could be used to control it. It is already possible to set up a network with today's computers and smart home networks could use identical technology and infrastructure.

It is estimated that some 38 per cent of households in the UK have more than one computer. This is not so much a sign of affluence as a reflection of how quickly computers become obsolete – in particular, too slow to run the latest software efficiently – and therefore have to be replaced. The old computer is then either put to one side or passed on to other members of the household. If someone

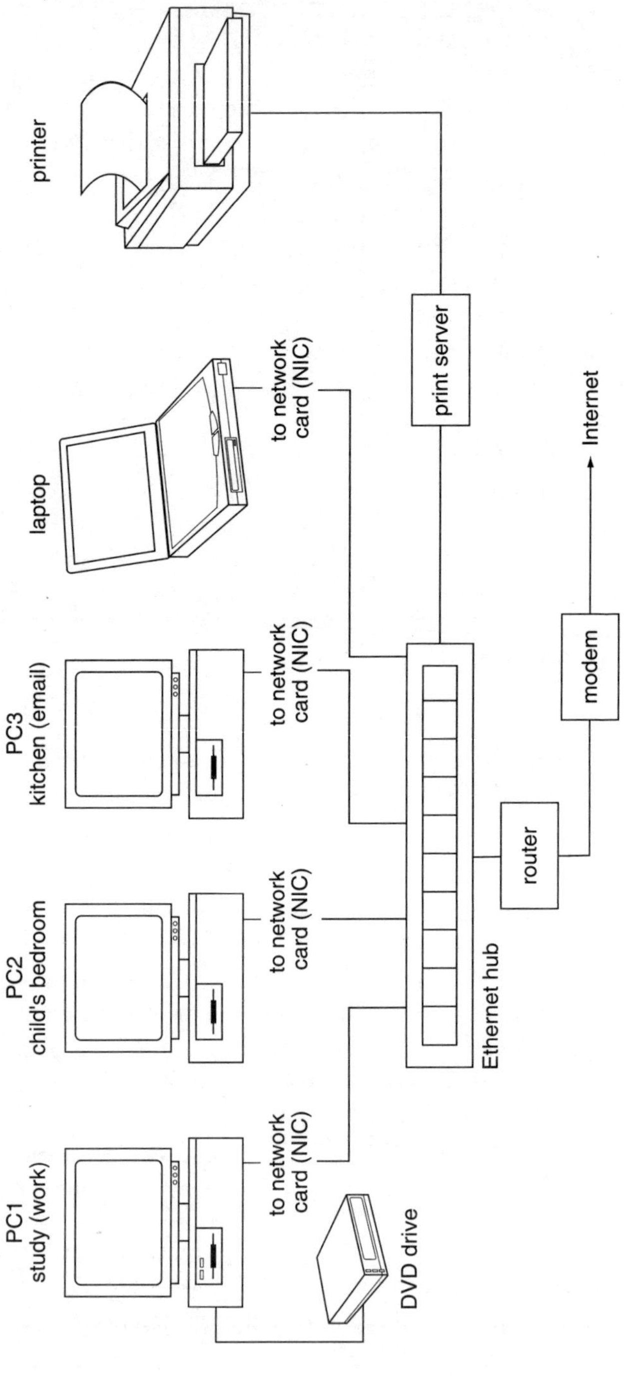

printer
laptop
PC3
kitchen (email)
PC2
child's bedroom
PC1
study (work)
to network card (NIC)
to network card (NIC)
to network card (NIC)
to network card (NIC)
print server
Internet
modem
router
Ethernet hub
DVD drive

A computer network

also has a laptop computer for work, that means there are three computers in one home – and this is by no means an unusual situation.

Already, a single computer cannot serve the needs of even a small family when it is required by more than one person at a time. The numbers of computers owned are likely to increase dramatically as it becomes the norm for all members of the family to have their own computer, for either work or school.

Families that connect their computers together will reap the benefits, because this means that they can share some of the costly peripherals such as printers, scanners, hard drives, software, modem and Internet access. Interconnecting the components of the system creates what businesses call a local area network (LAN); in the smart home it is being called the home area network (HAN).

There are various methods for networking computers but the most straightforward for domestic use, shown in the diagram, is known as a 'star network' (the alternative is a ring network). It uses a standard signalling system called Ethernet; the connecting cables are called CAT-5. Some property developers are installing CAT-5 cables as standard in new houses.

It is possible now to install your own HAN and, hence, the beginnings of a smart home. Each computer has to be fitted with a network interface card (NIC) and the printer also has to have a 'print server'. All the component parts are linked by a device called a hub. The data rate for this simple domestic network would be 10Mbps, which is about 20 times faster than a basic V90 Internet modem. Even faster networks are possible, running at 100Mbps.

If you want to share an Internet connection you will need to connect via a device called a router, which sorts out which bits of data belong to which of the computers. Devices such as DVD drives, scanners and hard-disk drives can be connected to one of the computers so that they can be accessed from any of the others (so long as the computer with these devices is also switched on). You can select which devices and which hard drives are available to other members of the family over the network and which can only be accessed 'locally', on a particular computer.

Domestic network kits, such as the Netgear Network Starter Kit, can be purchased (www.netgear.com). Other companies such as 3-Com* and Intel also produce domestic network systems.

In the future, a 100Mbps Ethernet signalling system could form the basis of the fully wired and intelligent home.

D-i-y home-automation systems

Even today it is possible to control remotely and to automate some of the more basic electrical appliances in the home, especially if you have some basic d-i-y skills.

The most common system uses a signalling protocol called X-10. This sends very simple digitally coded signals through the household mains wiring, without the necessity for complicated re-wiring. The various modules that are used to do the controlling simply plug into existing mains sockets. The system, which has been around since the late 1970s, has been particularly popular in the USA, where it has been easy to buy the various components. Today, several UK shops stock X-10 products that are suitable for use with UK mains wiring. A comprehensive catalogue of components can be found at www.laser.com (the web site of Laser Business Systems Home Automation). This site is part of a 'web ring' that comprises over 100 web sites dealing with X-10 home-automation systems, including some sites by private individuals extolling the virtues of their automated houses.

As with most hobbyist products, there seems to be no upper limit to how much you can spend on X-10 devices or how much time you can spend installing and programming them. A very simple beginner's kit can be bought for under £60 but all this will enable you to do is to switch on and off manually and remotely, a couple of electrical devices such as table lamps or heaters. To achieve a more sophisticated level of automation, which would enable you eventually to have all the electrical devices in your home controlled automatically, you will need to spend about £700 to begin with and several hundreds more over time for extras.

Some X-10 devices and beginners' kits are beginning to appear in some of the bigger d-i-y retail stores.

The X-10 system

The basic X-10 system simply sends digital coded signals through the domestic wiring; these codes are sent from the X-10 controller box and received by the X-10 switching modules throughout the house.

As all the X-10 modules in the house will be able to receive the commands sent by the controller(s), each module needs to be able to distinguish between commands meant for it and those meant for another module. If they cannot, chaos will reign as all the appliances switch on or off together. The solution is a system of unique addresses. The system uses 16 electronic 'house codes' designated by letters A to P and 16 'device' codes designated by numbers 1 to16. This gives a grand total of (16 x 16) 256 codes. Every module in the house is assigned one of these identification codes, usually by setting some thumbwheel-type switches on each module. The 256 codes should be enough for most homes – and enough to help prevent conflict with neighbours, should they be using the same system. This is important because X-10 signals on the mains wiring can 'leak' through to neighbouring houses via the main power lines in your house.

In the beginner's system shown in the diagram, the mini controller is plugged into a mains socket in the living room. Pressing one of the switches on the remote controller will send one of your digital codes – say, 'A1' – along the house wiring. This signal will be received by all the modules you have plugged into the mains sockets in other rooms. However, only the module you have set to recognise 'A1' will react and switch on whatever is plugged into it (the table lamp in our example); the coffee machine will remain off.

While this system might be a useful remote-control facility, it hardly constitutes home automation.

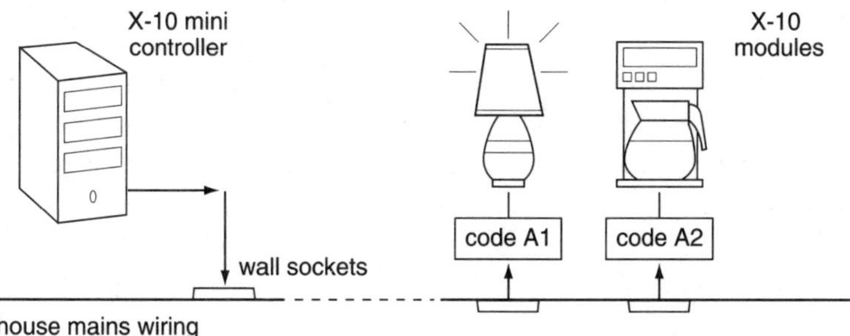

Beginner's system for home automation

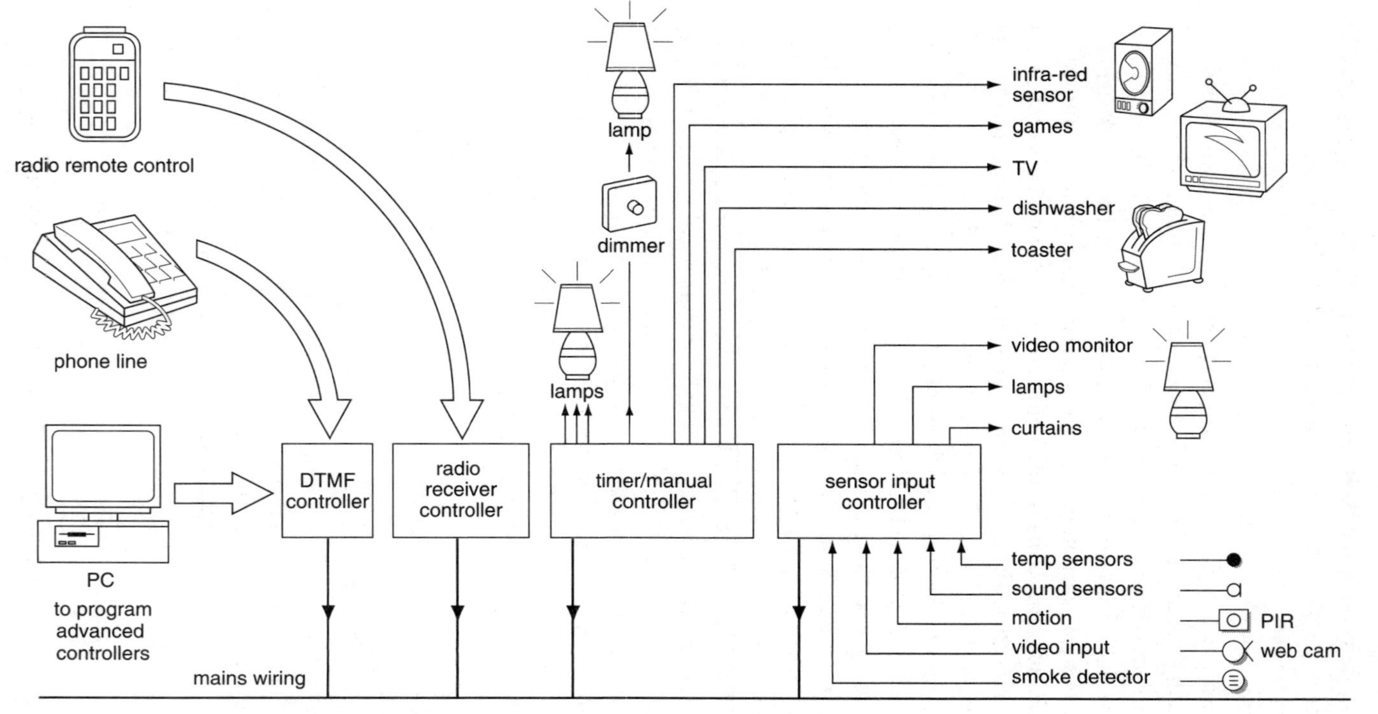

Schematic diagram of an advanced X-10 installation

The beauty of the X-10 system is that you can address several appliances together. For example, if all your downstairs lights are coded with house code 'A', then sending an 'A' will switch them all on, whereas sending A1 will just switch one of them on.

The diagram shows just some of the more advanced controlling that can be achieved using the X-10 system. With an advanced X-10 controller, it is possible to set things to switch on or off at prescribed times, lights can be dimmed and curtains can be drawn using a motorised system. Lighting and other appliances can be controlled by means of hand-held infra-red remote controls, radio-link control or even telephone dial-up, using the tone keypad to identify tasks.

The more sophisticated controllers can be programmed using a computer. These controllers can also be set to activate selected appliances according to temperature, sound or motion. One popular application is to set up a camera and motion detector at the front door. When the X-10 controller detects a visitor it can display a picture on your TV.

Beyond X-10 there are already a number of possibilities for creating the d-i-y smart home, which could appeal if you are a real enthusiast with plenty of time and, more importantly, money. Otherwise, unless you are thinking of building your own house, it would probably pay to wait a little: you may find that the smart home will gradually come to you, courtesy of one or more of the major utility, broadcasting or communications companies.

Intelligent home-automation systems of the future

The various gadgets and systems described above are really just individual elements for the smart home. They need to be integrated for the automated home to turn into a smart home. This integration also needs to be taken a step further – we need to be able to connect our home to the outside world. This requires a smart home 'gateway'.

Whether the fridge, or any other kitchen appliance for that matter, would be regarded as the best choice of device to be our intelligent home controller or our gateway to external services is open to question. Telecommunications companies, utility (gas and electricity) providers and broadcasting companies all see their products as being potential home controllers or gateways. Now that building the infrastructure for a smart home is both technically and financially viable, the provision of such an infrastructure is seen as a potential new source of business.

The business model for providing a smart home will not be the traditional one of *selling* consumers boxes full of electronics, such as televisions, hi-fis or set-top boxes. It is more likely to be the 'vertically integrated' business model of the type used by mobile phone companies and digital TV providers: the smart home will be sold to us as a means of getting us to sign up to services such as broadcasting, video on demand, pay-per-wash, monitoring and servicing of the central heating system, providing telephone and Internet access or supplying groceries. Under such a scenario, the hardware is usually heavily subsidised in the expectation that we will spend our money with the company in the future. Not surprisingly, several rival systems and standards for the infrastructure needed to integrate all these systems are available and being developed.

The X-10 system, and others like it, are too basic to meet the needs of the smart home. The data rate of the digital signals it sends down the mains wiring is far too slow to do anything other than obey simple on and off commands. What smart-home occupants will want to do is send relatively complex instructions to their appliances and have the system make intelligent decisions based on the information it receives back from those appliances. They will also want to distribute sound, video and interactive media throughout the house. These types of system need state-of-the-art digital technology to transmit the data.

The smart home should be more than just a home full of automatically controlled, labour-saving devices – it should be the result of a holistic approach to a house. Overall, then, a smart home should cater for our entertainment needs, control our physical environment, and look after our security and communications.

The sorts of facility we might want our smart homes to provide could be:

- increased versatility of domestic appliances such that they can not only be controlled remotely but can be relied upon to make intelligent decisions about when they need to carry out their tasks

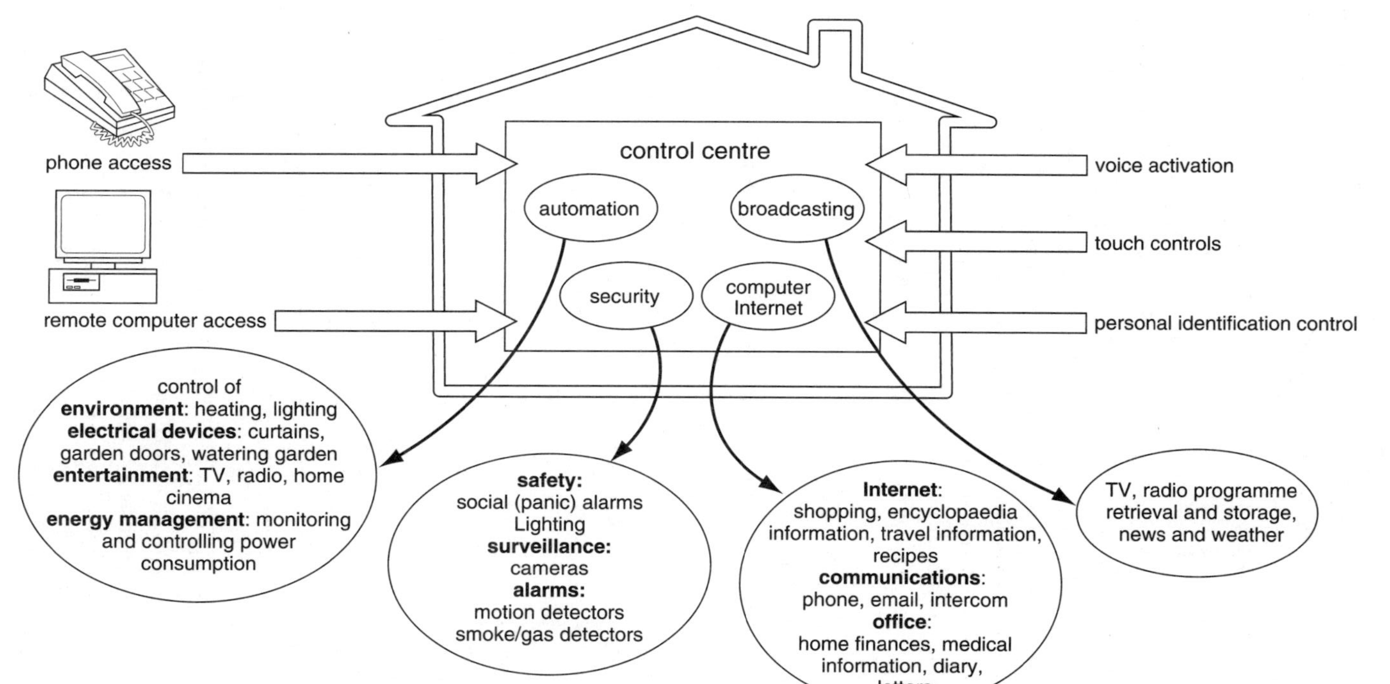

The components of a smart home

- voice activation of home electronic systems by spoken command, given either direct or via a telephone
- operation of a home security system, capable of distinguishing between intruders and legitimate visitors
- operation of a home monitoring system, checking smoke detectors, the state of the plumbing (burst pipes) and condition of our central heating boilers. It could also check that all your doors and windows are locked at night or when you are away.
- automatic control of the home environment and services such as central heating, hot water, lighting and air-conditioning; also, opening doors, closing curtains, etc.
- operate power-management systems to ensure our overall power consumption is kept to a minimum.
- communication with the outside world (bank, supermarket,

Smart-home systems

A bewildering number of different technical standards exists already for smart-home systems. In due course, it is hoped, common sense should prevail, sparing us another battle of the Betamax-*vs*-VHS kind – which would mean that your fridge spoke a different language from your toaster, as it were.

Systems such as X-10 that rely on existing home mains wiring are unlikely to feature significantly in the smart home, as this type of network cannot transmit complex instructions or data reliably. Instead, two different and co-existing distribution systems are likely to emerge. First, there will be **cabled systems**, which could use simple 'twisted pair'-type wires, special coaxial cables or even fibre optics. Whichever is chosen, it will mean re-wiring the home – a significant expense. Complete 'wired' systems are likely to be incorporated into new homes rather than fitted retrospectively into existing ones. Of the different systems currently being proposed, the main contenders appear to be the European Installation Bus – an official European standard; Echelon LonWorks and CEBUS, both American systems; Universal Plug and Play (UPnP), an American initiative supported by several large companies including Microsoft and Sony; Ethernet, the computer network standard described earlier in this chapter; and firewire (also called IEEE 1394, the official

electricity and other utility providers) for the purposes of financial transactions and replenishing grocery supplies
- access to information and to system status and system controls from remote locations such as a workplace. If your smart home had automatic pet-feeding equipment and you had to stay late at work, you could phone in to activate it remotely
- distribution of audio and video entertainment: for example, 'piping' music/video to any room in the home, and with the ability to follow us around it. A surround-sound system could automatically balance itself for best effect by detecting our location in the room
- organisation of entertainment: obtaining and saving TV programmes we want to watch, video-on-demand and multi-player games; the system should also manage ordering and payment, as appropriate

name given to it by the Institute of Electrical and Electronics Engineers). The last-mentioned system, IEEE1394, is particularly interesting as it is already in use in many households. It is the so-called firewire fibre optic connecting system used by digital camcorders and computers for transferring digital audio and video signals. The system is being adapted for the smart home under the name of HAVi (home audio and video interoperability) and it combines the audio and video distribution ability of firewire with extra-remote-control capability. Whatever system(s) is (are) chosen, the reasonably priced CAT-5 wiring mentioned earlier should be capable of distributing it.

There will also be **wireless systems** that will not require any modifications to the home. Again, several proposals are being weighed in the balance. The most promising candidates are HomeRF (American); IEEE802.11 – a wireless version of the computer Ethernet system; and Bluetooth, the low-power radio system that was launched in Europe in early 2001. An interesting aspect of all these systems is that while they operate in the microwave region (2.4GHz), they do not broadcast on a fixed frequency in this range in the way normal radio transmitters do. Instead they constantly hop about, changing frequency all the time. This 'spread-spectrum' system of transmission improves security and immunity from interference.

- access to the Internet and email from anywhere in and around the home from portable display devices and sharing of an Internet connection between computers and other devices such as mobile phones and PDAs
- intelligent forwarding of incoming telephone calls to multiple cordless handsets or voice mailboxes
- constant updates of news and requested information, wherever we are in the home
- networking of home computers, so that they can share programs, data, audio and video, and peripherals such as central hard disks, printers and remote display devices
- personal assistance, reminding us of what tasks we need to carry out, what items we need to buy, what appointments have been arranged; this facility should be able to distinguish automatically between different members of the household
- system diagnostics: by monitoring equipment performance, smart homes should be able to detect any likely malfunction in domestic appliances before they actually occur and arrange for them to be fixed or replaced
- tele-care: remote monitoring of elderly or otherwise vulnerable people via a link to his or her smart home, checking, for example, whether all the doors were locked at night, or more importantly, monitoring his or her medical condition
- communication with our cars – checking fluid levels, for example, and also the car's location, by means of GPS locations technology and general engine diagnostics.

Smart-home products in the marketplace

Two developments in smart-home technology are already past the drawing-board stage.

The multimedia home platform (MHP) is being developed by Pace,* the manufacturer of the UK digital TV set-top box, in conjunction with partners in the digital TV industry. In their view the set-top box is the logical choice of device to become the hub of the smart home, and in this respect they certainly have an advantage because digital TV has given them the crucial foot in the door.

Pace sees the development of the set-top box into the home network as being an evolutionary process. Acknowledging that the rewiring of existing homes will not be an attractive option for home-owners, it plans the development of wireless devices that can be connected to the set-top box and to other home devices such as a TV or computer, thereby establishing the beginnings of the networked home.

Wireless connection to the Internet or to portable, hand-held devices is also being developed. E-commerce (shopping online) is one of the economic driving forces behind this operation. Pace is developing a system, currently known as Shopping Mate, which will implement this. The device will have a screen and, potentially, a bar code reader. Through third-party links with retailers it will allow consumers to compile shopping lists and place orders without interrupting main-screen viewing.

Some of the other applications predicted by Pace, alongside digital TV and radio distributed around the home, are digital alarm clocks, Internet radio, management of power consumption requirements and home security systems.

Interestingly, the company does not initially plan to use one of the newer high-speed, 2.4GHz wireless technologies being developed specifically for this type of application (HomeRF, Ethernet or Bluetooth*). Instead it plans to use the digitally slower DECT digital cordless telephone system to do the data transmissions around the home and possibly also to transmit some of the simpler home automation signals through the mains wiring. The reasoning behind this is that it is established technology, already available at affordable prices.

Bluetooth

Principally developed by the Swedish mobile phone handset manufacturer Ericsson, which named the system after Harald Blåtand, a tenth-century Viking king, this technology has been adopted not only by other mobile manufacturers but by most of the world's major electronics manufacturers. Bluetooth is a wireless networking system with a difference, using very low power transmissions. This makes it suitable for fitting to portable devices such as mobile phones, laptop computers, PDAs, personal stereo systems, camcorders, headphones, and so on. The system automatically establishes a radio link between devices when two devices are within reception range – typically, within 10 metres, although a planned higher-powered Bluetooth could extend this to 100 metres if required.

The Bluetooth electronic circuits can be made very small and can therefore be fitted to just about any portable device without drawing too much power. A Bluetooth device has its own digital code that it can identify itself and transmit to any other Bluetooth device within range so the two (or more) devices can swap data. So, for example, if you were to walk into a room containing a Bluetooth-equipped Internet connection, your emails would automatically be available on the PDA you were carrying in your pocket. Alternatively, you could get your digital camera to transfer its images to your computer or direct to your printer simply by bringing it close and pressing a button. Bluetooth-equipped cash cards could be used to pay road tolls and bus fares as well as buying goods, without your even having to remove it from your wallet. Bluetooth technology could link your hi-fi and video equipment together without the need for any cables and the components could be moved from place to place without problems. All your electronic equipment could be operated with one Bluetooth remote control. And, if your fridge has any useful data to pass on to your toaster, Bluetooth would be the medium it uses. Bluetooth will in fact remove the need for connecting cables on portable equipment altogether.

One of the first Bluetooth devices to be marketed is deceptively simple – a mobile phone hands-free earpiece and microphone which links to the mobile phone using a Bluetooth radio link (no wires). As such it is not really a good example of what Bluetooth can do, but at least it shows the system works.

Bluetooth technology currently appears to offer slower data rates than some alternative wireless links, such as Ethernet, and there are reports that it causes interference to some other radio devices. However, Bluetooth has a lot of industrial support and its versatility could ultimately make it the most appropriate technology for use in intelligent home networks and beyond.

Who wants a smart home?

Technology is moving forward apace, and new products are emerging all the time. But does anyone want them?

To try to answer this question, as part of the work carried out for the *Smart Homes* report for the Joseph Rowntree Foundation and the Chartered Institute of Housing, Consumers' Association surveyed over 1,000 households, during 2000, to examine consumers' attitudes and interest in the smart-home concept.

First, interviewees were reminded of the situation in 1980, when perhaps very few people would have expected to own a car with features such as central locking or electric windows; yet today we take it for granted that from our driving seats we can open a back window (or the boot, or the petrol cap), adjust the far-side wing mirror, change a CD or pick up the latest traffic report. The smart home would in many ways reflect the convenience that we have grown used to in our cars.

The concept of the smart home used in the survey was presented as follows:

- **a smart home is one where you can have one button control of everything in your home** Many homes already have central heating, remote-controlled TVs, telephones, burglar alarms, computers and the like. A smart home is one which integrates all these and many other devices into one simple-to-operate system controlled by a single remote control
- **a smart home will be more convenient** With one remote control you can turn on the TV, start the dishwasher, open an upstairs window or lock all of the doors. You could also do all your grocery shopping from your armchair by accessing the Internet on your TV
- **a smart home will be more comfortable** In your smart home sensors would make sure rooms were automatically lit and heated when you were using them. And in cold weather sensors would ensure heating was activated to protect against frost. The system would also use energy more efficiently and save you money
- **a smart home will be more secure** Video cameras which are linked to TV or computers will enable you to see who is at the door before you open it. When you are on holiday, the system will set lights or music to come on and off at different times to deter burglars
- **a smart home will be safer** Devices can be programmed to react in emergency situations. In the event of a gas leak, electrical systems would be switched off, windows opened and the system would contact the emergency services and even phone you at work
- **a smart home means someone is at home when you are away** For example, if you forget to videotape a TV programme,

you could use your mobile phone to send a message to switch on the video player. The system could even phone you if there are any problems at home – such as its security being breached
- **a smart home will allow you to automate and set controls to run your home** You will have integrated control of every device in your home which means they will be able to work together to suit you and your lifestyle.

The results from the survey showed that there is an underlying public interest in smart-home technology that could be unleashed if the market develops. While views were mixed, about half of those surveyed expressed interest in the smart home concept (although 'interest' may not translate fully into willingness to pay). Generally, the results suggest that people fall into one of three groups:

- **interested** Those interested in living in a smart home (45 per cent of respondents) are most likely to be: people aged 15–34; family households; those with pay TV and home-entertainment systems (e.g. DVDs and video games consoles); those with PCs and/or Internet access; those on higher incomes; those who hold positive attitudes about new technology
- **ambivalent** Those who are neither interested nor uninterested in the idea (19 per cent) are well represented across all groups in the population, though marginally more likely to be older and on medium/low incomes
- **uninterested** Those not interested in living in a smart home (37 per cent) are most likely to be: aged 55 and over; households without children; households without PCs, pay TV or home entertainment systems; those who hold negative attitudes towards new technology.

Unsurprisingly, the smart home is most attractive to more pro-technology consumers, including the so-called early adopters vital to the preliminary development of high-technology markets. Households that reported the most positive attitudes towards new technology – and have greater ownership of newer technologies such as home-entertainment equipment and PCs – also demonstrated greater interest in living in a smart home.

Consumers' Association also surveyed the potential suppliers of smart homes. Here it found a general lack of enthusiasm on the part of construction and property industries, manufacturers and suppliers for pushing – or even properly promoting – the technology. The lack of common standards, an inappropriately skilled workforce and concern that 'it's just a fad' have been factors in preventing the smart-home market from developing sustainable momentum, despite significant interest from the consumer electronics industry.

On the plus side, organisations such as the Building Research Establishment and the European Intelligent Building Group are researching and promoting the intelligent- and energy-efficient-house concept and are having some success convincing property developers and housing associations of their importance.

Visiting a smart home

Unfortunately the few genuine smart homes that exist – as opposed to marketing gimmicks – are expensive, experimental systems and not open to the public. The Integer Programme, run by the European Intelligent Building Group, is responsible for a number of projects and in particular a purpose-built experimental smart home at the Building Research Establishment in Watford. You can have a virtual tour of this home at its web site, www.integerproject.co.uk. This site actually allows you to see inside the house by the use of webcams and to control some of the equipment in the house. Energy-saving is one of the key elements of the Integer project, and it is claimed that savings of up to 50 per cent have been made in energy and water consumption.

In early 2001 the telephone company Orange opened an experimental smart home based on various wireless distribution and control systems. You can have a virtual tour of this project at its web site, www.orange.co.uk/orangeathome. This site offers 360-degree views of each room and some video clips.

Chapter 7

Digital photography

This chapter looks at how digital technology has brought about changes to the world of amateur photography – both still photography and home movie-making. The new products include digital still cameras, computer software and television systems to view photographs on screen, digital camcorders and equipment to edit camcorder films digitally.

Although these developments do offer a certain versatility and convenience that the analogue methods struggle to compete with, they show no immediate signs of completely replacing traditional photography. The high quality and low cost of conventional film mean that it is still an attractive option, and many users are happy to continue using this medium – at least for the time being.

Still photography

Developments in electronics – in particular, the manufacture of chips that could capture an image focused on to their surface – in the mid-1980s began to make digital photography a possibility. These chips were called charged coupled devices (CCDs). At the same time, computer software that could be used to display and even alter 'digital' electronic images and printing machines that could handle digital colour images were being made. All the ingredients for digital still photography were coming together. By the early 1990s digital cameras using CCDs and digital image manipulation using computers were being used for industrial and scientific purposes and for professional photography. However, unless one went for the really expensive equipment, picture quality was a limiting factor. By the mid-1990s, digital cameras were made available for the consumer market but again picture quality was not their forte. The restricting factor was the amount of detail that the CCDs could capture.

CCDs are composed of an array of thousands of tiny light-sensitive elements. When an image is captured on a CCD, it is converted into an equal number of tiny dots known as pixels. Clearly, the more elements a CCD has, the more detail the photograph will have. In the early days it was not possible to make CCDs with enough elements to produce photographs of the quality of photographic film, so the first consumer digital cameras were not very good. When *Which?* magazine tested digital cameras even as recently as 1998, most of those tested had 640 x 480 pixel CCDs. This meant that they were fine for printing out small pictures, maybe to put into a newsletter, say, or for viewing on a computer so long as you did not want to fill the screen. *Which?* concluded that 'digital cameras don't tend to take great pictures'. Things have progressed rapidly since then, and CCDs with a million or more elements are being produced (leading to the sale of so-called mega-pixel cameras). Tests done by *Which?* in early 2001 concluded that the best digital cameras in the shops are comparable with conventional film.

How a digital camera works

Like a conventional automatic camera, a digital camera has electronic exposure control, usually with manual override, a zoom lens, built-in flash and auto-focusing. One advantage digital cameras have is that they can automatically adjust the colour balance to compensate for lighting, whereas with conventional cameras this adjustment is made by selecting an appropriate film or using filters.

The main difference between analogue and digital cameras is that whereas the latter projects the image on to a semi-conductor CCD panel, the former projects it on to a frame of film. The typical dimensions of this rectangular 'chip' are only 6.4 x 4.8 mm. On early models, and cheap ones even today, the number of the light-sensitive elements on the chip is limited, hence the image resolution is poor. An image comprising 640 x 480 dots (or pixels) will look satisfactory on a 15-inch computer monitor as part of a web page or if you reproduce it as a small picture. The lower quality will become apparent only when you want to print or display a larger version, perhaps on a sheet of A4 paper or on your computer monitor. For this type of use you will need a camera with a better-quality CCD – say, a mega-pixel model.

As well as a conventional viewfinder a typical digital camera has a small liquid crystal display (LCD) screen on the back which can also be used to compose the picture. This screen also enables you to 'replay' pictures you have taken which is a useful way to check that your pictures are satisfactory. You can choose to delete pictures that do not meet your approval.

When you press the shutter button, the image being focused on the CCD is captured and stored in the memory module.

The advantages of a digital camera

If digital cameras have struggled to compete with conventional film cameras, what is the point of them? The answer is that they are more versatile – in several ways.

They do not use film: instead they store the image on small removable memory cards. These cards can be transferred to a computer or suitably equipped ink-jet printer, so you can print images yourself. The film does not have to be processed, which saves time and money, and is more environmentally friendly.

Producing the image in digital form means that, by using a computer with the right computer software, you can improve the image before you print it out. For example, you could crop the picture to cut out a lamp-post at the side of the picture that you had not spotted. You can straighten the image if it suffers from camera tilt. You can brighten or colour-correct the picture if the lighting had not been quite right. With a bit of practice, you can even 'paint out' parts of the picture itself, maybe to remove the unknown person in the

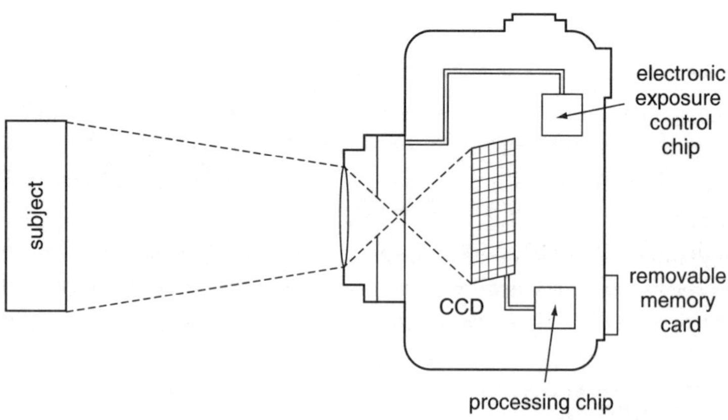

Basics of a digital camera

background that you had not spotted when you had pressed the shutter.

Having digital images means it is easy to insert them into computer documents such as newsletters, memos or web pages or send them in emails to family and friends.

Choosing a digital camera

You can buy a digital camera for as little as £35 and for as much as £1,300: the difference in price reflects both the quality of the final print and the performance of the camera lens. Unfortunately, the expense does not end there. A digital camera is virtually useless unless you also have a good computer (costing, say, £1,000 or more) or at least a special digital photographic printer, such as the Hewlett Packard* HP1000, which costs about £300.

Although you will have no ongoing film and processing costs, digital cameras do tend to eat up batteries at quite an alarming rate, particularly if you like to make use of the small colour LCD monitor screen on the back of the camera to compose or play back your pictures. (It is a good move to buy a camera with an optical viewfinder – not only does it save on batteries but it is easier on the eye than an LCD screen, which is difficult to see in bright sunlight.)

At first glance, a digital camera looks very similar to a conventional camera, although it can be much smaller because it has no need for all the mechanics associated with winding on the film. The diagram shows the basics of a digital still camera.

Most digital cameras have a zoom lens, often a 2x or 3x zoom. In addition, some boast an extra 'digital' zoom, but this is less satisfactory because it works by using pixels closer to the middle of the image. It inevitably reduces the resolution and can therefore give disappointing results.

When you buy a digital camera it comes with a memory module of typically 8Mb, which is usually large enough to store about 20 high-quality, high-resolution images. Extra and higher-capacity memory modules are available, but they can be expensive. You should also check compatibility of the higher-capacity memory modules with your computer and camera before you buy.

As for most types of digital technology several different systems are associated with digital cameras. Three kinds of memory modules are available. Some manufacturers, principally Kodak, Canon,

Nikon and Epson, use a square 'compact flash' memory card; others, such as Sanyo, Fuji and Olympus, use the wafer-thin 'smart media' card; and Sony uses its 'memory stick' system. All three kinds of cards can be compatible as storage devices in other equipment such as MP3 players and PDAs so long as you 'format' the cards for this use. As always, check compatibility before you buy.

Digital compression of images

Before an image is stored in the memory module of the camera, it is electronically processed, or compressed, to reduce the amount of data space it takes up in memory. If all the million or more pixels were stored in the memory module, you would have space for only a few pictures, so it is desirable to reduce the number of pixels by digital compression.

The system usually employed, called JPEG, is a highly mathematical process, similar to that used for digital TV transmissions (see Chapter 1). The system works by dividing the image into a large number of little squares. Each of these squares is analysed by the digital electronics to see if it contains much picture or colour detail. If the square is fairly featureless (a patch of sky, for example) the process does not have to send every pixel in that square – it can send a 'shorthand' version. If the square contains a lot of detail, changes in colour or contrast, it has to send more or all of the pixels. Using this method, the size of the image can be significantly reduced, without too much loss in quality, thus allowing a reasonable number of images to be stored in one memory module.

Some digital cameras give the user the option of selecting one of three different amounts of compression that can be applied, thus enabling more images to be stored. However, choosing more compression will reduce the picture quality and you might start to see some odd clunky or jagged-edge effects on your pictures if you select maximum compression (lowest quality). Mega-pixel cameras also allow you to lower the picture resolution by reducing the number of pixels they use to record the image, thus allowing more images to be stored at the cost of picture detail.

The JPEG image format is compatible with computers and image-processing software.

Transferring the photos to a computer

Once you have your pictures stored on your memory card, what do you do with them? Without a computer, or at least a special printer, you cannot do very much at all. The images have to be transferred to a computer before they can be displayed (on a computer monitor) or printed out (using a computer printer).

> **Tip: Viewing your pictures without a computer**
> Most (not all) digital cameras have an analogue video output signal that can be plugged in to your TV or VCR. This means that you can view your pictures on a TV and store them on videotape. TVs and especially VCRs are low-resolution systems, which is particularly noticeable with still photography, so you will not be getting the best from your digital camera. However, it does provide a cheap and convenient option for instant viewing of your pictures and a neat alternative to handing round a photo album.
>
> Some shops such as Boots and Kodak Express* will make real prints from your memory cards. If your camera has a feature called digital print order format (DPOF), it will send instructions to the printing machine about which images you want printed.

There are two ways of transferring the images from your camera to the computer. You can do so via your computer's serial (on older or cheaper computers) or USB port, if you have one spare, using software supplied with the camera for this purpose. Alternatively, you can do it by removing the memory module and plugging it directly into your computer via a special memory card reader. These card readers are not supplied with cameras and have to be bought separately as an accessory. When buying a reader for your computer make sure it is designed for the type of memory card used by your camera.

The serial-port method is obviously cheaper but it is annoyingly slow. The card-reader method is almost instantaneous and is similar to accessing files on one of your computer's disk drives. Some card readers require some connections to be made inside your computer, while others use the USB port. If you have an older

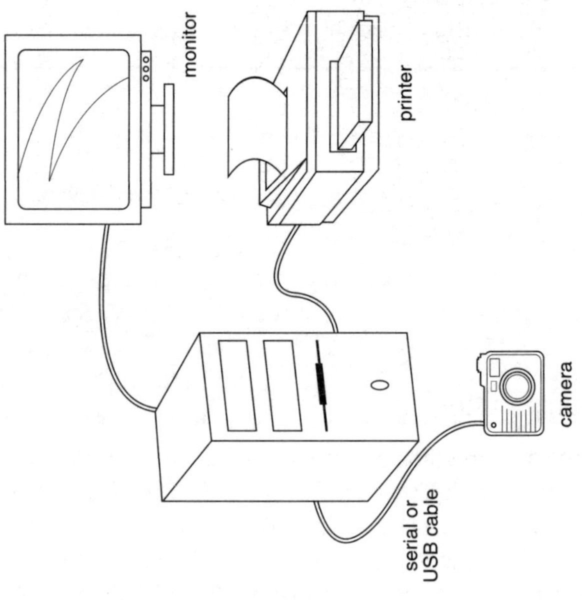

Transferring your pictures by direct connection

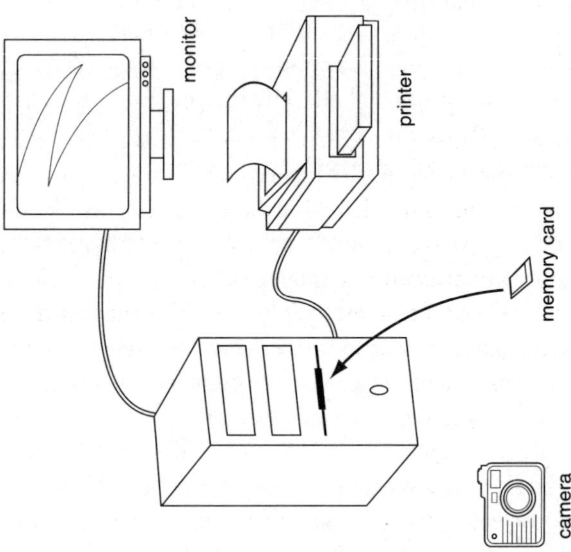

Transferring your pictures using memory card reader

computer and do not fancy opening it up, you can buy a type of reader for the 'smart media' cards that simply slots into your floppy-disk drive.

Sony produces digital cameras that store their pictures on conventional 1.4Mb floppy disks. This is very convenient as far as transferring the images to a computer goes, but the cameras are more bulky and the image quality and resolution has to be relatively low to fit them on to the disk. Sony also makes a camera that stores the pictures on to a recordable CD, which can hold many more pictures. Other manufacturers, such as Agfa, produce cameras that record the images on to special 40 Mb 'Clik' computer disks, which offer better value for money than equivalent-sized memory cards. The images are transferred to computers using a USB connection that gives faster transfer than using a serial port.

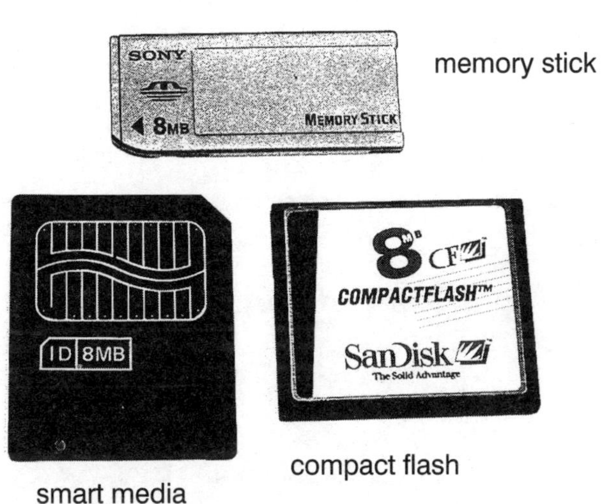

The three different memory card systems used in digital cameras

Adjusting photos

Once the pictures are safely stored in your computer as JPEG images, you can print them out. Most cameras are supplied with software that enables you to display and print the images.

It is also possible to buy image-editing software that can be used to enhance or adjust your photographs before you print them out. Such programs range in price from about £10 for something basic up to several hundred pounds for a professional product. A product called PhotoSuite by MGI Software* is one of the most popular for domestic use and sells for approximately £35. Another popular product is the more advanced PaintShop Pro, which costs about £90. With this type of software you can carry out basic modifications such as cropping and resizing photos, or you can improve the image by adjusting the colour, brightness, sharpness or contrast. You can even go further and start manipulating the image content by cutting and pasting parts of the image or even carrying out a bit of 'touching up' using the paint tools.

The software can then be used to display your photos on the screen as a slide show or to print them out. The picture below shows how this software appears on the screen in editing mode.

Photographic images take up a lot of hard-disk space, even in the compressed JPEG form, so if you are thinking of doing a lot of digital photography it is worth considering other forms of storage. Removable high-capacity disks such as Iomega zip disks or recordable CD-ROMs are two popular methods of storing photographic images.

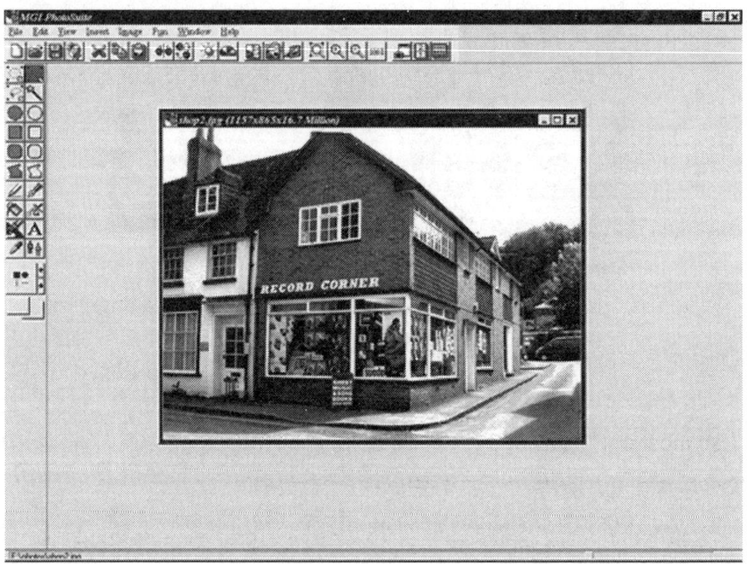

A picture being edited in MGI Photosuite (the editing tools are down the left-hand side)

An interesting new product that came on to the market in early 2001 is the digital wallet. It is a hard-disk storage device but because it is battery-operated you can store images in it without the need for a computer. This means that when your memory card fills up with pictures you can simply 'dump' them into the digital wallet and then carry on taking pictures with the memory card. You can then transfer the pictures on to your computer when you return home. Although a digital wallet is useful, it is so expensive that unless you expect to be taking over 200 pictures in each session you are better off buying half-a-dozen spare memory cards.

Printing photos

It is possible to get good-quality prints with a colour inkjet printer. Nowadays, even the cheapest of these can give satisfactory results, but it is probably worth spending at least between £150 and £200 if you want to achieve a sensible balance between price and quality. The quality of paper you print out on is important. The special photo-quality paper recommended by the manufacturer of the printer should give good results, but the expensive photo-quality 'glossy' paper will give the best results. Remember to set up your printer driver software to match the type of paper being used. The best glossy paper will give disappointing results if the printer is set for plain paper!

Tip: Printing photos without a computer

You do not need to have a computer to take advantage of a digital camera. It is possible to buy special colour inkjet printers with built-in memory card readers for one or more types of memory cards. The Hewlett Packard HP1000 and Fuji NX500 are examples of this type of printer. By plugging in the memory card from your camera, you can directly print out your photos. However, you have no opportunity to alter the photographs or adequately preview them, so most of the advantages of digital photography are lost.

Digital photography from your traditional 35mm or APS camera

If you do not have a digital camera, you can still take advantage of the developments in technology and have digital images made from your conventional camera. When you take your film to be processed, you can ask the processor to digitise your images and put them on to a computer CD-ROM. The resulting digital images can then be loaded into a computer, adjusted and printed out as described above. The Kodak 'Picture CD' system is probably the most convenient method of doing this, and the images are stored ready in JPEG format. The older Kodak 'Photo CD' system is more expensive but offers much higher-quality images using a special PCD format. Both systems work by using a very high-resolution, high-quality digital scanner that scans each negative and converts it to a digital image.

It is also possible to scan conventional photos with a domestic computer and scanner. The resolution from most conventional 'flatbed' computer scanners would not be good enough to scan something as small as a slide or negative. Resolutions of 600 dots per inch (dpi) would not provide much detail from something as small as a 35mm slide, so you would be better off making a conventional photographic print first and then scanning this in. You can buy special slide and negative scanners, which have a small scanning area but with a greater resolution over this area, typically 1,800 or 2,400 dpi. However, these can cost more to buy. Resolution is not the only parameter that affects the final picture quality: other optical properties, such as contrast and colour range, play a role too. Of course, as already noted, how good the resolution needs to be will depend on what you want to do with the results. Pictures for a newsletter, to be sent by email, or to be put on your web page may not require the high-resolution options.

Digital camcorders

Analogue camcorders can give quite disappointing results unless you buy one of the Hi-band SVHS-C or Hi-8 models. The basic analogue system can often give a low resolution and grainy picture. A digital camcorder, on the other hand, guarantees good results, but at a price. The cheapest system on the market costs about £500, while the best 'amateur' models can cost as much as £1,800. A digital camcorder does not need a computer. You can play back your recordings directly on to your TV, but the tapes will not play back on your regular VHS video recorder.

Two types of digital camcorder are available to consumers. Most use a tape format known as digital video (DV). DV tapes are small in size and sold in recording lengths of 60 and 80 minutes in 'standard play' or double this time in 'long play' mode. You can also buy versions of these tapes with a micro-chip in them that can store information about what has been recorded on the tape.

A range of Sony digital camcorders are available in a format known as Digi-8. The advantage of this format is that it uses the same tapes as analogue Hi-8 camcorders and is also able to play back previously recorded 8mm and Hi-8 tapes. This gives useful compatibility for existing 8mm users. Using a 90-minute Hi-8 tape, you can record 60 minutes of digital video.

Both digital formats use the same, MPEG compressed, digital recording technique as is used by digital TV (see Chapter 1 for technical details of this process). The picture quality you can get from a good domestic digital camcorder can be on a par with, if not better than, that from commercial broadcasters, the lens and exposure accuracy being the limiting factors.

DV-format camcorders can be made very small. However, if you are attracted to a model because of its size, make sure you are not paying for the miniaturisation at the expense of something else, the lens quality, for example. The smaller models can also be more expensive to repair if things go wrong – indeed, servicing any camcorder tends to be expensive.

Digital camcorders have all the automatic features you would expect from analogue models: auto exposure, focusing and colour balance (for different lighting conditions). How well these work usually depends on how much the camcorder cost. One particularly good feature of digital camcorders is the 'anti-shake' system that reduces the jerkiness of the picture that is typical of hand-held shots, especially when at or near full zoom. The system does not eliminate the shake but it makes the motion smoother and less noticeable.

Camcorders come with zoom lenses. Generally, the transition from wide angle to zoom is produced optically, by the lens. Some digital camcorders offer extra 'digital' zooms, giving zoom ratios of up to 50x. This effect is not produced optically: instead, the digital picture is expanded electronically, thereby enlarging a smaller area of the overall picture. Because a camcorder uses a CCD imaging device (see 'Basics of a digital camera', above), this results in fewer of the CCD elements being used to produce the picture, which in turn means a lower-resolution image. This effect rapidly becomes unacceptable as you approach maximum zoom and so generally you should regard 'digital' zoom ratios with some scepticism and go by the quoted optical zoom range.

As digital camcorders use the same type of CCD imaging technology as do still cameras, many of them can double as still cameras. The still image may be stored 'on tape' or, preferably, on one of the standard memory cards. Generally, a camcorder does not need to have the same picture resolution as a still camera (TV pictures are relatively low-resolution) so the camcorder's CCD may not necessarily be as good as that of a good digital still camera. If you want your camcorder to double as your still camera, you should check out the claimed resolution (that is, the number of pixels).

Digital camcorders offer all the advantages of digital image technology with all the disadvantages of a using tape. In the near future, we should be able to buy optical disc camcorders, probably based on the digital versatile disc (DVD) standard, which will offer instant access to any scene and easy editing of video clips.

Editing camcorder recordings

Editing analogue camcorder recordings has not been a very satisfactory process for the average home user. The cheap method simply means copying the selected clips, one at a time, from the camcorder to the VHS VCR. The procedure is simple enough, but the loss of quality that results from copying the analogue signals is disappointing. More expensive models, with 'auto assemble edit' features, help automate this process, and the even more expensive Hi-band models go some way towards reducing the quality loss. However, the end result of this assemble editing is often disappointing and lacks the professional touch. More advanced editing is possible using special video-mixing equipment or a computer, but the gear is expensive and is intended for the enthusiast. Moreover, the loss of quality resulting from copying is still a problem. The tangle of audio and video cables is also enough to put all but the real enthusiast off.

Copying from a digital camcorder to a standard analogue VCR gives results as good as the VCR can manage, and copying from a digital camcorder to another digital recorder can mean virtually no loss in quality at all. With a computer fitted with the latest interface cards and software you can achieve professional results.

There are two approaches to editing camcorder recordings with a computer.

You can copy directly from your camcorder to your analogue or digital VCR but under the control of the computer. The main audio and video signal path goes directly from one VCR to the other, while you view a low-quality version of your video on the computer screen to assist you. This is known as linear editing. The computer controls the two VCRs using a combination of an infra-red sender, connected to a spare serial port, which stops, starts and winds the VCRs, and a video interface box, connected to a parallel port, which controls the video signal. With this equipment and supplied software, you can carry out 'assemble editing' on your video clips and patch them together using a selection of cut-and-fade effects, giving them a professional touch. This type of system is quite cheap, assuming you already have a computer, but it does need quite a lot of connecting up to get it going. One of the most popular kits for this is the Pinnacle* Studio 400.

A more advanced system is one where all the video editing is done digitally, directly *on* the computer. This is known as non-linear editing. For this you will need a video editing software package such

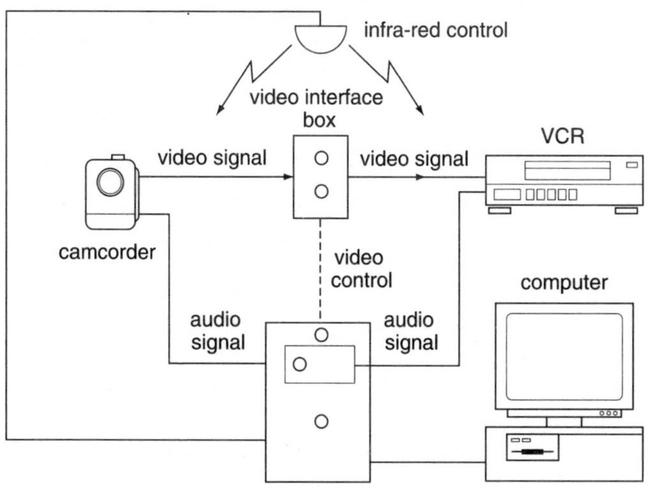

Schematic diagram of 'linear' editing system

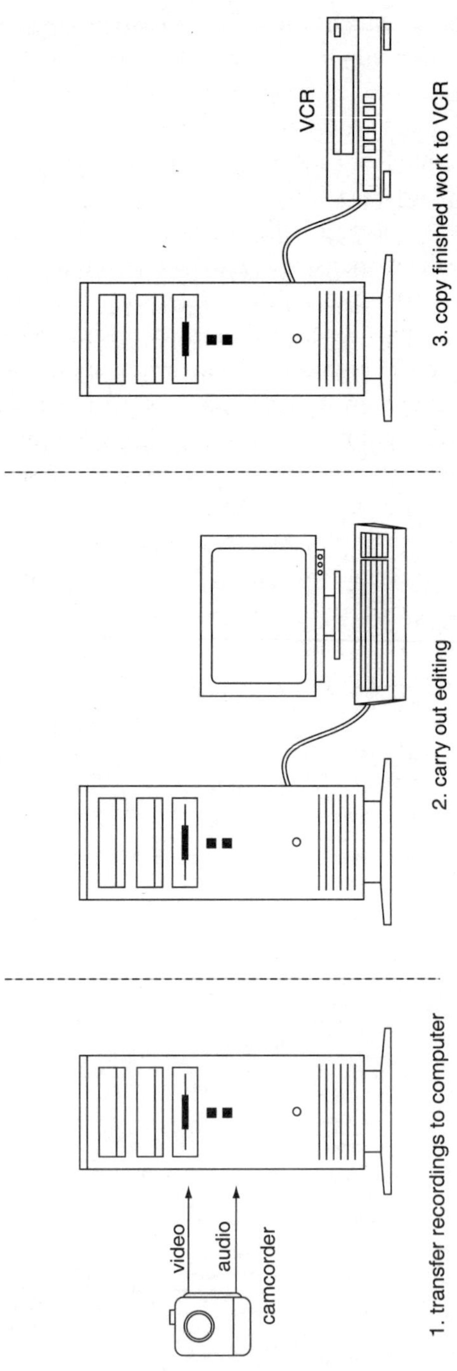

Schematic diagram of 'non-linear' editing system

as MGI VideoWave, which costs about £60, and a video capture card with digital firewire input. You will also need a video output of some sort, to copy your work back to the camera or to a VCR, so the firewire card should have an output as well. Alternatively you could use a computer graphics card that has an analogue video output, to copy it to a standard VHS VCR.

Because all the editing is to be done on the computer, it is possible to carry out the work using just the one camcorder acting as the source of the material and its final destination.

All your video clips are loaded on to the computer's hard drive via the digital firewire connection. The software then allows you to edit the clips without any need to wait for tapes to wind and rewind – the stop and start points can be found almost instantly – and the results can be previewed before you make a final decision. The software provides a wide range of editing tools and special effects, and professional results are possible with the minimum of effort and just a little practice. Once you are happy with your work, you can save it to disk or copy it back to the camcorder or VCR. This type of editing allows you to be more creative and is fun to do. However, you may find you end up spending hours working with the system, perfecting your work.

This system of editing is both more convenient and more versatile than the linear set-up but it requires a high-specification computer and plenty of hard-disk space.

If you wish to edit your clips on the computer and put the results back on to digital tape, you will have to copy them back to the camcorder. You must therefore make sure that when you buy a camcorder that it not only has a firewire socket (most do), but that the socket acts as an input as well as an output (some do not). If the camcorder's firewire socket cannot be used as an input, you can still copy your edited work by using analogue video connections.

Alternatively, if your computer is fitted with a recordable CD drive (CD-writer) you can save your finished work on a video CD-ROM. This can then be played on other computers. When computer DVD recorders become more affordable you could put your finished work on a DVD-video. However, different recordable DVD formats are being talked about now, so it might be worth waiting until the issue has been resolved before rushing out to buy one of these.

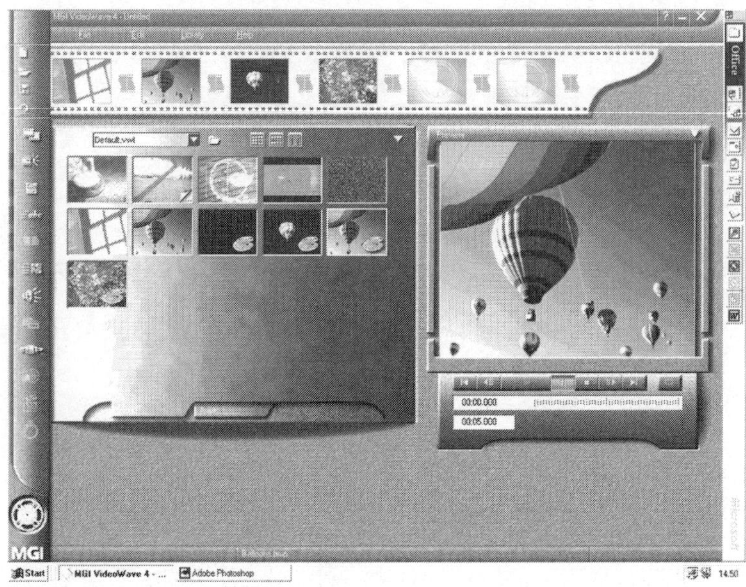

MGI VideoWave software

Recordable DVDs

If using a computer to edit your digital camcorder recordings seems like too much trouble, the new, stand-alone DVD recorders, due for launch in the UK at the end of 2001, could be the answer. Judging from an early example from Japan, these machines can be very versatile for simple editing. All you have to do is to copy all your digital camcorder recording on to a blank DVD and then use the DVD recorder's editing options to select which sequences you want and what order you want them in. The DVD player then plays back the memorised sequence. Anyone familiar with mini-disc editing menus will know how simple this is. All the original material is retained on the DVD and differently edited sequences can be selected and saved separately. You can do all this easily and with very few connecting cables. Recordable DVDs could be the answer to the prayers of home-movie makers.

Chapter 8

Other digital equipment in the house

This chapter brings together some additional ideas, gadgets and services that the world of digital electronics has to offer in and around the home. Developments in this area have led to the growth of the home-office, enabling many people to work from the comfort of their own domestic environment. Other digital inventions – such as universal remote controls – have helped solve niggling everyday problems.

Digital aids for running your own business

Whether you are running your own small business, working as a freelancer or consultant, or tele-working, digital services and products are essential tools. The modem is perhaps the gadget that has done the most to facilitate the growth of the home office. Together with the computer and the Internet, it has opened up various possibilities for those who want or need to work from their own premises.

If you are considering setting up your own business or working from home, this section will give you an idea of what digital equipment and services you will need and why, and how to use them to your advantage.

Essential digital gadgets and services

People who run their own business or work out of their own homes need, in addition to any specialist equipment central to their line of business, means of communicating with the outside world (telephone, fax machine, modem) and tools to help them work efficiently (computer and peripherals, personal digital assistant). Chapters 4 and

5 look at most of these appliances in detail; here the role of the computer and the fax machine is explored.

A computer and peripherals

A computer is an essential in any modern workplace. Even if your business is such that it does not require the use of one (e.g. a hairdressing salon), you will find a computer indispensable when it comes to doing all the paperwork and finances. A computer can handle tax and accounts and, in the long term, should help save you money because you can do away with the services of an accountant for the more routine tasks. Scheduling appointments and tasks, word-processing documents, keeping track of correspondence and preparing publicity material for your business are just a few of the jobs a computer can help with. If you are likely to travel a lot, you should consider buying a laptop computer too.

A printer is also a necessity – a basic inkjet type will suffice in most cases, but if you expect to be doing a lot of printing you should invest in a laser printer.

A computer is also a means of gaining access to the outside world. Communicating by email is invaluable as it saves time and money. A connection to the Internet provides an opportunity to create a web site to advertise your business or even to operate a virtual shop.

Software for the computer

Professional software is expensive but, unless you are really confident about what you are doing, it is probably worth paying extra for well-known packages. One advantage of doing so is that you will be more able to get support when things go wrong. Moreover, you will find that the software is more compatible with that of your clients and suppliers. Do not copy someone else's software – it is illegal. Moreover, you will not get any authorised technical support for pirated software.

The basic packages you may need are listed below.

- **Word-processing software** enables you to write documents and incorporate simple graphics and photos into them. Good word processors also have spell checkers and grammar checkers built in. Your word processor will also come in handy for composing advertisements and printing business cards.

- The data you input into a **spreadsheet**, which you can use as the basis of your cashbook and sales ledger, can be turned into tables and graphs.
- **Database software** is used for storing large amounts of information and records, such as the names and addresses of your customers and suppliers, and stock lists. A database program allows you to sort the data in any order or to search for entries.
- A **personal information manager** (PIM) is a computer-based diary. It can be used to book appointments, remind you of them and print out your daily schedule. Not all office suites have good PIMs, so you could considering buying a stand-alone one. Microsoft's *Schedule Plus* is one of the most advanced. Lotus's *Organiser* is less expensive and neat: it is made to look like a Filofax and it also acts as an address book.
- **Presentation software** will enable you to make your presentations or lectures more professional. What a presentation package allows you to do is to store your whole slide sequence electronically. You need to check that the venue for your presentation has either a computer with compatible software (Microsoft's *PowerPoint* being the most commonly used) or an overhead video projector into which you can plug your laptop.

All, or combinations of, the applications described above can be bought as part of a complete office suite of software. The advantage of doing this is that the programs can share information more easily. For example, your address database can be mail-merged into the word processor so you can send out customised mail shots, or graphs and tables from your spreadsheet can be incorporated into reports.

Professional office suites from Microsoft or Coral are quite costly (£200–£300) but they are very versatile. The other advantage of these packages is that they are more likely to be compatible with other companies' software, particularly in the case of Microsoft. Microsoft Office 2000 comprises *Word* (word processor), *Excel* (spreadsheet), *Access* (database), *Outlook manager* (email) and *PowerPoint* (presentation) and several other programmes.

If your requirements are more modest, you can get simpler but still very good office suites for under £100, such as Claris Works and Microsoft Works.

If you are considering publishing a newsletter, you should perhaps buy desktop-publishing (DTP) software, such as Microsoft's *Publisher* or GSP's *Power Publisher*. This will enable you to produce more ambitious documents in terms of the layout than a word-processing package would.

A specialist accounts package will be very useful. Products such as *Quicken* and Microsoft Money are popular and compatible with some online banks' electronic statements and other data. They both have business versions, which can handle multiple bank accounts and VAT returns. Accounting packages from Sage Software are also popular, particularly with accountants. The Consumers' Association's *Taxcalc*★ is useful for those who have to fill in an annual tax return.

A web-publishing package may be required if you want to put your business on the Internet. Microsoft's *FrontPage* and Macromedia's *Dreamweaver* are two examples of such packages.

A modem

You need a modem to enable you to get online for both World Wide Web access and email. For more modest business ventures, a simple 56Kbps (V90 or V92) modem could be sufficient – it is relatively inexpensive but slow. For more adventurous operations that rely heavily on Internet access for information-gathering or e-commerce, you should consider one of the high-speed Internet options offered by the broadband access technologies. These include special integrated services digital network (ISDN) telephone lines, and the newer asynchronous digital subscriber line (ADSL) system, which uses conventional telephone lines. However, they come at a cost: usually you have to pay an initial installation charge as well as a higher monthly rental. The modem itself is also more expensive and would have to be fitted to or into your computer. (Normal V90 modems are already built into new computers.) An ISDN or ADSL connection can provide a normal telephone line and an Internet connection simultaneously, so it can be cost-effective solution.

A fax machine

Fax machines are an easy and convenient means of transmitting documents, so if you run your own business you will almost certainly need one. The more inexpensive models use special thermal paper; plain-paper fax machines usually use inkjet printer technology. An alternative to a stand-alone fax machine is a combination of a computer, a fax/modem and a scanner. See Chapter 4 for details.

Digital aids for home entertainment

Most major digital innovations in the home, such as digital TVs and DVD players, open up a market for new gadgets. Some of them are needed to solve unforeseen problems (e.g. scart lead distribution or expansion boxes), others improve products (e.g. the PVR boxes discussed in Chapter 1), and yet others are gimmicks that serve no great purpose (e.g. the TV viewing chair with a built-in cool box).

Universal remote controls

As digital-home entertainment systems grow, people inevitably end up with an array of remote controls which become increasingly harder to keep track of. As it is going to be some years before the smart homes described in Chapter 6 become common, the best solution to the problem of multiple remote controls now is a universal remote control, which can be programmed to operate all the components of a home-entertainment system.

There are two types of universal remote controls. The cheaper kind comes pre-loaded with the necessary remote commands for all the popular items. All you have to do is enter codes which tell it which model of TV, VCR, amplifier, and so on you have. This type of remote control can be bought to operate just a couple of devices or up to 12 devices as required. The only disadvantage of this kind of system is that it may not have the name of one of your pieces of equipment in its pre-loaded list – this can happen with unusual items or those that are either very old or very new – or that even if it does contain the required item, it may not perform all the functions that you want. For example, some of these devices do not allow you to access all the TV teletext features or programme your VCR. Check before you buy such a remote control whether it does all that you want it to.

More versatile universal remote controls can 'learn' from your existing controls what commands you use. You simply put the universal control into 'learning' mode, point it at one of the original controls so they face each other and transmit each command in

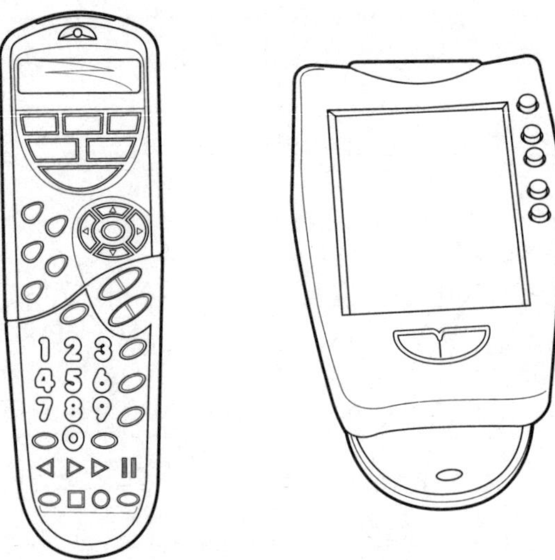

Universal remote controls – simple and advanced

turn. This can be quite a lengthy process but at least you can be sure that all the commands you want are copied over. Some more advanced versions of this type of control can learn whole sequences of commands (so-called macro commands), so with one button push you could switch on the TV and hi-fi system and start playing a DVD, for example. The ultimate in this type of universal control is one that has a touch-sensitive LCD screen instead of buttons. This can display different control layouts for each item selected.

Infra-red remote extenders

One problem with remote controls is that, because they work using infra-red light, they function only in the room where the equipment you want to control is situated. However, you may be in your kitchen, listening to music being played on your CD player, which is in your lounge. How can you control the CD player without having to go from one room to another? The answer is by using an infra-red signal extender. As the diagram below shows, this device simply uses a radio link to re-distribute the infra-red commands. Tests for *Which?* magazine have shown that these devices work well throughout the rooms of most houses, but they may have difficulty in a very large house.

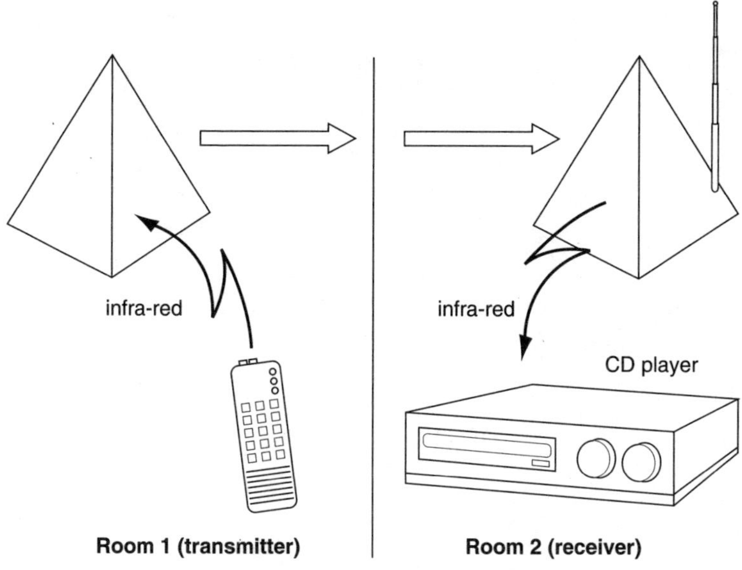

The pyramid-styled Powermid infra-red remote extenders being used to control a CD player from another room using an infra-red extender. The devices are just 10.5cm high.

Video-distribution transmitters

Many people in the UK have more than one television in their house – perhaps in a bedroom or the kitchen in addition to the lounge. If you use a set-top aerial to pick up the signal they will work well, but what if you want a better-quality picture or to watch programmes from your digital TV set-top box or video player in another room? You could run video and audio cables throughout the house, but a much neater solution is the video-sender. This uses a radio transmitter and receiver to distribute the picture and sound throughout the house. When they were first developed, these devices used unauthorised frequencies and caused interference to TVs in neighbours' houses. Modern video-senders are legal and use low-power microwave frequencies. They usually incorporate an infra-red remote extender so you can control remotely the source set-top box or VCR.

Again, tests for *Which?* magazine showed that these devices worked well throughout the rooms of most houses, but they had some difficulty in very large houses.

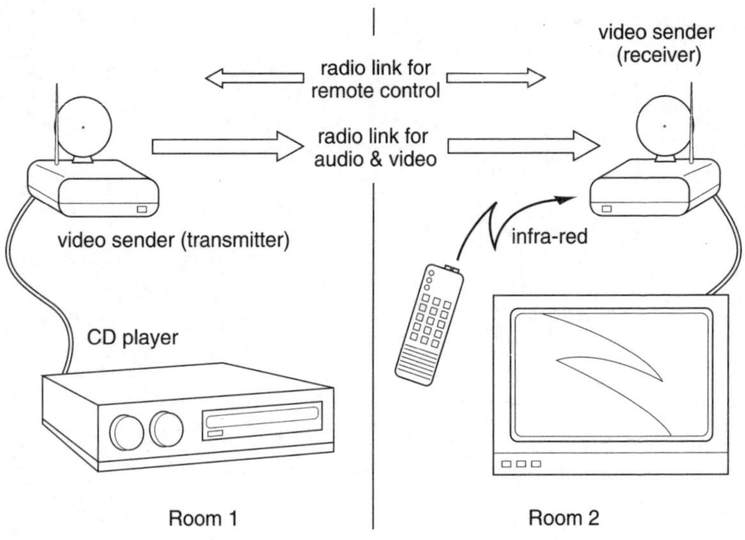

Video sender

Flat TV screens

Television *aficionados* who want to have large projection TV sets in their house may find that they are costly and bulky. Moreover, the inherent low resolution of TV transmissions and the fact that large projection TVs designed for domestic use are dull, mean that the results are disappointing and you do not gain anything in terms of picture quality. These devices also tend to have a restricted viewing angle so you have to ensure that you orient yourself towards the centre of the screen. Good-quality projection TV screens are used for public displays (for open-air events and in pubs, say), but they are expensive.

Flat-panel TV 'plasma' or LCD screens that can be hung on the wall are also very expensive, but modern ones can offer very good picture quality. Instead of having a conventional glass TV tube, they use a panel of a million-or-so tiny semiconductor light-emitting elements. These types of screens are difficult to manufacture as it takes only one faulty element to ruin the effect. They also consume a lot of power. The latest examples of this type of device from manufacturers such as Sony, Philips and Sharp give excellent results on screens of about 42 inches, but again the inherent low resolution of

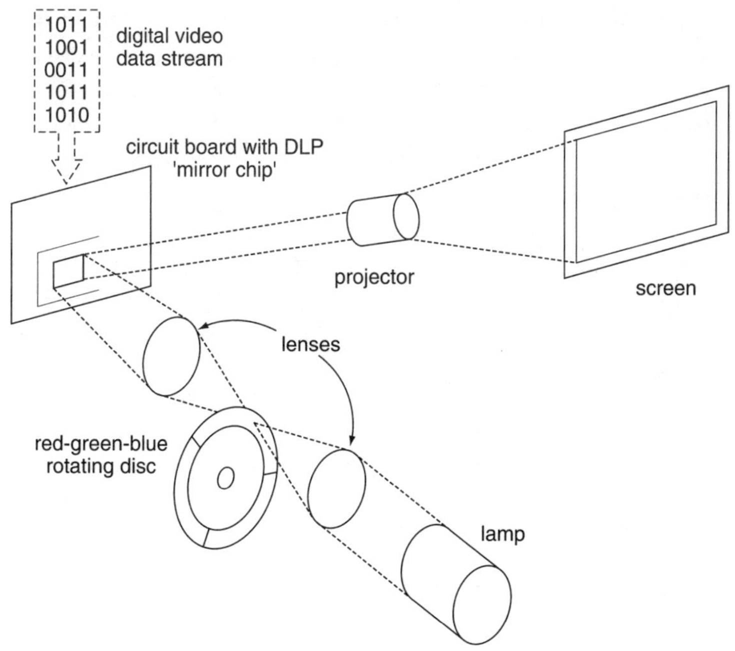

How the Texas Instruments digital light processing technology works

TV transmissions means that you do not gain much in terms of picture quality. If and when high-definition television (HDTV) becomes available, this type of display will produce superb results.

An alternative technology could do an even better job than the plasma screen. Developed by the US semiconductor company Texas Instruments, it is called digital light processing (DLP) and is a strange mix of old and new technology. It is already being used in some cinemas in the UK. At the heart of this system is a semiconductor chip, which has a million or more microscopic mirrors on its surface. Each of these mirrors can be individually tilted slightly by an electrical signal sent to it. As shown in the diagram, this means that the chip can be used as part of a TV or film projector. As in a conventional film projector, the picture brightness is governed by the source of light, so large and bright displays can be created. The resolution is governed by the number of mirrors on the chip. Manufacturers claim that it is not difficult to make these devices.

In the cinema, the film Toy Story 2 was not only created entirely digitally, but was in a few cinemas projected using a DLP projector. The resulting picture quality was better than that from a conventional film print, the clarity of colour being the most noticeable improvement. Several conventionally made films are being transferred into digital mode so they can be projected using DLP. It is claimed that cinema-goers will experience a quality that is as good as the *master* print. Another advantage of using digital projectors in the cinema is that it will no longer be necessary to process and distribute expensive reels of film. Instead the digital signal can be distributed over telephone lines or via satellite to cinemas. This will save money and so, naturally, will result in lower prices for cinema seats!

Unusual digital developments

Some digital gadgets have new and unique applications. They tend to be exciting and capture the public imagination. Not all of the products discussed below are easily accessible in terms of availability and cost, but they could be in the near future.

GPS – knowing where you are

During the 1980s the US Department of Defense launched a fleet of 24 low-orbit satellites. They are regularly spaced and circle the earth such that at least four satellites are above the horizon at any point on the earth. The precise position of each satellite is known because each one contains an atomic clock, a computer and a radio transmitter which constantly broadcasts its position and time. The system can be used to pinpoint a position on the earth's surface to an accuracy of within 100 to 10 metres, depending on the equipment used. For military use an accuracy of 1 metre is possible.

If you want to know your exact position on the earth, your GPS receiver needs to pick up the signals from three satellites. By comparing these signals (using triangulation) it can calculate where you are. On simple receivers, this position is read out as map references or longitude and latitude coordinates. If the receiver can pick up four satellite signals, it can also work out your altitude. More advanced receivers are equipped with an LCD screen and a map, on

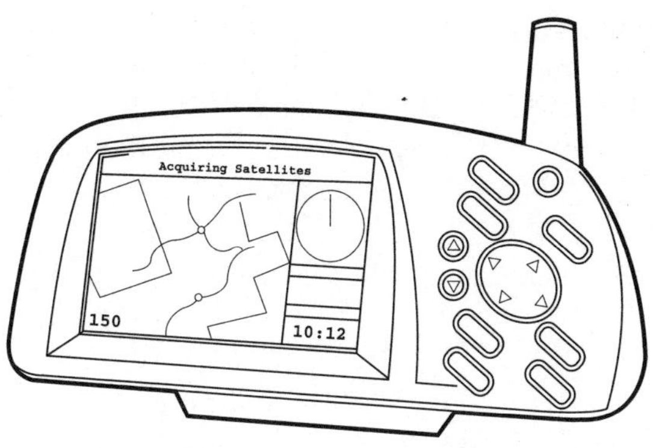

A GPS receiver

which your location can be displayed. Simple GPS receivers are used by hikers and for other outdoor activities.

A more advanced application of this system can be found in the route planners fitted to top-of-the-range cars. These systems comprise a GPS receiver and a CD-ROM containing a detailed road map of the UK. Before you set off on a long journey, you tell the system where you want to go and it plans the route. A voice tells you when to turn left or right and because the GPS is always tracking your position it can re-route you should you take a wrong turn. In the best systems, the CD-ROM contains details of one-way streets and other features and needs to be updated regularly. Some systems, such as Philips Carin, can be fitted to any car, but they cost about £1,000–£2,000.

Another motor-car application of GPS enables you to track your car if it has been stolen. For this, you have to have a car fitted with a GPS receiver and an automatic mobile phone. You also need, at your home or in the office, a computer, a modem and a program containing a detailed road map of the UK. If the car is lost you dial-up the car's mobile phone from your computer's modem. The car replies, sending its location from the GPS receiver. The computer then displays the car's location on the road map. This location is very precise – you can even tell where on a road the car is located. A system using this technology is available from Carbug.* It is expensive and so would normally be used only by owners of expensive cars or company fleet-car departments.

Digital walkie talkies

Mobile phones have transformed the way we communicate while we are on the move. But they are not the only digital communications device on the market – for about £100 you can buy a pair of digital walkie talkies. These operate on a small range of frequencies at around 446MHz (i.e., just below the television broadcast band).

Old-style analogue walkie talkies, particularly the CB (Citizens Band) radio devices, were bulky and consumed batteries at an alarming rate. Their quality and range could also be poor unless users went in for the more expensive models. Toy walkie talkies were also generally very disappointing as they operated in a very small range.

The new digital walkie talkies are quite a revelation. They are not much bigger than a mobile phone, have a range of 2 kilometres or more, do not incur call charges and are reasonably modest on battery consumption. These devices are popular in the USA, particularly for family use. In the UK, they have not caught on in such a

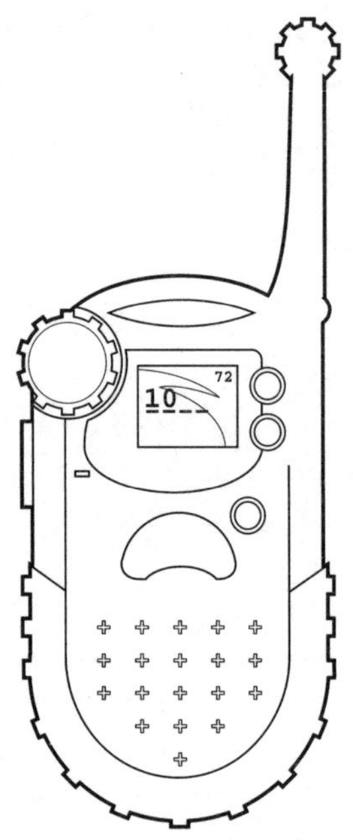

A digital walkie talkie

big way, even though they can be bought from most high-street electrical shops and mobile phone shops.

As with a mobile phone, each device consists of a radio transmitter and a receiver. The receiver has 8 groups of 38 channels. The large number of channels reduces the chances of interference problems that was always a problem with CB but it does make searching the band for someone impractical, so you have to agree with other users in advance which channel you are going to use. Another drawback is that the system does not offer privacy because anyone can tune in.

Robots

Chapter 6 touched briefly on two types of robot-type devices – the vacuum cleaner and the lawn mower. The desire to have domestic robots is another science-fiction dream that could come true, although we may find the idea of having a number of bulky mechanical robots in your house rather alarming, particularly if they need to be mobile. It would be ideal if we could have a single, multi-purpose robot, like Robbie the Robot from *Forbidden Planet*, but researchers in this area point out that this would be impractical, and that domestic robots are more likely be small and discreet. It may be that we will have a number of little, specialist robots distributed around the house performing manual tasks for us. However, it is more likely that a robot could also be a smart robot, able to constantly re-build itself to perform many different tasks ranging from routine maintenance to cleaning. So, in the future smart home, our meals are likely to be prepared and served not by a life-sized humanoid-type robot but by a cluster of tiny 'nano-robots'. This technology is still a long way off – or is it?

Appendix I

Digital signals

This book has explored the idea that our world will be *digital* in the future – entertainment, work and communications will all be conducted digitally. But what exactly do we mean when we say something is digital?

The brief explanation of digital signals in this appendix will help you appreciate the fundamental difference between the digital and analogue worlds and why digital engineering can offer us so much more.

The digital alphabet

Digital technology offers a very simple and efficient way of transmitting and storing text characters.

If you wanted to send a letter to a friend as quickly and efficiently as possible, how would you do it? Writing it and then posting it is a slow process. Communicating its contents by reading it over the radio or telephone, or pointing a camera at it and sending it on TV would make the transmission quicker, but these methods are inefficient and costly.

A simple, quick and cheap way of sending the text characters in the letter is to fax it – that is, to use a digital process. Take just one character, say, the capital letter 'A' . This could be written or typed on to paper. The fax machine would scan this image by dividing it up into a number of square sections, as shown below. These squares could then be transmitted one at a time, in sequence, down a telephone line. When the square is black a tone of a certain pitch is sent, and when the square is white a tone of another pitch is sent. This is a very simple digital system – it allows us, in this example, to send simple black or white. It does not allow us to send grey. Also, as the example shows, the number of squares, or 'samples' we choose to divide the original character up into will determine how accurately the received image will be seen. A grid of 7x9 squares (see diagram) is usually sufficient for us to recognise alphabetical characters, so we need to send at least 63 samples per character.

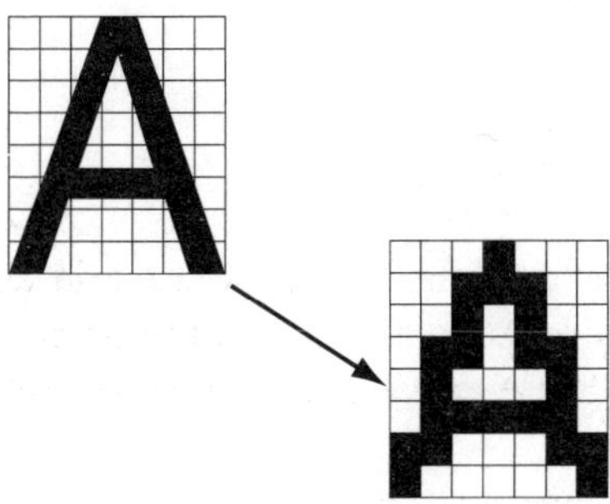

How the letter 'A' is transmitted by using a facsimile (fax) method

In our example, as in reality, we are using analogue tones down an analogue phone line to do the transmitting. So we have a partial digital solution here, but it is still quite slow and uses a number of analogue elements.

There is another approach. If we can *create* the letter 'A' in digital form in the first place, we can transmit it more efficiently. A digital signal comprises only '1's and '0's. To assign a digital *code* to our letter 'A', we use a binary number. According to the internationally recognised ASCII standard, the 8-bit binary number 01000001 is the code for the upper-case letter 'A'. So we can send or store our letter 'A' electronically using this digital signal. When this signal is received or restored it is recognised as an 'A' and so the character 'A' is shown on the screen or printed out as required. The interesting thing in this case is that the size or typeface of the original 'A' could be quite different from the one on the receiving equipment. This 'fine detail' is not sent or stored, as it is not necessary for sending plain text. The final size and typeface will be that selected as suitable for display on the receiving equipment. It is very easy and quick to send or magnetically store these '1's and '0' and the 8-bit code is very efficient. This is why plain-text documents do not take up much space on a computer's hard drive compared with some other files, and also why they appear more quickly on the screen than do pictures when web pages are being downloaded from the Internet.

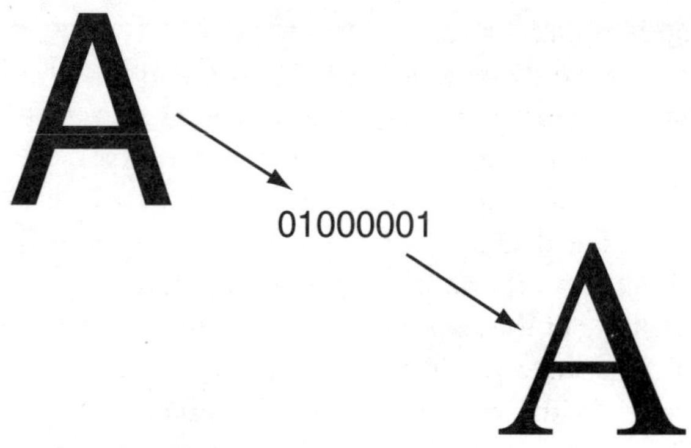

How the letter 'A' is transmitted using the 8-bit ASCII code

Digital music

Digitising music or pictures is somewhat different. The accuracy of the transmission is more important than efficiency – we do not want the receiving equipment to put its own interpretation on the music in the way that digital text transmissions do.

First, let us consider the drawbacks of simple analogue music signals.

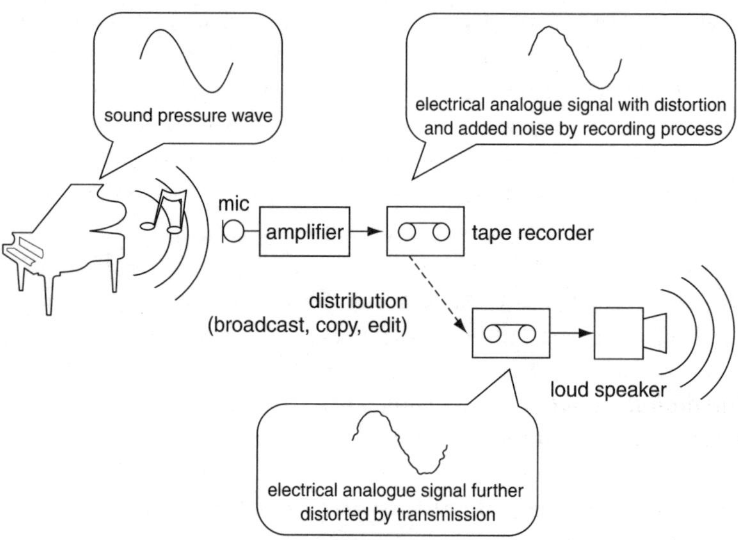

How music is transmitted by analogue signal

The analogue signal

The diagram above shows how we might record a sound using traditional analogue techniques. The sound of middle C from the piano is produced by the vibrations of strings in the piano. These vibrations are transferred into sound waves in the air which we hear with our ears. The diagram shows how this sound wave varies as it travels through the air, producing a steady variation of pressure. To make a recording of the sound we use a microphone – an electrical device which acts in a very similar manner to our ears. The sound pressure wave in the air causes the microphone's diaphragm to vibrate. The diaphragm's movement is converted into an electrical signal, which is an analogue of the pressure variation. The electrical voltage of the signal varies in the same way as the air pressure varies. To preserve this electrical signal so we can play it pack later we use electronics to amplify it. This amplified signal can be used to cut a vinyl gramophone record, or put on to a magnetic tape or on to a radio wave to be broadcast.

The problem with this system is that the analogue signal gets corrupted on its journey from the microphone onwards. For example, the electronic and mechanical processes in the microphone, the amplifiers and the recording, cutting or transmitting processes are not perfect – they corrupt the signal, distorting it slightly. Furthermore, all these systems have inherent background noise which interferes with the signal (for example, the 'hiss' heard frequently on tapes). The analogue signals are also vulnerable to external interference (for example, the crackles on AM radio, which can result from electrical appliances being switched off or on nearby or from thunderstorms many miles away). Also, in the case of tapes and gramophone records, these problems actually get worse as the devices age.

Analogue recording systems tend to be large, to minimise the effects of mechanical damage, and analogue radio and TV transmitters have to use high transmitter powers to overcome interference.

The digital signal

Digital audio recording can virtually eliminate these problems. The diagram below shows, in simple terms, how the piano's middle C is digitised into a voltage signal of only '1's and '0's.

First, the electrical analogue signal from the microphone is electronically dissected. This is done by rapidly registering it many times

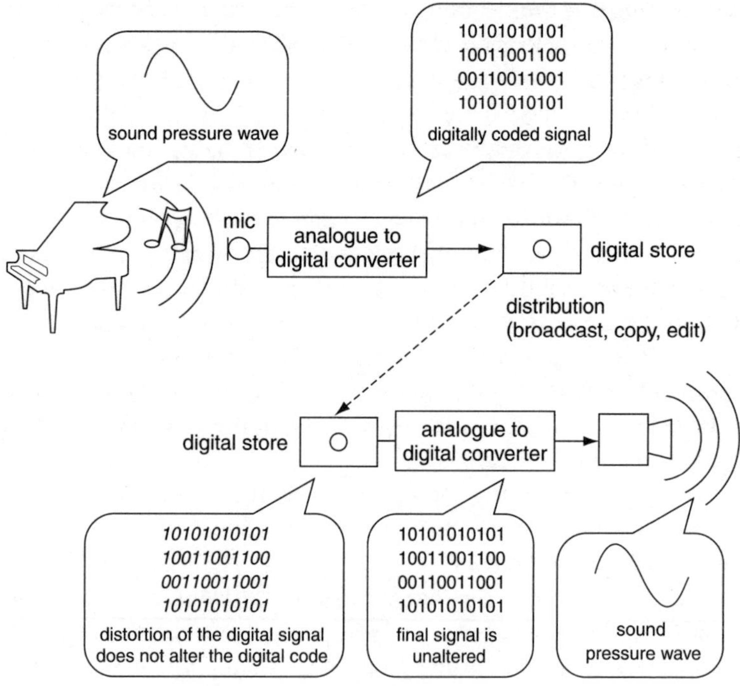

How music is transmitted by digital signal

a second as it progresses. On a compact disc, for example, this is done 44,100 times a second (44.1KHz). The process is called 'sampling' and is so fast that the human ear cannot detect that it has been done. At each sampled point the specific analogue voltage level that the signal has reached is measured. This voltage is then converted into a digital (binary) code by being passed through another circuit called an 'analogue-to-digital converter'. For hi-fi-quality reproduction, this binary number consists of 16 '1's or '0's, and so is referred to as a 16-bit code. By using as many as 16 bits in a code we can mathematically produce over 65,000 different numbers. In other words, we can resolve over 65,000 different voltage level steps in our audio signal. This is sufficient resolution for the demands of hi-fi quality. Hence, by sampling at 44.1KHz and coding at 16 bits the music can be converted into a high-quality digital signal. This signal, comprising '1's and '0's can then be stored or transmitted as required. Clearly, sampling at this high frequency and simultaneously coding the voltage level means that the electronic processes involved are having to take place very quickly to get it all done. Because of this, digitally encoded music takes up a lot more storage space or transmitter bandwidth than the equivalent analogue signal would. There is no way all this extra information could be stored on vinyl or a slow-moving audio cassette. Instead, 'optical' storage or fast-moving magnetic tape or disc systems have to be used. Similarly, to transmit all this fast-moving digital data much higher radio frequencies are needed.

When a person listens to the music, the digital signal undergoes the reverse process. It is passed through a digital-to-analogue converter that reconstitutes the original voltage levels. The 44.1KHz sampling frequency is detected and used to control the timing of the whole operation, so that the final music signal is reconstituted with the correct timing.

The quality of the final decoded signal is governed by two things: the sampling frequency and the number of 'bits' used to code the signal. These are 44.1KHz and 16 bits respectively for a standard audio CD (generally regarded as being hi-fi quality). If you do not require such high quality, you can use a reduced sampling frequency and a lower number of bits. A sampling frequency of 10KHz and an 8-bit system would be perfectly acceptable for speech reproduction, for example.

So, why does using a digital signal help us to get better quality sound? A digital signal is not worried by extraneous interference and distortions that are present in the electronics, storage or transmission paths. Of course, a digit (1) or a lack of a digit (0) can be distorted or have noise added in the same way as an analogue signal can, but this does not matter. When the signal is de-coded it is reconstituted as being just a '1' or a '0', without any of the distortion it might have picked up en route. So, in being able to reconstitute the original signal as if nothing had happened, the system is much more immune from problems than the analogue system.

When is an error not an error?

Of course, if a digital signal is so seriously corrupted that a digital bit can no longer be identified as being a '1' or '0', problems can occur. However, during the de-coding process it is possible to deal with even this type of eventuality – the so-called error-correction technique is an important aspect of digital signal processing of all types.

A music CD you paid £15 for probably has hundreds or thousands of digital 'errors' on it owing to manufacturing defects – fortunately, however, your CD player can spot them and work out what the signal should be. In fact the error is completely corrected and so ceases to be an error. Of course, there is a limit to this, and if the CD has been manufactured with more errors than the specification allows, or it has become too scratched, the CD player cannot cope with it.

Digitising pictures

The process for digitising pictures is fairly similar to the process described above for audio signals but more complex. To digitise a picture you need to be able to digitise all the colour information in the picture, so brightness, hue and saturation all need to be sampled and digitally coded.

Too much of a good thing?

The digital audio compact discs use the basic digital process described above. However, as electronics became faster and engineers became more well-versed in digitising techniques, the processes became more refined. With computer-type electronic circuits engineers can now very accurately modify the stream of data. They can reduce the number of data bits by simply removing unnecessary sections (bits you will not see or hear) and apply short-cut codes to the signal when it becomes repetitive or predictable. This allows them to fit more data into a given space and it is one reason why they can now fit a whole film on to one DVD disc compared with just 74 minutes of music on the old-style audio CD. They can also interleave several streams of digital data from two totally separate sources into one stream and then separate them out again. These 'multiplexing' or 'packeting' techniques are the bases of many broadcasting and telecommunications systems, including the Internet, and ensure that transmission systems are used to their maximum capacity and efficiency.

Appendix II

Digital equipment and power consumption

Because digital systems have greater immunity than do analogue systems to external interference, it is possible to transmit digital signals using less power. With optical storage and semiconductor storage techniques, digital devices can be made physically smaller and mechanically less complex. This sounds like good news for the environment – that we will be using less power and fewer resources in the digital home. Although this may happen some time in the future, now, ironically, the opposite is true.

Owing to digital innovation and the number of new devices (computers, fax and answering machines, larger and digital TVs, cordless phones, etc.) that have entered our homes, we are consuming more power than ever before. These gadgets draw power when in use, of course, but that is only part of the story. More and more of our entertainment and communications equipment uses power when not being used, and it is this hidden power consumption that is the problem.

Energy-conscious devices

Manufacturers of washing machines, refrigerators and some other 'white goods' have been grappling with the power-consumption issue for a few years. When you buy one of these items now you will find a European Union 'energy label' on it, giving information on how energy-efficient the product is. Manufacturers now take the issue of power consumption seriously when they design new products.

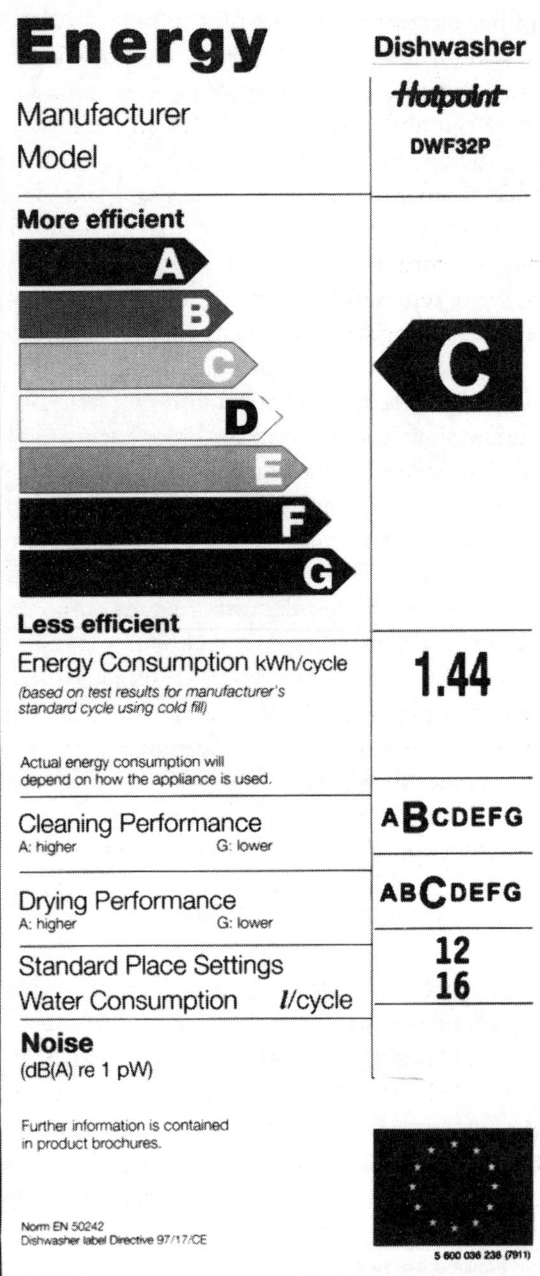

Energy label

Much of our electronic equipment is never switched off, it just goes into a 'standby mode'. Some gadgets, such as TVs or hi-fi systems, draw a small amount of power when they are in this standby mode, so they can 'wake up' when you point a remote control at them. Other items, such as VCRs, have to be in a permanent standby mode in order to keep their clocks going and to record programmes you have set up in advance. Digital TV set-top boxes and personal video recorders are permanently on so the broadcasters can access them remotely to update the electronic programme guides and check billing status. Many items such as cordless phones and answering machines are permanently powered up in order to work or to keep their batteries charged up.

In addition to all this, some products draw standby power for no reason at all – mobile phone chargers, for example, are often left plugged in to the mains even when they are not being used. Other wall-mounted power supplies, such as those used for portable radios or games machines, are always drawing a small amount of power – just feel them, if they are warm, they are using power.

It is true that in many cases we are talking about very small amounts of standby power – perhaps fewer than 3 watts per item, but the problem is that it all adds up. Of course, the effect it has on your electricity bill is quite small too, maybe £11 per year for the average household. When multiplied by the 25 million households in the UK, that adds up to a lot – and the wasted consumption is actually the equivalent of the full output of two new power stations!

Excessive standby power taken by idle wall adapters, TVs and VCRs is an avoidable waste of energy. New power-supply technologies, coupled with government legislation or voluntary agreements with industry, are significantly reducing this waste. However, the rapid development and take-up of digital television reception platforms will soon compromise any savings made. It is estimated that by 2005 digital TV reception equipment will in effect double the amount of electricity used by electronic equipment in the home. The average household will be using more electricity for electronic equipment than for fridges and freezers combined.

Each digital TV reception platform will consume approximately 400Kwh of electricity per year, costing the UK an additional £17 million-worth of electricity and leading to an increase in atmospheric pollution of 5 million tonnes of carbon dioxide. If every household in Europe eventually has digital TV reception, the rise in annual electricity consumption over today's level will be the equivalent of the total consumption of Denmark, at a cost of £4.2 billion and an increase in atmospheric pollution of 24 million tonnes of carbon dioxide per year.

The Consumers' Association's Research and Testing Centre (CARTC) is contributing advice to UK and European Union expert groups who are developing systems to reduce the power required by future generations of digital TV reception systems through power-management systems. These systems make sure that the digital reception platform uses only the power that is required for the activity requested at any one time. Eventually this intelligent power management will be extended to all the peripheral devices connected to the digital receiver, even washing machines, heating systems, lights etc.

Industry has already been making some improvements. Take, for example, digital TV set-top boxes. When CARTC first measured the power consumption of set-top boxes, the standby consumption of the worst models was 27 watts. Recent design improvements have reduced this, and the latest boxes, such as those made by Pace, draw only 11 watts. Unfortunately, this will inevitably increase again as extra features, such as video distribution or video-recording devices such as PVR, are added to new models. Special electronic power-management systems need to be incorporated in such equipment to manage this consumption.

It is proposed that by 2010 power-management systems in Europe will reduce the power required by all digital TV reception systems and intelligent home multi-media digital platforms by up to 40 per cent, creating a reduction in electricity costs of £1.7 billion and a reduction in atmospheric pollution of 9.5 million tonnes of carbon dioxide.

How to reduce hi-tech power consumption

Here are some tips on how to be energy-efficient at home.

- Get into the habit of switching off (or at least to standby) hi-fi and video equipment which is not being used.
- Switch off the battery chargers for your mobile phone or personal stereo when not in use.

- When you buy a new domestic appliance make sure you know how energy-efficient it is.
- Configure your computer so it automatically goes into standby mode and blanks the screen when not being used.
- Install some 'intelligent' lighting in your home. Motion detectors or X10 systems (see Chapter 6) can control your room lighting by turning it on only when it is needed, thereby saving a significant amount of power. Also, the use of low-energy light bulbs helps save power in the long run.

Glossary

3-G (third generation) A reference to the forthcoming mobile phone system that will provide always-on, fast Internet access and services

AAC (advanced audio codec) An audio file system which is an alternative to MP3 (q.v.)

AC3 (or Dolby digital) A digital audio system for providing home-cinema surround sound

ADSL (asymmetric digital subscriber line) Broadband telephone system that provides a fast, always-on Internet service from homes, using standard telephone lines

ASCII (American standard code for information interchange) The traditional coding standard for text files in computers and on the Internet. Each alphabetic, numeric and special character is represented by a binary number (a string of eight '0's or '1's)

bandwidth Information or programme material transmitted by radio waves or distributed on a cable is usually described as being broadcast at a certain frequency (e.g. 100MHz). In fact, the information has to spread a certain amount on either side of this 'centre' frequency. The amount by which it spreads, or is allowed to spread, is the bandwidth. In digital data, the greater the bandwidth, the faster the data can travel

bit In digital electronics the name given to a single digit (often mathematically represented as '1')

broadband A broadband transmission system is one with a greater bandwidth (q.v.) compared with a standard system

byte A group of eight bits (q.v.), roughly one character of text

CAT-5 (category 5) The physical wiring used for connecting computers at home or in the office. It is possible to send over 100 million bits per second with this type of cabling

CCD (charged coupled device) Light-sensitive semiconductor device used to record the image in a digital camera

CD-ROM (compact disc read-only memory) A disc, physically identical to a music CD, which stores computer data instead of music. It is called 'read-only' because you can only read data from the disc – you cannot 'write' data to it

chip Slang expression for an integrated circuit. Can be used for any circuit from a simple amplifier to a complex microprocessor. The name derives from the small piece (chip) of silicon housed inside the black plastic casing on to which the circuit is etched

compact flash A type of small, removable, memory card used to store data, typically in digital cameras and MP3 players

DAB (digital audio broadcasting) The name for the digital radio service

DECT (digitally enhanced cordless telecommunications) Domestic digital cordless telephones

digital compression When a video, graphics or audio signal has been digitised, there is often far too much data for it to be transmitted or stored economically. Digital compression is used to reduce the amount of data before transmission

DLP (digital light processing) Developed by Texas Instruments, this is a digital display system that uses an integrated circuit with millions of tiny mirrors on its surface. It can be used for cinema or domestic TV projection

Dolby Pro-Logic An analogue audio system for providing home-cinema surround sound

DTMF (dual tone, multi-frequency) The 'musical' tones you hear when you press the keypad on a telephone. They can be used to send simple signalling messages down the phone line

DTS (digital theatre system) A digital surround-sound system, similar to but incompatible with AC3 (q.v.)

D-VHS A digital video-recording system that uses tapes similar to analogue VHS tapes

DV (digital video) In digital camcorders, the small cassette-tape format used by most manufacturers

DVD (digital versatile disk) A disk similar to a compact disc but holding much more information. DVD-ROMs contain computer programs or data and DVD videos contain films

e-commerce Buying and selling goods and services over the Internet

ensemble A group of radio stations digitally mixed together to share one radio channel, same as 'multiplex'

EPG (electronic programme guide) The on-screen menu on digital TV showing all the channels and programmes being broadcast. The EPG may also give programme synopses

Ethernet The most commonly used system for connecting computers together at home or in the office. Designed to a standard, IEEE 802.3, Ethernet was originally developed by Xerox. Typically it refers to a wired network but can also be used for a radio-linked network

FAQs (frequently asked questions) Lists of (allegedly) frequently asked questions together with answers, typically found in web sites, newsgroups or instruction books

firewall A security system that protects a computer, or network of computers, from viruses or other unwanted material from the Internet. Typically used by companies to protect their computer network, firewalls will be increasingly needed for domestic use as home-users adopt fast, always-on Internet access

free-to-air TV channels that you do not have to subscribe to. More specifically the term refers to the BBC and ITV channels that are covered by the TV licence in the UK

FTP (file transfer protocol) A method of transferring files from one computer to another across the Internet. It is commonly used to download large files or to load documents into a web site

fuzzy logic A computer-based decision-making process based on 'degrees of truth' rather than the simple 'true or false' ('1' or '0') decision. Typically used in domestic appliances where a number of parameters need to be taken into account (e.g. wash cycle for a washing machine)

GPS (global positioning system) A system which can be used to pinpoint a position on the earth's surface remarkably accurately; it uses a network of satellites and individual receivers

GPRS (general packet radio service) A variation on the basic GSM (q.v.) digital mobile-phone system, which provides faster, always-on access to the Internet and other services. This system precedes the 3G, the third-generation phones (q.v.)

GSM (global system for mobile communications) The basic digital mobile-phone system

HAN (home area network) A variation on LAN (local area network, q.v.), HAN is a network of computers in a home

HDTV (high-definition television) A TV system that offers greater picture detail than the current service. HDTV usually refers to a system that uses 1,050 or 1,250 lines to make up the picture, as opposed to the 525 or 625 used presently. Limited HDTV transmissions are available in Japan and the USA

HSCD (high-speed circuit-switched data) A higher-speed system for digital mobile phones used by the Orange network in the UK as an alternative to GPRS (q.v.)

hypertext Text (or a picture) that provides a link to another related page on a web site or, say, a CD-ROM encyclopaedia

ICRA (Internet content rating association) An organisation that supervises the system of tagging web pages to categorise their content for the purposes of filtering by, say, concerned parents. *See also* Internet filter

iDTV (integrated digital television) A TV with the digital TV receiver built into it – i.e. a normal TV with the set-top box inside

infra-red Energy in the region of the electromagnetic radiation spectrum at wavelengths longer than those of visible light, but shorter than those of radio waves. In the home this is used for remote controls, but being similar to visible light it works only for 'line of sight' applications

interactive A general term used to imply that the user can interact with a system or service. For example, watching a TV program is normally not 'interactive' whereas the TV teletext service is, because you can select specific items from a menu. Watching a DVD video can also be interactive because you can select different scenes from a menu and call up additional information about the video

ISDN (integrated services digital network) A telephone line system that provides faster data rates (e.g. faster Internet access) than the standard dial-up system. Data rates of up to 128Kbits per second are possible, as are simultaneous voice and data connections

ISP (Internet service provider) An organisation that connects its computers to the Internet and then allows its customers (both corporate and domestic) to connect to these, thus linking to the Net indirectly

Internet filter A software program on an Internet terminal (e.g. computer or TV) that blocks certain web pages and other content that the user regards as socially unacceptable

JPEG (joint photographic experts group) A standardised digital compression (q.v.) system for still images (typically photos). With graphic interchange format (GIF) and portable network graphics (PNG) file formats, JPEG is a commonly used format on the World Wide Web, usually with the file suffix of '.jpg'. JPEG images are also used in domestic digital photography

LAN (local area network) A small network of computers linked together, usually at a place of work. *See also* CAT-5, Ethernet and HAN

LNB In satellite TV reception, the small box of electronics that is positioned in the centre of the receiving satellite dish. It converts and amplifies the very-high-frequency satellite signal to a lower-frequency signal that can be sent down a cable

mini disc A small 7cm disc for recording audio. It is more versatile and of a higher quality than the analogue cassette tape. Suitable for home hi-fi use and portable players

modem (modulator-demodulator) A box of electronics that changes the digital signal from your Internet terminal (e.g. computer or TV) into an analogue signal suitable to be sent down a telephone line and *vice versa*

modulation The process of superimposing a programme signal (e.g. a TV broadcast or a stream of digital information) on to a high-frequency carrier wave (e.g. a radio-frequency signal) so that it can be transmitted

MP3 (MPEG audio layer 3) A digitally compressed audio format originally used in digital video but now widely used on the Internet for distributing and playing audio files

MPEG (motion picture experts group) The body that lays down standards for digital audio and video formats. MPEG2 is the system used for digital TV

multimedia A service that offers graphics, photographs, sounds and video clips in one presentation

multiplex In digital broadcasting and telecommunications, a group of several separate digital signals mixed together so they can be transmitted together in one digital channel. *See also* ensemble

netiquette A set of unofficial rules of etiquette for users of email and newsgroups

newsgroup An Internet service, similar to email, for the public to post messages on a wide variety of subjects. Each topic has its own newsgroup and anyone can participate

packet switched A type of network in which relatively small units of data called packets are routed through a network based on the destination address contained within each packet. Most data over the Internet use packet switching. *See also* streaming

PC (personal computer) Often used to mean any computer, but more accurately a computer that complies with the IBM PC system (as opposed to, say, Apple Macs)

PDA (personal digital assistant) A small, hand-held computer and data storage device

PDC (programme delivery control) A service provided by the five main terrestrial analogue TV services in the UK to instruct a VCR when to start and stop recording a TV show that the user has programmed into the VCR's memory. It means shows that are running late are recorded in full

PIM (personal information manager) A computer software program that acts as a diary, address book, etc.

pixel TV pictures and digital images generally are made up of tiny dots called pixels (short for 'picture element'). The greater the number of pixels in an area, the greater the picture detail. On a TV screen there are red, green and blue pixels which together can produce a wide range of colours

plasma display A type of video screen used for large-screen TVs. Like LCD displays they are costly. *See also* DLP

PPV (pay per view) TV service that allows you to watch particular programmes for a fee. You make the payment via your phone bill or credit card. This is distinct from 'subscription' TV, where you pay a monthly subscription for all programmes

PVR (personal video recorder) Also known as a PTV, or personal television, this is the new magnetic hard-disk video recorder that allows time-shift recording of TV programmes. It uses an electronic programme guide to select programmes to be recorded. The TiVo system was the first to be sold in the UK but future systems are likely to be built into the digital TV receivers

RDS (radio data system) The digital data system used on analogue FM radio to transmit additional programme information and instructions. Special RDS-equipped radios use this system to display station names and other details

RGB (red, green and blue) A video signal in which the colour information is transmitted as three separate 'components' to give a better-quality picture

router On the Internet, a device that determines the next network point to which a data packet should be forwarded

RSACi (Recreational Software Advisory Council) Now known as ICRA (q.v.)

scart A multi-pin plug and socket found at the back of modern TVs and VCRs in Europe. It enables standard and high-quality video signals and stereo sound to be connected with one single cable

SDMI (secure digital media initiative) A method of digitally encoding audio files such that the number of times they can be 'copied' can be controlled

search engine A software tool on the Internet that helps you to locate information you want. Owing to the uncoordinated way in which the Internet works, search engines have varying degrees of success and results are often governed by how intelligently the user asks the questions

smartmedia A type of small, removable memory card used to store data, typically used in digital cameras and MP3 players

SMS (short message service) A service for sending messages of up to 160 characters to GSM mobile phones

Spam Unsolicited, unwanted, nuisance email on the Internet

spreadsheet Originally, a sheet of paper that showed accounting or other data in rows and columns; nowadays, on a computer a piece of software that simulates the paper spreadsheet by capturing, displaying and manipulating data arranged in rows and columns

SSL (secure sockets layer) An Internet protocol for managing the security of a message transmitted over the Internet

STB (set-top box) A box of electronics that plugs into a TV to provide extra services. In digital TV reception, set-top boxes contain the extra receiving circuits required by your analogue TV to be able to receive the digital transmissions

streaming Certain types of data sent over the Internet are not suited to packet switching (q.v.). Live video and audio feeds have to be 'streamed', and special software 'plug-ins' are needed to view or listen to them

surfing The process of visiting World Wide Web pages or sites by using hyperlinks (q.v.)

S-video (or S-VHS) Originally called Super-VHS, a system by which a video signal is sent as two separate components which can be thought of as separate colour and black and white. Like RGB (q.v.) this gives a better-quality picture than standard composite video

TiVo A brand name for a particular personal video recorder (q.v.)

UMTS (universal mobile telecommunications system) The transmission system to be used for the third-generation mobile phones

URL (uniform resource locator) The address of an Internet page or file

USB (universal serial bus) A versatile computer 'plug-and-play' connection for conveniently connecting peripherals such as audio players, joysticks, keyboards, scanners, cameras and printers

V90 Along with V92, V34, etc., an international standard for dial-up modems. V90 is the version used in most houses for dialling the Internet. It gives data speeds of up to 56Kbps receiving data and 33.6Kbps sending data

VCR (video cassette recorder) A device that allows you to record programmes from a television

WAP (wireless application protocol) A standardised specification for sending Internet (web-based) information so that it can be received on specially equipped digital mobile phones

web clipping The automatic retrieval of specific pre-selected information from the World Wide Web. Unlike web 'surfing' (q.v.), this is an efficient and cost-effective way for users with mobile Internet access and PDA displays to obtain important information

widescreen A TV picture whose width-to-height dimensions are in the ratio 16 units by 9 units. Standard TVs have a ratio of 4x3. In the case of cinema films, widescreen means much wider ratios

WMA Microsoft Windows' Media Audio, a system for digitally encoding audio files

X-10 A simple home-automation system that uses mains power wiring to send instructions to automated appliances

Addresses and useful web sites

Chapter 1: Entertainment

Digital radio

BBC Digital Radio
Room 5661
Broadcasting House
Portland Place
London W1A 1AA
email:digitalradio@bbc.co.uk

BBC Reception Advice
Television Centre
Wood Lane
London W12 7RJ
Tel: (08700) 100123
Web site:
www.bbc.co.uk/digitalradio
(to check to see if your area has digital radio coverage)

Confederation of Aerial Industries Ltd (CAI)
Fulton House Business Centre
Fulton Road
Wembley Park
Middlesex HA9 0TF
Tel: 020-8902 8998
(for installation and advice on roof aerials)

Digital One
UK National Commercial Digital Radio Network
20 Southampton Street
London WC2E 7QH
Tel: 020-7288 4600
Web site:
www.ukdigitalradio.co.uk

Hirschmann Electronics Ltd
St. Martins Way
St. Martins Business Centre
Bedford MK42 0LF
Tel: (01234) 345999
(for installation and advice on car aerials)

Psion Wavefinder
Tel: (0990) 134224
Web site: www.wavefinder.com

Radio Authority
Holbrook House
14 Great Queen Street
London WC2B 5DG
Tel 020-7405 7058
Web site:
www.radioauthority.org.uk/

Roberts Radio Limited
PO Box 130
Mexborough
South Yorkshire S64 8YT
Tel: (01709) 571722
Web site:
www.robertsradio.co.uk

UK Digital Radio Forum
4th Floor, Landseer House
19 Charing Cross Road
London W1V 7DI
Tel: 020-7753 0348
Web site: www.dab.org

World DAB Forum
Wyvil Court
Wyvil Road
London SW8 2TG
Tel: 020-7896 9051
Web site: www.worlddab.org

Digital television

BBC Reception Advice
See Digital radio
(to check if your area has digital television coverage)

BSkyB
Tel: (08702) 424242
Web site: www.sky.com

Channel 4 digital channels
Channel 4 Television
124 Horseferry Road
London SW1P 2TX
Tel: (0800) 441234/
020-7306 8333
Minicom: 020-7306 8691
Web sites: www.channel4.com, www.e4.com, www.film4.com

Digital Television Group
Liss Mill
Liss
Hampshire GU33 7BD
Tel: (01730) 893144
Web site: www.dtg.org.uk
(has a list of publications, some free, and provides information for the installation of digital TV for multiple dwellings)

Home Choice
Tel: (0800) 092 4444
Web site:
www.homechoice.co.uk

Independent Television Commission
33 Foley Street
London W1W 7TL
Tel: 020-7255 3000
Web site: www.itc.org.uk

ntl
Tel: (0800) 052 1815 (new customers)
Tel: (0500) 941 940/
(0800) 052 7888 (existing customers)
Web site: www.askntl.com

ONdigital
Customer Services
PO Box 4
Plymouth PL1 3XU
Tel: (0808) 100 0101/(0870) 600 9696
Web site: www.ondigital.com

Telewest
Tel: (0500) 500 100
Web site: www.telewest.co.uk

TiVo
Tel: (08702) 418486
Web site: www.uk.tivo.com

Other

British Audio Dealers Association (BADA)
PO Box 229
Redhill
Surrey RH1 1YG
Tel: (01737) 760008
(for details of local hi-fi retailers who meet BADA quality standards)

Dolby Digital
Dolby Laboratories
Hammersley House
4th Floor, 5-8 Warwick Street
London W1B 5LX
Web site:
www.dolby.com/digital

Kerbango
Web site: www.kerbango.com

RealPlayer
Web site: www.real.com

Chapter 2: Sources of information

Altavista
Web site: www.altavista.com

AOL
Web site: www.aol.com

Electronic Arts
PO Box 835
Slough
Berkshire SL3 8XU
Web site: www.ea.com,
http://shop.ea-europe.com
(*makers of* Sim City *games*)

Encyclopaedia Britannica
Britannica.co.uk Ltd
16 Golden Square
London W1F 9JQ
Tel: 020-7862 4000
Web site:
http://corporate.britannica.co.uk

GSP Software
Meadow Lane
St Ives
Huntingdon
Cambridgeshire PE27 4LG
Tel: (01480) 496575
Web site: www.gspltd.co.uk

ICRA
Web site: www.icra.org

Intuit
'Quicken' financial software
Intuit Services Centre
PO Box 2093
Swindon SN5 8TR
Tel: (0800) 585058
Web site: www.intuit.co.uk

Kidznet
Web site: www.kidz.net

Microsoft Software
Microsoft Limited
Microsoft Campus
Thames Valley Park
Reading RG6 1WG
Tel: (0870) 601 0100
Minicom: (0870) 503 0400
Web site:
www.microsoft.com/uk/

Net Nanny
Web site: www.netnanny.com

Safe Surf
Web site: www.safesurf.com

Solid Oak
Web site: www.solidoak.com

Yahoo
Web site: www.yahoo.com

Chapter 3: E-commerce

DTI Enquiry Unit (Consumer Affairs)
1 Victoria Street
London SW1H 0ET
Web site:
www.dti.gov.uk/cacp/ca/
(a government web site covering many consumer issues including the new Distance Selling Directive, Sale of Goods Act, etc. A very useful source of information and points of contact)

ONnet
ONdigital Customer Services
PO Box 4
Plymouth PL1 3XU
Web site: www.ondigital.co.uk

OPEN
34-35 Farringdon Street
London EC4A 4HJ
Tel: (0870) 606 0808
Web site: www.open-here.co.uk
(the interactive shopping arm of BSkyB's digital television service)

Railtrack
Web site: www.railtrack.co.uk

TrustUK
Web site: www.trustuk.org.uk

Which? Web Trader
Web site:
www.which.net/webtrader

Chapter 4: Communications

Internet service providers

There are many ISPs to choose from in the UK. The addresses of those mentioned in the main text are listed below.

America on Line (AOL)
Tel: (0800) 376 5432
Web site: www.aol.co.uk

British Telecom
Tel: (0800) 800 152
Web site: www.bt.co.uk

BT Openworld
Tel: (0800) 169 6922
Web site:
www.btopenworld.com
(ADSL provider)

CIX
Tel: (0845) 355 5151
Web site: www.nextra.co.uk

Compuserve
Web site:
www.compuserve.com

Which OnLine
Castlemead
Gascoyne Way
Hertford X, SG14 1YB
Tel: (0845) 983 0240
(provides exclusive access to consumer information and Which? *magazines and some books)*

Internet phone companies

Deltathree
Web site: www.deltathree.com

Mediaring
Web site: www.mediaring.com

Net2phone
Web site: www.net2phone.com

Other

ADSL
Web site:
www.broadband.bt.com
(lists all the companies that provide ADSL lines in the UK)

ntl
See Chapter 1

Ricability
30 Angel Gate
326 City Road
London EC1V 2PT
Tel: 020-7427 2460
Web site: www.ricability.org.uk/
(for a comprehensive booklet explaining social alarms and reviewing all the main models)

Phone bills
Web site:
www.phonebills.org.uk
(enables you to discover the most competitive tariff for you)

Telewest
See Chapter 1

Chapter 5: On the move

Avantgo
Web site:
https://avantgo.com/setup/teaser.html
(an information service for PDAs)

Department of Health
Richmond House
79 Whitehall
London SW1A 2NS
Tel: 020-7210 4850
Minicom: 020-7210 5025
Web site:
www.doh.gov.uk/mobilephones
(for mobile phone safety leaflet)

Olympus Optical Co (Europa) GmbH
'Eye-Trek'
Wendenstr. 14-16
20097 Hamburg
Germany
Web site: www.eye-trek.co.uk/

Panasonic
Tel: (08705) 357357
Web site: www.panasonic.co.uk

Sharp Electronics (UK) Ltd
Sharp House
Thorp Road
Manchester M40 5BE
Tel: 0161-205 2333
Web site: www.sharp.co.uk

Sony
Tel: (08705) 111999
Web site: www.sony.co.uk

Chapter 6: Smart homes

3-Com
220 Wharfedale Road
Winnersh
Wokingham
Berkshire RG41 5TP
Tel: (01189) 278300
Web site:
www.3com.co.uk/solutions/personal/index.html

Bluetooth
Web site: www.bluetooth.com
(official web site with all the latest news)

Dyson Ltd
Tetbury Hill
Malmesbury
Wiltshire SN16 0RP
Tel: (0870) 5275105
Web site: www.dyson.co.uk

Electrolux
Web site:
www.electrolux.co.uk/screenfridge

Ericsson
Web site: www.ericsson.co.uk/technologies.shtml

Husqvarna Forest and Garden UK
Oldends Lane
Stonehouse
Gloucestershire GL10 3SY
Tel: (01453) 822382
Web site: www.husqvarna.co.uk

Laser Equipment
16 Garthland Drive
Barnet
Hertfordshire EN5 3BB
Tel: 020-8441 9788
Web site: www.laser.com
(X-10 home automation)

Lets Automate
Tel: 020-8326 6649
Web site:
www.letsautomate.com
(X-10 home automation)

LG Electronics
Tel: (01753) 500400
Web site: www.lge.co.uk
(Internet fridge)

Netgear
Web site: www.netgear.com

Orange
Web site: www.orange.co.uk/orangeathome

Pace
Victoria Road
Saltaire
Shipley
West Yorkshire BD18 3LF
Tel: (01274) 532000
Web site: www.pace.co.uk/networked-home/index.asp
(multimedia home platform – set-top boxes)

Robomow
Friendly Robotics UK Ltd.
65 Park Street
Thame
Oxfordshire OX9 3HT
Tel: (01844) 261653/
(0800) 028 2836

Chapter 7: Digital photography

Club 35 (Kodak Express)
121-123 The Broadway
West Ealing
London W13 9BE
Tel: 020-8840 4850
Web site: www.club35.co.uk

Fuji Photo Film (UK) Ltd
Unit 10a St Martins Way
St Martins Business Centre
Bedford MK42 0LF
Web site: www.fujifilm.co.uk

Hewlett Packard
Tel: 020-7512 5202

MGI
Norfolk House
110 Saxon Gate West
Milton Keynes
Buckinghamshire
MK9 2DN
Tel: (01908) 278100/
(0800) 973830
Web site: www.mgisoft.com

Pinnacle Software
The Teardrop Centre
London Road
Swanley
Kent BR8 8TS
Tel: (01322) 665652
Web site:
www.pinnaclesys.de/uk/
(video-editing software)

Chapter 8: Other digital equipment in the house

Carbug
Tel: 020-7222 7284
Web site: www.carbug.co.uk

Garmin
Unit 5, The Quadrangle
Abbey Park Industrial Estate
Romsey
Hampshire SO51 9AQ
Tel: (01794) 519944
Web site: www.garmin.com
(manufacturers of GPS receivers)

Thomson Multimedia Sales UK Ltd
30 Tower View
Kings Hill
West Malling
Kent ME19 4NQ
Tel: (01732) 520920
(manufacturers of video senders)

Which? Taxcalc
Which? Software
Castlemead
Gascoyne Way
Hertford SG14 1SH
Web site: www.taxcalc.com

Index

Page numbers in *italics* indicate where an illustration is to be found.

WHICH? BOOKS

The following titles were available as this book went to press.

General reference (legal, financial, practical, etc.)

Be Your Own Financial Adviser	432pp	£9.99
420 Legal Problems Solved	304pp	£9.99
150 Letters that Get Results	288pp	£9.99
What to Do When Someone Dies	160pp	£9.99
The Which? Computer Troubleshooter	192pp	£12.99
The Which? Guide to an Active Retirement	530pp	£12.99
The Which? Guide to Changing Careers	288pp	£10.99
The Which? Guide to Choosing a Career	336pp	£9.99
The Which? Guide to Choosing a School	336pp	£10.99
The Which? Guide to Computers	336pp	£10.99
The Which? Guide to Computers for Small Businesses	256pp	£10.99
The Which? Guide to Divorce	352pp	£10.99
The Which? Guide to Doing Your Own Conveyancing	208pp	£9.99
The Which? Guide to Domestic Help	208pp	£9.99
The Which? Guide to Employment	304pp	£10.99
The Which? Guide to Gambling	288pp	£9.99
The Which? Guide to Getting Married	224pp	£9.99
The Which? Guide to Giving and Inheriting	240pp	£9.99
The Which? Guide to Going Digital	272pp	£10.99
The Which? Guide to Home Safety and Security	198pp	£9.99
The Which? Guide to Insurance	320pp	£10.99
The Which? Guide to the Internet	304pp	£10.99
The Which? Guide to Money	448pp	£9.99
The Which? Guide to Pensions	336pp	£9.99
The Which? Guide to Renting and Letting	336pp	£10.99
The Which? Guide to Shares	256pp	£9.99
The Which? Guide to Shopping on the Internet	272pp	£10.99
The Which? Guide to Starting Your Own Business	288pp	£10.99
The Which? Guide to Working from Home	252pp	£9.99
Which? Way to Buy, Own and Sell a Flat	288pp	£10.99
Which? Way to Buy, Sell and Move House	320pp	£10.99
Which? Way to Clean It	256pp	£9.99
Which? Way to Drive Your Small Business	240pp	£10.99
Which? Way to Manage Your Time -- and Your Life	208pp	£9.99
Which? Way to Save and Invest	464pp	£14.99
Which? Way to Save Tax	352pp	£14.99
Wills and Probate	224pp	£10.99
Make Your Own Will	28pp	£10.99

Action Pack (A5 wallet with forms and 28-page book inside)

Health

Understanding HRT and the Menopause	256pp	£9.99
The Which? Guide to Children's Health	288pp	£9.99
The Which? Guide to Complementary Medicine	270pp	£9.99
The Which? Guide to Managing Asthma	256pp	£9.99
The Which? Guide to Managing Back Trouble	160pp	£9.99
The Which? Guide to Managing Stress	252pp	£9.99
The Which? Guide to Men's Health	304pp	£9.99
The Which? Guide to Personal Health	274pp	£9.99
The Which? Guide to Women's Health	448pp	£9.99
Which? Medicine	528pp	£12.99

Gardening

The Gardening Which? Guide to Growing Your Own Vegetables	224pp	£18.99
The Gardening Which? Guide to Patio and Container Plants	224pp	£17.99
The Gardening Which? Guide to Small Gardens	224pp	£12.99
The Gardening Which? Guide to Successful Perennials	224pp	£17.99
The Gardening Which? Guide to Successful Propagation	224pp	£12.99
The Gardening Which? Guide to Successful Pruning	240pp	£12.99
The Gardening Which? Guide to Successful Shrubs	224pp	£12.99

Do-it-yourself

The Which? Book of Do-It-Yourself	320pp	£14.99
The Which? Book of Plumbing and Central Heating	160pp	£13.99
The Which? Book of Wiring and Lighting	160pp	£16.99
Which? Way to Fix It	208pp	£12.99

Travel/leisure

The Good Bed and Breakfast Guide	672pp	£14.99
The Good Food Guide	768pp	£15.99
The Good Skiing and Snowboarding Guide	592pp	£15.99
The Good Walks Guide	320pp	£13.99
The Which? Guide to Country Pubs	608pp	£13.99
The Which? Guide to Pub Walks	256pp	£9.99
The Which? Guide to Scotland	528pp	£12.99
The Which? Guide to Tourist Attractions	512pp	£12.99
The Which? Guide to Weekend Breaks in Britain	528pp	£13.99
The Which? Hotel Guide	736pp	£15.99
The Which? Wine Guide	496pp	£14.99
Which? Holiday Destination	624pp	£12.99